Even at the Doors

(Jesus, Israel, and the End-Times)

"EVEN AT THE DOORS"

(Jesus, Israel, and the End-Times)

by

JAMES J. JACKSON

Even at the Doors (Jesus, Israel, and the End-Times)

Cover design by Heather Clark Designs
(heatherclarkdesigns@yahoo.com)

Published through "Lulu Enterprises, Inc."
3131 RDU Center, Suite 210
Morrisville, NC 27560

ISBN: 978-0-6151-7310-8

The scripture quotations used in this book are from the King James Version of the Bible. I have modernized a few of the words in some of the quoted passages, yet none of these changes affect the original meaning of any of the Bible verses that I use.

For more information from the author, please go to the web site at http://www.iesouschristos.com or http://www.evenatthedoors.com

This book is dedicated to my beautiful wife

Crystal

whom God used to bring me back onto
His paths of righteousness
and
to my children whom God gave to me
to care for and love

William, Matthew, and Camille

CONTENTS

Preface

The last question Jesus answered while He was still on the earth had to do with the timing of His second coming to the people of the earth.[1] He was standing on the Mount of Olives on the eastern side of Jerusalem waiting to ascend into heaven. His disciples asked Him, *"Lord, will You at this time restore again the kingdom to Israel?"* Jesus replied and said unto them, *"It is not for you to know the times of the seasons which the Father has put in His own power."*[2] Earlier, during the Passover week of Jesus' crucifixion, He had told these same disciples that *"of that day and hour knows no man, no, not the angels of heaven, but My Father only."*[3]

The apostle Paul stated something similar concerning the second coming of Jesus in his first letter to the Christians in Thessalonica. The Thessalonians were concerned that they had missed the return of Jesus and asked Paul about it. He told them that *"of the times and seasons, brethren, you have no need that I write to you. For you yourselves know perfectly that the day of the Lord comes as a thief in the night...But you, brethren, are not in darkness that that day should overtake you as a thief. You are all the children of light and the children of the day."*[4]

Thus, is it possible for Christians to know the exact timing of Jesus' return to the earth? The answer to that is an unequivocal "*NO*". There have been many cults and misguided individuals that have given various dates for the return of Jesus Christ but all of them have been wrong.

Is it possible to know whether the second coming of Jesus Christ is getting nearer? Should we know if the time is approaching? I believe the answer to both these questions is *"yes"*. In response to His disciples' queries on the Mount of Olives before His crucifixion concerning the timing of His second coming, Jesus told them about the various troubles and deceptions that were going to come upon the earth before that event would take place. He then finished this part of His teaching by telling the disciples, *"So likewise you, when you shall see all these things, KNOW that it is near, even at the doors. Truly I say unto you, this generation shall not pass till all these things be fulfilled."*[5]

Earlier in His ministry Jesus had rebuked the religious leaders for not knowing the timing of the coming of the Messiah (I will deal with this issue more specifically in Chapter 5). Jesus said that these leaders should have *known* that He was fulfilling many of the Messianic prophecies because they had received them centuries before in the Old Testament. Likewise, Jesus told His followers that there will be signs that the end is approaching and that they should *know* when it is near, even at the doors.

The times that we are living in are full of confusion and strife. People are looking for answers to the problems that arise in their everyday lives. They are looking for hope. I am writing this book so that those individuals who read it may find the only *true* peace that is available to humankind in these troubled times. The apostle Paul wrote in a letter to a Christian named Titus that Christians should be *"looking for that blessed hope and the glorious appearing of the great God and Savior Jesus Christ."*[6] Christians have a hope that, tragically, the world does not share.

I want people to know that the Bible does tell us that there are signs and prophecies that indicate Jesus' second coming to earth may be nearer than we think. The Day of the Lord should not overtake Christians or *"children of the light"* as Paul calls them like a thief in the night.

Therefore, the purpose of this book is to give an overview of the prophecies concerning the first and second comings of Jesus Christ. In addition, it is my intent to show the timing of the end-time events as they relate to the near future.

I will use the Bible as the source for the theme of this book. It is the prophetic book that lays out God's entire plan for humankind. It is said that the Bible is an anvil that has worn out many a hammer. Archaeology has proven time after time that the Bible is historically accurate contrary to the opinions of many of its "learned" critics. In Part One of this book, I will show that it is also prophetically accurate. Just as the events the Bible predicted to occur over two thousand years ago came to pass, so too the prophecies that predict the future *will* also come to pass. As God declares in His Word: *"Remember the former things of old: for I am God, and there is none else; I am God, and there is none like Me, Declaring the end from the beginning, and from ancient times the things that are not yet done, saying, My counsel shall stand, and I will do all My pleasure."*[7]

I would like to point out a couple of literary notes that I will be using in this book. When I quote scriptures I will capitalize the names of God and Jesus and any pronouns that refer to Them. My purpose in this is twofold. The first is to give God the honor that He deserves. The second is so that it will be clear for the reader as to whom the quoted passages are referring to. I will also be italicizing the Bible verses I quote to set them apart from the main text of this book.

Additionally, I will be quoting New Testament scriptures to show how Jesus fulfilled and will fulfill the prophecies concerning the Messiah. These scriptures will be quotations of the people who saw, heard, and knew Jesus. They had not only their lives changed by their experiences with Him but also their souls. Many of them gave up their lives because of their belief that He was indeed the Messiah.

---

[1] The apostle Paul on the road to Damascus asked Jesus some questions after His ascension but Jesus was answering from heaven. *(Acts 9: 1-9)*

[2] *Acts of the Apostles 1:6-7*

[3] *Matthew 24:36*

[4] *II Thessalonians 5:1-2, 4-5*

[5] *Matthew 24:33-34*

[6] *Titus 2:13*

[7] *Isaiah 46:9-10*

May God bless this book and your reading of it

- James Jackson, 2006

Part One

The First Coming Of The Messiah

1 - The Promised Messiahs?

The earthly ministry of Jesus confused the people of His day. This confusion was not only shared by the people and the religious leaders but even Jesus' own disciples along with John the Baptist were confused as to the nature of the Messiah.

The nation of Israel had long been looking for the Messiah to set them free from the oppression of the various nations that had conquered them since the days of Moses. Their religious leaders had told them that when the Messiah came He would cast off the yoke of bondage that foreign governments had put upon them. When the Jewish people proclaimed Jesus as Messiah on Palm Sunday, they expected Him to defeat the Roman government and set up His kingdom on earth at that time. Instead, the Romans crucified Jesus and the people became disheartened and rejected Him as the Messiah. The problem was that the Jewish religious leaders had not understood *all* of the prophecies that Old Testament revealed concerning the Messiah. Where did this confusion concerning the Messianic prophecies come from?

The Old Testament did indeed speak of the Messiah as a conquering savior for His people. It also spoke of a suffering Messiah who would be punished for the sins of His people. The late Orthodox Jewish Talmudic scholar and later a believer in Yeshua (i.e., Jesus), Rachmiel Frydland, wrote, "There are two very distinct lines of prophecy in the Scriptures concerning the Messiah. One line portrays him as a humble suffering-saviour. The other line of prophecy depicts him as a conquering king-redeemer. Talmudic and other Jewish sources recognize these two competing functions of the Messiah. One explanation invoked to resolve this dilemma was that there would be two Messiahs: one who would suffer and be humbled and one who would rule and be exalted."[1]

The Jewish leaders tried to explain this seeming discrepancy with various theories. One stated that if the Jewish people were living righteously before God then He would send the conquering Messiah. Conversely, if the Jewish nation was in rebellion against the laws of God then they would be sent the suffering Messiah. It seems however, the one theory they did not envision was that God would send His Messiah twice.

The first time was to save the people from their sins by suffering for them. The second time was to set up His earthly kingdom so that the people would live as God had intended for them all along.

One reason that there would be a delay between His two comings was to not only give the Jews a chance to be reconciled to God through the forgiveness of their sins but also to give the Gentiles a chance to be reconciled to a God they did not know. Jesus stated in the aforementioned Olivet Discourse, *"And this gospel of the kingdom shall be preached in all the world for a witness unto all nations and THEN shall the end come."*[2]

In this chapter, I will discuss the foundational Messianic prophecy given by God in the Old Testament.

The "Prophet" Prophecy

Moses uttered an unmistakable prophecy concerning the Messiah. He declared to the Jews:

> *"The Lord thy God will raise up unto you a Prophet from the midst of you, of your brethren, like unto me, unto Him you shall listen. I will raise them up a Prophet from among their brethren, like unto you, and will put My words in His mouth and He shall speak unto them all that I shall command Him."*
>
> *- Deuteronomy 18:15, 18*

God had ordained Moses to be His representative for the Jewish nation after the Egyptians had enslaved them. God had told him to go to the Egyptian Pharaoh and tell him to set the Jews free from the bondage of slavery so that they could serve their God. There was reluctance on Moses' part to do the Lord's bidding in this endeavor. He was concerned that he was not an eloquent man along with a few other reservations that he had regarding himself. God told Moses that He would put the words in his mouth that he was to speak and that would lead to the salvation of the Jews through their deliverance from bondage. Thus, Moses did obey the Lord and the Lord did deliver the Jewish people from bondage through His messenger.

It was after the Jews had left Egypt when Moses prophesied to them that God would raise up a Prophet like Moses and that He would speak the words of the Lord.

The Jewish people of Jesus' day were familiar with this prophecy. When John the Baptist was preaching in the wilderness, they asked him, *"Who are you? ...Are you Elijah? ...Are you that Prophet?"*[3] John's response was no but that he was preparing the way for the Prophet/Messiah.

When Jesus was teaching in the Jewish Temple in Jerusalem during the Feast of Tabernacles, the Jews listening to Him were amazed at His words. So much so that they declared, *"Of a truth this is the Prophet."*[4]

Was Jesus this Prophet/Messiah spoken of by Moses? The New Testament is unequivocal in its claims that He was. Jesus said, *"I am come in My Father's name and you receive Me not...Do not think that I will accuse you to the Father: there is one who accuses you, Moses, in whom you trust. For if you believed Moses you would have believed Me because he wrote of Me. But if you believe not his writings how shall you believe My words."*[5] Indeed Jesus was identifying Himself as the Prophet/Messiah spoken of by Moses.

This prophecy states that the Messiah would be like Moses and that God would give Him the words that He was to speak. God spoke to Moses and said, *"Come now therefore and I will send you unto Pharaoh that you may bring forth My people, the children, of Israel out of Egypt."*[6] So the task that God gave to Moses was to deliver the people from the bondage of slavery. Likewise, the Messiah's mission was to deliver the people from their bondage to sin by giving His life as a sacrificial offering to God. The writer of Hebrews declares that Jesus did fulfill this task: *"But we see Jesus, Who was made a little lower than the angels for the suffering of death...that He by the grace of God should taste death for every man...Forasmuch then as the children are partakers of flesh and blood, He also Himself likewise took part of the same, that through death He might destroy him that had the power of death, that is, the devil; and deliver them who through fear of death were all their lifetime subject to bondage."*[7]

The other part of this prophecy was that the Messiah spoken of by Moses was to speak the words that God put in His mouth. When the Jewish religious leaders asked Jesus who He was He replied, *"Even the same that I said unto you from the beginning. I have many things to say and to judge of you, but He that sent Me is true and I speak to the world those things which I have heard of Him...When you have lifted up the Son of man, then shall you know that I am He and that I do nothing of Myself but as My Father has taught Me I speak these things."*[8]

There are a couple of other interesting parallels between Moses and Jesus that the Bible records. The first is that the governing rulers tried to have each killed at birth.[9] As we will see in later chapters, I believe that just before God initiates a major prophetic event Satan[10] tries to destroy the means by which God plans to use in fulfilling His will. I believe that such an event took place within the recent past.

The second one is that Moses was reluctant to take on God's difficult mission because he did not think he would be able to see it through to the end. Jesus, while praying in the Garden of Gethsemane, also asked God if there was some other way the mission could be accomplished. Nevertheless, Jesus did submit to God's will.

In the next few chapters, I will discuss those prophecies that Jesus fulfilled with His first coming. I will show how the New Testament clearly illustrates that He indeed was the suffering Messiah that was prophesied in the Old Testament. Later I will list the prophecies that Jesus did not fulfill...yet. They pertain to those passages in the Old Testament that describe a royal Messiah. Jesus will fulfill them with His second coming, a time which I believe His followers will recognize as approaching nearer, even at the doors.

[1] "What the Rabbis Know About the Messiah", Rachmiel Frydland, p.51 (Messianic Publishing Co. 1991, 1993)

[2] *Matthew 24:14*

[3] *John 1:19, 21*

[4] *John 7:40*

[5] *John 5:43, 45-47*

[6] *Exodus 3:10*

[7] *Hebrews 2:9, 14-15*

[8] *John 8:25-26, 28*

[9] *Exodus 1:15-2:10; Matthew 2:1-18*

[10] The Bible indicates that Satan has general if not specific knowledge of God's prophetic plans for the future. In Chapter 9 of this book, I discuss the Tribulation Period in detail and point out that it will last seven years. In the Book of Revelation, John sees Satan cast out of heaven at the midpoint of the Tribulation Period. In response to this event, a voice from Heaven cries out:

> *"Therefore rejoice, ye heavens, and ye that dwell in them. Woe to the inhabiters of the earth and of the sea! for the devil is come down unto you, having great wrath, because he knows that he has but a short time."*
>
> *- Revelation 12:12*

According to this passage, Satan *knows* that the Tribulation Period is a short period of time and realizes his time is almost up according to God's prophetic plans. At the end of the Tribulation, God is going to restrain Satan for a thousand years and then judge him for eternity. This knowledge of future events has enabled Satan to try to hinder God's plan for the human race throughout history.

2 - The Divinely Human Messiah

Some biblical scholars have ascertained that there are more than three hundred prophecies in the Old Testament that pertain to the Messiah of Israel. I will discuss a representative few of them and show the fulfillment of these prophecies by Jesus Christ according to the New Testament. I will start with those passages that predict the birth of the Messiah on earth. The next chapter will deal with those prophecies that describe His life and the chapters after that will finish with the prophecies that predict His suffering and death.

As any Journalism 101 class would teach, a writer must answer six questions when he is reporting the facts of this story. In the subject at hand they are: Who is the Messiah? Why is the Messiah coming? How will the Messiah come? Where will the Messiah be born and live His life? What will the Messiah do? When will the Messiah come? Part One of this book will answer each of these questions.

The Messiah: In the Beginning

At the very beginning of the Bible God let mankind know that He would send a special person to redeem humans from the sinful evil that will become their lot in life. In the third chapter of Genesis God warns the Devil, who had just beguiled humans into sinning against Him, that He will send a being that will overcome him. God said:

> *"And I will put enmity between you* [i.e., the Devil] *and the woman, and between your seed and her seed; it shall bruise your head and you shall bruise His heel."*
>
> *- Genesis 3:15*

God announces that the seed or child of a woman will vehemently oppose the works of Satan. This passage has some very interesting wording in it. God specifically said that it would be the *seed* of a woman who would do God's work in defeating the Devil. Biology has taught us that it is the seed or semen of a man that results in the birth of a human being. Here though, God makes clear that no man will be involved in the birth of this child. This is the first hint that the birth of God's Savior of mankind will have a very unique birth.

This child will do fatal damage to the Devil and his works as is made clear by the phrase *"bruise your head"*. Conversely, Satan will only *"bruise"* this child's heel. Both of these expressions are referring to the crucifixion of Jesus through which He gained the victory over sin and death.

I believe this prophetic verse is the first mention in the Bible that the Devil will attack God's Savior unsuccessfully. The fulfillment of this prophecy will have eternal consequences.

Fulfillment by Jesus Christ:

> *"He that commits sin is of the devil; for the devil sinned from the beginning. For this purpose the Son of God was manifested that He might destroy the works of the devil."*[1]

> *"Forasmuch then as the children are partakers of flesh and blood, Jesus also Himself likewise took part of the same; that through death He might destroy him that had the power of death, that is, the devil;"*[2]

These New Testament passages give us the answers to the questions of *who* the Messiah is and *why* He came. Jesus, the Son of God, defeated the Devil with His sacrificial death and resurrection.

As you will read in Chapter 6, Jesus Christ is not only the Son of God but He is also God the Son. Yet, as God, He came to earth as a human being in order to die for the sins of every human being that has ever lived.

Now let us look at *how* the Messiah would come.

The Virgin-Born Messiah

God gave to the prophet Isaiah the task of warning not only the nation of Israel concerning its sins but of also giving them hope that would come in the form of God's Messiah. In the Book of Isaiah, the prophet seems to give contradictory descriptions of what the Messiah would be like. There are passages that describe a suffering Messiah and others that deal with a royal Messiah. The prophecy that I will discuss here concerns the nature of the birth of the Messiah and also His humanity.

> *"And he said, Hear ye now, O house of David; Is it a small thing for you to weary men, but will ye weary my God also? Therefore the Lord Himself shall give you a sign; Behold, a virgin shall conceive, and bear a son, and shall call His name Immanuel."*
>
> \- *Isaiah 7:13-14*

God is promising the House of David (i.e., Israel) that He would give to them a sign in the form of a "virgin-born" child. There has been some controversy concerning the Hebrew word "almah" which is translated here as *"virgin"*. The primary meaning of this word is "young woman". Two facets of this issue should shed some light as to which interpretation is correct.

The first is rather obvious. Young women have been giving birth to children since the dawn of humanity. How could any young woman giving birth to a child be a *sign* that God used special intervention in her case?

The second reason rests upon a Greek translation of the Old Testament that was written almost three hundred years before the birth of Jesus Christ. This translation was completed by Jewish scholars of that era. In Isaiah 7:14 they specifically used the Greek word *parthenos* to translate the Hebrew word *almah*. This Greek word can only mean a "virgin". It would seem then that these Jewish scholars understood the intent of this prophetic verse to mean that this child would be born under unique circumstances.

Therefore, it is clear that God was promising to send a special child to Israel. God hints at the nature of this child in that He said His name shall be Immanuel, which means *God with us* or *God is with us*. Thirty-nine verses after this one God offers more attributes of this child: *"For unto us a Child is born, unto us a Son is given: and the government shall be upon His shoulder: and His name shall be called Wonderful, Counselor, The mighty God, The everlasting Father, The Prince of Peace. Of the increase of His government and peace there shall be no end, upon the throne of David, and upon his kingdom, to order it, and to establish it with judgment and with justice from henceforth even for ever. The zeal of the LORD of hosts will perform this."*[3]

This second passage confirms that Isaiah 7:14 is clearly a Messianic prophecy. The New Testament also refers to this scripture and its deeper meanings.

<u>Fulfillment by Jesus Christ</u>:

> *"Now the birth of Jesus Christ was on this wise: When as His mother Mary was espoused to Joseph, before they came together, she was found with child of the Holy Ghost. Then Joseph her husband, being a just man, and not willing to make her a public example, was minded to put her away privately. But while he thought on these things, behold, the angel of the Lord appeared unto him in a dream, saying, Joseph, thou son of David, fear not to take unto you Mary your wife: for that which is conceived in her is of the Holy Ghost. And she shall bring forth a Son, and you shall call His name JESUS: for He shall save His people from their sins. Now all this was done, that it might be fulfilled which was spoken of the Lord by the prophet, saying, Behold, a virgin shall be with child, and shall bring forth a son, and they shall call his name Emmanuel, which being interpreted is, God with us."*[4]

The Messiah was to be born of a human woman without a man's involvement. The Gospel of Matthew makes it evident that the Holy Spirit accomplished this by conceiving the Messiah inside her.

One other aspect of this prophecy begs further examination. Why did God require that His Messiah be born of a virgin? Both the Old and New Testament together give the answer to this question.

God made it known very early on that human life and blood is interwoven on both a physical level and a spiritual level. In the Law that God gave to the children of Israel He said, *"For the life of the flesh is in the blood: and I have given it to you upon the altar to make an atonement for your souls: for it is the blood that makes an atonement for the soul."*[5] The writer of the Book of Hebrews wrote, *"And almost all things are by the law purged with blood; and without shedding of blood is no remission."*[6] God has declared in these passages that blood and man's sinful nature are inseparable.

The apostle Paul, in discussing the sinful nature of man, wrote, *"Wherefore, as by one man [Adam] sin entered into the world, and death by sin; and so death passed upon all men, for that all have sinned."*[7] Paul is saying that the sin nature passed through the bloodlines of Adam to all men.

As noted above, God required the shedding of blood to make atonement for human sin. In the Law, God commanded the Jews to sacrifice certain animals every year in order to fulfill this requirement. One of the prerequisites was that the animal had to be perfect (i.e., unblemished). The problem is that these animal sacrifices only *covered* man's sins. Again, the Book of Hebrews declares, *"For the law having a shadow of good things to come, and not the very image of the things, can never with those sacrifices which they offered year by year continually make the comers thereunto perfect. For then would they not have ceased to be offered? because that the worshippers once purged should have had no more conscience of sins...For it is not possible that the blood of bulls and of goats should take away sins."*[8]

Therefore, God had to send a Messiah who had not been tainted by humanity's sinful blood. He accomplished this by having His Holy Spirit conceive the Messiah in the womb of a virgin. The New Testament affirms in the Book of Acts that this is what took place: *"Take heed therefore unto yourselves, and to all the flock, over the which the Holy Ghost has made you overseers, to feed the church of God, which He has purchased with His own blood."*[9] It was God's *own* blood that ran through Jesus' veins. In addition, Paul writing to the Roman Christians, declared, *"[Jesus] Whom God has set forth to be a propitiation through faith in His blood, to declare His righteousness for the remission of sins that are past, through the forbearance of God."*[10] That Jesus met God's requirement that a sacrifice had to be perfect is spoken of in the New Testament: *"Seeing then that we have a great High Priest, that is passed into the heavens, Jesus the Son of God, let us hold fast our profession. For we have not an high priest which cannot be touched with the feeling of our infirmities; but was in all points tempted like as we are, yet without sin."*[11]

Jesus was sinless (and therefore "unblemished") and thus was an acceptable sacrifice to God on behalf of humankind. Chapter 4 of this book will more fully explore this aspect of the Messiah.

Next, I will discuss *where* the Messiah would come.

The Christmas Gift That Keeps On Giving

God gave a prophecy concerning another aspect of the Messiah's birth by revealing to the Jews where He would be born. Many people who celebrate Christmas have at one time sung the Christmas carol "O Little Town of Bethlehem". This song describes the fulfillment of a prophecy written over 2600 years ago:

> *"But thou, Bethlehem Ephratah, though thou be little among the thousands of Judah, yet out of thee shall He come forth unto Me that is to be Ruler in Israel; whose goings forth have been from of old, from everlasting."*
>
> \- *Micah 5:2*

Micah was a prophet sent by God to the nation of Israel to preach not only judgment of them for their apostasy but also their deliverance by the hand of the Messiah. This prophecy deals with their deliverance.

God tells the Jewish people that the Messiah, whom Moses prophesied of a long time before, will be born in Bethlehem. It was this prophecy that the religious leaders of King Herod's day referenced in response to his inquiry as to where the Messiah was to be born.

Fulfillment by Jesus Christ:

"Now when Jesus was born in Bethlehem of Judea in the days of Herod the king, behold, there came wise men from the east to Jerusalem, Saying, Where is He that is born King of the Jews? For we have seen His star in the east, and are come to worship Him. When Herod the king had heard these things, he was troubled, and all Jerusalem with him. And when he had gathered all the chief priests and scribes of the people together, he demanded of them where Christ should be born. And they said unto him, In Bethlehem of Judea: for thus it is written by the prophet, And thou Bethlehem, in the land of Judah, art not the least among the princes of Judah: for out of thee shall come a Governor, that shall rule My people Israel."[12]

The Gospel writer Luke also wrote of Jesus' birth in Bethlehem:

"And it came to pass in those days, that there went out a decree from Caesar Augustus that all the world should be taxed...And all went to be taxed, every one into his own city. And Joseph also went up from Galilee, out of the city of Nazareth, into Judea, unto the city of David, which is called Bethlehem; (because he was of the house and lineage of David) to be taxed with Mary his espoused wife, being great with child. And so it was, that, while they were there, the days were accomplished that she should be delivered. And she brought forth her firstborn Son, and wrapped Him in swaddling clothes, and laid Him in a manger; because there was no room for them in the inn."[13]

One interesting side note to this event is that in order to fulfill this prophecy God worked through the most powerful man on earth at that time, Caesar Augustus, the emperor of the Roman Empire.

There is another point to discuss (and relevant to the purpose of this book) concerning this prophecy of the place of the Messiah's birth. As mentioned earlier, Satan was determined to stop the will of

God by hindering His plan for the deliverance of the Jews from the bondage of slavery. Satan[14] incited the Pharaoh of Egypt to kill all of the Hebrew male babies in order to stop the deliverer Moses from living. Moses' parents thwarted this diabolical plan by hiding him in a basket and floating it in the Nile River where Pharaoh's daughter found him and raised him.[15]

Likewise, Satan inspired King Herod, the king of Judea at the time of Jesus' birth, to try to kill Jesus as an infant in order to stop God's plan for the deliverance of mankind from their bondage to sin. Herod was an evil man who had killed many members of his own family along with many of the Jewish citizens of Judea. Once again, God used the parents to save their son by having them take Him from Bethlehem to Egypt out of Herod's reach.[16]

I believe that Satan has already tried to stop God's plan to bring about the second coming of Jesus Christ. In Part Three of this book I will discuss this issue further.

Why Israel?

One other question that I would like to bring up is why did God send the Messiah to the nation of Israel? God created the world and all the inhabitants thereof and there have been many great countries and empires in world history. Yet He chose to bless the world through the Jewish people of Israel. God said to Abraham, the patriarch of the Jews, *"I will bless those who bless you, and him who curses you I will curse; and by you all the families of the earth shall bless themselves."*[17] This blessing came in the form of His Son Jesus Christ.

God declares in the Old Testament that He has bestowed His divine favor upon the Jews. In the Book of Deuteronomy, Moses writes concerning them:

> *"For you are a holy people unto the LORD your God: the LORD your God has chosen you to be a special people unto Himself, above all people that are upon the face of the earth. The LORD did not set His love upon you, nor choose you, because you were more in number than any people; for you were the fewest of all people: But because the*

> *LORD loved you, and because He would keep the oath which He had sworn unto your fathers, has the LORD brought you out with a mighty hand, and redeemed you out of the house of bondmen, from the hand of Pharaoh king of Egypt."*[18]

It is because of this passage that the world refers to the Jews as the "chosen people". God loves the Jews and therefore sent His Messiah to redeem and reconcile them to Himself. When a Gentile woman approached Jesus for help, He said to her, *"I am not sent but unto the lost sheep of the house of Israel."*[19] Of course Jesus did help this woman but He was making a point concerning the primary focus of His mission. Later on, He said that the Gentiles would be included in God's plans: *"And other sheep I have, which are not of this fold: them also I must bring, and they shall hear My voice; and there shall be one fold, and one Shepherd."*[20] But while Jesus was on the earth, He allowed God's chosen people to have the first opportunity to accept Him as the Messiah.

The apostle Paul also spoke of this when he said, *"For I am not ashamed of the gospel of Christ: for it is the power of God unto salvation to every one that believes; to the Jew first, and also to the Greek* [i.e., non-Jew or Gentile]*."*[21]

Therefore, God's plan from the beginning was to send His Messiah to Israel where the Jews lived on the land that He had granted to them. God let them know that the Messiah would be born in Bethlehem as one of the many signs that He gave to them so that they would recognize Him as their Deliverer. Of course, some of the Jews did accept Jesus as the Messiah but as a nation they rejected Him.

The next chapter will examine the life of the Messiah as prophesied by God. This will answer the question as to *what* the Messiah was going to be like when He came to earth the first time.

---

[1] *I John 3:8*
[2] *Hebrews 2:14*
[3] *Isaiah 9:6-7*
[4] *Matthew 1:18-23*

[5] *Leviticus 17:11*

[6] *Hebrews 9:22*

[7] *Romans 5:12*

[8] *Hebrews 10:1-2, 4*

[9] *Acts 20:28*

[10] *Romans 3:25*

[11] *Hebrews 4:14-15*

[12] *Matthew 2:1-6*

[13] *Luke 2:1, 3-7*

[14] That Satan was behind the plots to prevent both the birth of Moses and Jesus can be shown by looking at the scriptures in the Bible that describe the purpose and nature of Satan. The name Satan means adversary or opponent. Satan is an adversary to both humans and God. The Book of Revelation calls Satan that *"old serpent" (Revelation 12:3-4, 7-9),* which is a reference to the serpent in the Garden of Eden who deceived Adam and Eve into sinning against God. The apostle Paul in writing about the Antichrist who is going to be possessed by the Devil states that he *"opposes and exalts himself above all that is called God" (2 Thessalonians 2:3-4).* In the Old Testament it states *"And Satan stood up against Israel, and provoked David to number Israel"* which resulted in disaster for the Jewish people *(1 Chronicles 21:1-7).* Each of these verses show clearly that Satan is opposed to God and intent on harming God's people by hindering His plans. Moses' birth and life resulted in the earthly salvation of the Jewish people. Jesus' birth and life resulted in the salvation of all mankind. That Satan would not be interested in opposing God on such a monumental scale that involved millions and millions of people is beyond comprehension and would require a suspension of all logical belief.

[15] *Exodus 1:8-22; 2:1-10*

[16] *Matthew 2:1-16*

[17] *Genesis 12:3*

[18] *Deuteronomy7:6-8*

[19] *Matthew15:24*

[20] *John 10:16*

[21] *Romans 1:16*

3 - The Earthly Messiah

There was a misunderstanding among the Jews of biblical times (and continues to this day for the majority of Jews) as to what the Messiah would be like when He came to earth. Many prophecies foretold of a conquering king who would free the Jewish people from oppression. However, there were also prophecies that spoke of a different kind of Messiah. It is these latter prophecies that I will discuss in this and the next chapter.

God gave the prophet Isaiah many prophecies concerning the Messiah. He refers to the Messiah in various places as the "Branch" of the Lord and the "Servant" of the Lord. I will deal with the former appellation in this chapter and Chapter 7 and the latter in the next chapter.

I will be quoting two sections of prophetic passages from the Book of Isaiah. They are representative of the prophecies concerning the Messiah's life on earth.

Isaiah wrote:

> *"And there shall come forth a rod out of the stem of Jesse, and a Branch shall grow out of his roots: And the Spirit of the LORD shall rest upon Him, the spirit of wisdom and understanding, the spirit of counsel and might, the spirit of knowledge and of the fear of the LORD."*
>
> \- *Isaiah 11:1-2*

The first part of this verse declares that the Messiah will be of the lineage of King David whose father was Jesse. It goes on to say that the Messiah will have God's Holy Spirit dwelling inside Him and that it will be manifested through Him. This can only mean that there will be something unique about Him. God will clearly be seen as working in the Messiah. He will have God's Spirit, God's wisdom, God's understanding, God's power, God's knowledge, and an understanding of whom God is.

Fulfillment by Jesus Christ:

> *"The book of the generation of Jesus Christ, the son of David, the son of Abraham...And Jesse begat David the king...And Jacob begat Joseph the husband of Mary, of whom was born Jesus, who is called Christ."*[1]

The Gospel of Matthew gives an abbreviated genealogy of Jesus that shows He descended from Jesse and his son King David. The next passage will demonstrate that God's Spirit was indeed manifested in Jesus:

> *"Then came Jesus from Galilee to Jordan unto John, to be baptized of him...And Jesus, when He was baptized, went up straightway out of the water: and, lo, the heavens were opened unto Him, and he saw the Spirit of God descending like a dove, and lighting upon Him: And lo a voice from heaven, saying, This is My beloved Son, in Whom I am well pleased."*[2]

> *"And Jesus being full of the Holy Spirit returned from Jordan, and was led by the Spirit into the wilderness, being forty days tempted of the Devil...And Jesus returned in the power of the Spirit into Galilee and there went out a fame of Him through all the region round about."*[3]

The people of Jesus' day recognized that He had the fullness of God's Spirit residing in Him. They also clearly saw God's wisdom working through Jesus.

Jesus had gone to the Temple in Jerusalem during the Feast of Tabernacles and was teaching the multitude. As He finished speaking the Jewish Temple guard sought to arrest Him but instead were in awe at the wisdom of His words:

> *"So there was a division among the people because of [Jesus]. And some of them would have taken Him; but no man laid hands on Him. Then came the officers to the chief priests and Pharisees; and they said unto them, Why have ye not brought Him? The officers answered, Never man spoke like this man."*[4]

Even the enemies of Jesus recognized that God was speaking through Him. It was after this divisive teaching that some of the Jews declared Jesus to be the Prophet spoken of by Moses.

That Jesus had the wisdom, understanding, and knowledge of God was revealed to those who did not believe in Him:

> *"But there were certain of the scribes sitting there, and reasoning in their hearts, Why does this man thus speak blasphemies? Who can forgive sins but God only? And immediately when Jesus perceived in His spirit that they so reasoned within themselves, He said unto them, Why reason you these things in your hearts?"*[5]

> *"Then went the Pharisees, and took counsel how they might entangle Him in His talk. And they sent out unto Him their disciples with the Herodians, saying, Master, we know that Thou art true, and teach the way of God in truth, neither care Thou for any man: for Thou regardest not the person of men. Tell us therefore, What thinkest Thou? Is it lawful to give tribute unto Caesar, or not? But Jesus perceived their wickedness, and said, Why tempt ye Me, you hypocrites?"*[6]

Jesus understood exactly what others were thinking and feeling. This type of knowledge is only possible by the Spirit of God.

Jesus manifested the might or power of God in many ways. I will mention only a couple of them.

"And a certain woman, which had an issue of blood twelve years, And had suffered many things of many physicians, and had spent all that she had, and was nothing bettered, but rather grew worse, When she had heard of Jesus, came in the press behind, and touched His garment...And straightway the fountain of her blood was dried up; and she felt in her body that she was healed of that plague. And Jesus, immediately knowing in Himself that power had gone out of Him."[7]

Only the power of God can *miraculously* heal health problems that human beings have suffered since the beginning of man's history. This woman had been to many doctors yet in this case, they had been unable to heal her. She was healed by simply touching Jesus' garment because of who He was.

Jesus exhibited another aspect of God's power that resided in Him while He was with the disciples in a boat on the Sea of Galilee:

"And when He was entered into a ship, His disciples followed Him. And, behold, there arose a great tempest in the sea, insomuch that the ship was covered with the waves: but He was asleep. And His disciples came to Him and woke Him, saying, Lord, save us: we perish. And He said unto them, Why are you fearful, O ye of little faith? Then He arose, and rebuked the winds and the sea; and there was a great calm. But the men marveled, saying, What manner of man is this, that even the winds and the sea obey Him!"[8]

There is a saying that everyone complains about the weather but no one does anything about it. In the verse above, eyewitnesses saw Jesus miraculously change the weather, an act that is only possible by the power of God.

Events such as these led the disciples of Jesus to believe that He had the power of God and was the Messiah. The New Testament records many miracles that Jesus performed while He was on the earth. The apostle John mentions many miracles that Jesus did that were not written down, *"This is the disciple which testifies of these things, and wrote these things: and we know that his testimony is true. And there are also many other things which Jesus did, the which, if they should be written every one, I suppose that even the world itself could not contain the books that should be written"*[9] It was the miracles that Jesus' followers had personally observed that caused them to willingly die for these beliefs because they *knew* they were true.[10]

The last point on this section has to do with Jesus' knowledge of God, knowledge that Isaiah prophesied the Messiah would have.

Jesus had just finished miraculously feeding a multitude of more than five thousand men, women, and children with just five loaves of bread and two fish. This miracle once again led some of the Jewish people to declare that Jesus was the Messiah spoken of by Moses: *"Then those men, when they had seen the miracle that Jesus did, said, This is of a truth that Prophet that should come into the world. When Jesus therefore perceived that they would come and take Him by force, to make Him a king, He departed again into a mountain Himself alone."*[11] The next day Jesus and His disciples crossed the Sea of Galilee where He once again taught the multitudes. He is telling them about His relationship with God, His Father:

> *"For I came down from heaven, not to do Mine own will, but the will of Him that sent Me...No man can come to Me, except the Father which has sent Me draw him: and I will raise him up at the last day. It is written in the prophets, And they shall be all taught of God. Every man therefore that has heard, and has learned of the Father, comes unto Me. Not that any man has seen the Father, except He which is of God, He has seen the Father."*[12]

In the Old Testament Moses had made a request of God to see His glory. God responded: *"I will make all My goodness pass before you, and I will proclaim the name of the LORD before you; and will be gracious to whom I will be gracious, and will show mercy on whom I will show mercy. And He said, You can not see My face: for there shall no man see Me, and live."*[13] Jesus was born of a human woman yet He was able to see the Father and live. As I pointed out in the last chapter, there was a divine aspect to the birth of Jesus. He had come down from heaven where He had seen and *known* the Father.

The following verses illustrate that Jesus had a unique knowledge of God such as the Messiah would have according to Isaiah:

> *"I am one that bears witness of Myself, and the Father that sent Me bears witness of Me. Then said they unto Him, Where is thy Father? Jesus answered, You neither know Me, nor My Father: if you had known Me, you should have known My Father also."*[14]

> *"Then said they unto Him, Who art thou? And Jesus said unto them, Even the same that I said unto you from the beginning. I have many things to say and to judge of you: but He that sent Me is true; and I speak to the world those things which I have heard of Him. They understood not that He spoke to them of the Father. Then said Jesus unto them, When you have lifted up the Son of man, then shall you know that I am He, and that I do nothing of Myself; but as My Father has taught Me, I speak these things. And He that sent Me is with Me: the Father has not left Me alone; for I do always those things that please Him. As He spoke these words, many believed on Him."*[15]

> *"As the Father knows Me, even so know I the Father: and I lay down My life for the sheep."*[16]

> *"If I do not the works of My Father, believe Me not. But if I do, though you believe not Me, believe the works: that you may know, and believe, that the Father is in Me, and I in Him."*[17]

> *"Jesus said unto Him, I am the way, the truth, and the life: no man comes unto the Father, but by Me. If you had known Me, you should have known My Father also: and from henceforth you know Him, and have seen Him."*[18]

Jesus had knowledge of God unlike anyone before or since He came to earth. After hearing Him and seeing the miracles that He performed, many people did indeed declare Him the Messiah.

Another prophecy of Isaiah foretold of the acts that the Messiah would perform when He came to earth:

> *"The Spirit of the Lord GOD is upon Me; because the LORD has anointed Me to preach good tidings unto the meek; He has sent Me to bind up the brokenhearted, to proclaim liberty to the captives, and the opening of the prison to them that are bound; To proclaim the acceptable year of the LORD, and the day of vengeance of our God; to comfort all that mourn; To appoint unto them that mourn in Zion, to give unto them beauty for ashes, the oil of joy for mourning, the garment of praise for the spirit of heaviness; that they might be called trees of righteousness, the planting of the LORD, that He might be glorified."*
>
> *- Isaiah 61:1-3*

As we saw in the first prophecy listed above, the Spirit of God was to be manifested through the Messiah. Here again Isaiah prophesies that the Spirit of God would be seen in the Messiah.

The interesting wording of this passage is written in such a way that the Messiah is speaking in the first person here. The key phrase is *"the LORD has anointed Me"*. The word "anointed" is translated from the Hebrew word "mashach" which is the root of the Hebrew word "mashiach". It is from this second word that we get the English translation "Messiah". The translation of this latter word into Greek is "christos" from which we get the English word "Christ".

According to this passage, the Messiah will preach the good news (i.e., "gospel" in the New Testament) to the humble. He will also heal those that are hurting and proclaim freedom to those who are in bondage. He will give hope to those who are downcast and grieving. He will announce that the time of God's will for suffering humanity is at hand.

Fulfillment by Jesus Christ:

At the beginning of His earthly ministry, Jesus Christ quoted this prophecy in a synagogue in Nazareth:

> *"And [Jesus] came to Nazareth, where He had been brought up: and, as His custom was, He went into the synagogue on the Sabbath day, and stood up for to read. And there was delivered unto Him the book of the prophet Isaiah. And when He had opened the book, He found the place where it was written, The Spirit of the Lord is upon Me, because He has anointed Me to preach the gospel to the poor; He has sent Me to heal the brokenhearted, to preach deliverance to the captives, and recovering of sight to the blind, to set at liberty them that are bruised, To preach the acceptable year of the Lord. And He closed the book, and He gave it again to the minister, and sat down. And the eyes of all them that were in the synagogue were fastened on Him. And He began to say unto them, This day is this scripture fulfilled in your ears."*[19]

The last line of this verse was earthshaking to the Jewish listeners in the synagogue. Jesus was clearly claiming that He was the fulfillment of this Messianic prophecy. This did not sit well with the Jews who were there. Their wrath and indignation welled up within them and they grabbed Him and led Him to a nearby cliff to throw Him off the edge. The Gospel writer merely states that Jesus was able to depart from the midst of them and go His way.

The New Testament testifies clearly that the Spirit of the Lord was upon Jesus. As I already noted, Jesus had been conceived by the Holy Spirit[20] and thus was always full of the Spirit during His life. However, it seems that God gave Him a special anointing of the Holy Spirit at His baptism to begin His ministry: *"Then Jesus came from Galilee to the Jordan to John, to be baptized by him. John would have prevented him, saying, "I need to be baptized by you, and do you come to me?" But Jesus answered him, "Let it be so now; for thus it is fitting for us to fulfill all righteousness." Then he consented. And when Jesus was baptized, He went up immediately from the water, and behold, the heavens were opened and He saw the Spirit of God descending like a dove, and alighting on Him; and lo, a voice from heaven, saying, "This is My beloved Son, with whom I am well pleased."*[21]

After this episode, Jesus went about accomplishing the things that Isaiah spoke of. He started His ministry in Galilee which was the fulfillment of another prophecy given to Isaiah, *"Nevertheless the dimness shall not be such as was in her vexation, when at the first he lightly afflicted the land of Zebulun and the land of Naphtali, and afterward did more grievously afflict her by the way of the sea, beyond Jordan, in Galilee of the nations. The people that walked in darkness have seen a great Light: they that dwell in the land of the shadow of death, upon them has the Light shined."*[22]

> *"Now when Jesus had heard that John [the Baptist] was cast into prison, He departed into Galilee; And leaving Nazareth, He came and dwelt in Capernaum, which is upon the sea coast, in the borders of Zabulon and Nephthalim...From that time Jesus began to preach, and to say, Repent: for the kingdom of heaven is at hand."*[23]

It was in Galilee where Jesus started preaching the *"good tidings"* to the people and started healing *"the brokenhearted"* and delivering *"the captives"* from sin and sickness:

> *"And Jesus went about all Galilee, teaching in their synagogues, and preaching the gospel of the kingdom, and healing all manner of sickness and all manner of disease among the people. And His fame went throughout all Syria: and they brought unto Him all sick people that were taken with divers diseases and torments, and those which were possessed with devils, and those which were lunatics, and those that had the palsy; and He healed them."*[24]

The Gospels in the New Testament are full of healing miracles that Jesus performed while He was on the earth. However, I will not take the time to list them here. Suffice it to say, there were many eyewitnesses to miraculous deeds that Jesus did.

I do want to mention one other event that took place to illustrate how religious leaders of that day misunderstood Jesus' mission on earth. It pertains to the last section of the prophecy under discussion here which states that the Messiah will: *"...comfort all that mourn; To appoint unto them that mourn in Zion, to give unto them beauty for ashes, the oil of joy for mourning, the garment of praise for the spirit of heaviness; that they might be called trees of righteousness...".*

There was a tragic woman who was overcome by the sins that she had committed in her life. She came to Jesus distraught by the life that she had lived. The Gospel writer Luke relates the story:

> *"And one of the Pharisees desired Him that He would eat with him. And He went into the Pharisee's house, and sat down to meat. And, behold, a woman in the city, which was a sinner, when she knew that Jesus sat at meat in the Pharisee's house, brought an alabaster box of ointment, And stood at His feet behind Him weeping, and began to wash His feet with tears, and did wipe them with the hairs of her head, and kissed His feet, and anointed them with the ointment. Now when the Pharisee which had bidden Him saw it, he spoke within himself, saying, This man, if He were a prophet, would have known who and what manner of woman this is that touches Him: for she is a sinner. And Jesus answering said unto him, Simon, I have somewhat to say unto you. And he said, Master, say on. There was a certain creditor which had two debtors: the one owed five hundred pence, and the other fifty. And when they had nothing to pay, he frankly forgave them both. Tell Me therefore, which of them will love him most? Simon answered and said, I suppose that he, to whom he forgave most. And He said unto him, You have rightly judged. And He turned to the woman, and said unto Simon, Seest thou this woman? I entered into your house, you gave Me no water for My feet: but she has washed My feet with tears, and wiped them with the hairs of her head. You gave Me no kiss: but this woman since the time I came in has not ceased to kiss My feet. My head with oil you did not anoint:*

but this woman has anointed My feet with ointment. Wherefore I say unto you, Her sins, which are many, are forgiven; for she loved much: but to whom little is forgiven, the same loves little. And He said unto her, Your sins are forgiven. And they that sat at meat with Him began to say within themselves, Who is this that forgives sins also? And He said to the woman, Your faith has saved you; go in peace."[25]

The saddest part of this story is that the religious leader, Simon, did not see past his own understanding of what the Messiah would be like. He, like most of the religious leaders, was probably expecting the Messiah to come and triumph over the Roman government. He ignored or rationalized prophecies such as this one in Isaiah that spoke of the Messiah being merciful and compassionate to the downtrodden.

There were however, those people who did see in Jesus' ministry the work of the promised Messiah:

"And many of the people believed on Him, and said, When Messiah comes, will He do more miracles than these which this man has done?"[26]

Throughout His earthly ministry, Jesus manifested the wisdom of God, the knowledge of God, the power of God, the mercy of God, and the love of God. All of these characteristics were a fulfillment of the Messianic prophecies given in the Old Testament.

In the next chapter, I will show that not only would the Messiah not come in triumph the first time but also that He would suffer and be killed at the hands of humanity.

---

1 *Matthew 1:1-16*
2 *Matthew 3:13, 16-17*
3 *Luke 4:1-2a, 14*
4 *John 7:43-46*
5 *Mark 2:6-8*
6 *Matthew 22:15-18*
7 *Matthew 5:25-27, 29-30*

[8] *Matthew 8:23-27*

[9] *John 21:24-25*

[10] -The New Testament records the death of the apostle James, son of Zebedee: *"Now about that time Herod the king stretched forth his hands to vex certain of the church. And he killed James the brother of John with the sword" (Acts 12:1-2).*

-The Jewish historian, Josephus, described the death of James, the brother of Jesus: "...Ananus, who, as we have told you already, took the high priesthood, was a bold man in his temper, and very insolent; he was also of the sect of the Sadducees, who are very rigid in judging offenders, above all the rest of the Jews, as we have already observed; when, therefore, Ananus was of this disposition, he thought he had now a proper opportunity [to exercise his authority]. Festus was now dead, and Albinus was but upon the road; so he assembled the sanhedrim of judges, and brought before them the brother of Jesus, who was called Christ, whose name was James, and some others, [or, some of his companions]; and when he had formed an accusation against them as breakers of the law, he delivered them to be stoned" ["Antiquities of the Jews", Book XX, Ch. IX, Sec. 1].

-The early church historian Eusebius (ca. 300 A.D.) wrote of the apostle Peter's death: "Meanwhile the holy apostles and disciples of our Saviour were dispersed throughout the world ...Peter appears to have preached in Pontus, Galatia, Bithynia, Cappadocia, and Asia to the Jews of the dispersion. And at last, having come to Rome, he was crucified head-downwards; for he had requested that he might suffer in this way" ["History of the Church", Book 3, Sec. 1].

-The secular Roman historian Tacitus recorded the persecution of the early Christians by Nero who made them the scapegoat for the fire that burned Rome in 64 A.D.: "But all human efforts, all the lavish gifts of the emperor, and the propitiations of the gods, did not banish the sinister belief that the conflagration was the result of an order [i.e., by Nero]. Consequently, to get rid of the report, Nero fastened the guilt and inflicted the most exquisite tortures on a class hated for their abominations, called Christians by the populace. Christus, from whom the name had its origin, suffered the extreme penalty during the reign of Tiberius at the hands of one of our procurators, Pontius Pilatus" ["The Annals", Tacitus, ca. 109 A.D.]

[11] *John 6:14-15*

[12] *John 6:38, 44-46*

[13] *Exodus 33:19-20*

[14] *John 8:18-19*
[15] *John 8:25-30*
[16] *John 10:15*
[17] *John 10:38*
[18] *John 14:6-7*
[19] *Luke 4:16:21*
[20] *Matthew 1:20*
[21] *Matthew 3:13-17*
[22] *Isaiah 9:1-2*
[23] *Matthew 4:12-13, 17*
[24] *Matthew 4:23-24*
[25] *Luke 7:36-50*
[26] *John 7:31*

4 – The Death of Messiah?

The greatest obstacle for the Jews of today concerning Jesus is that they reject the idea that the Messiah was supposed to be killed. They, like the Jews of biblical times, expect the Messiah to come in triumphal glory. They cannot accept the idea that God's plan included two comings of the Messiah nor that the Messiah would be killed. Nevertheless, the Old Testament clearly points out that the Messiah was to be a suffering servant of humanity at some point in time. This chapter will highlight some of those prophecies and show how Jesus fulfilled the role of the suffering Servant. I want to mention that there have been Jews who have accepted Jesus as the Messiah because of the preciseness of these prophecies.

There are several writers of the Old Testament that foretell of the suffering Messiah. We turn first to the Book of Isaiah to start this discussion:

> *"Behold, My Servant shall deal prudently, He shall be exalted and extolled, and be very high. As many were astonished at You; His visage was so marred more than any man, and His form more than the sons of men: So shall He sprinkle many nations; the kings shall shut their mouths at Him: for that which had not been told them shall they see; and that which they had not heard shall they consider. Who has believed our report? and to whom is the arm of the LORD revealed? For He shall grow up before Him as a tender plant, and as a root out of a dry ground: He has no form nor comeliness; and when we shall see Him, there is no beauty that we should desire Him. He is despised and rejected of men; a Man of sorrows, and acquainted with*

grief: and we hid as it were our faces from Him; He was despised, and we esteemed Him not. Surely He has borne our griefs, and carried our sorrows: yet we did esteem Him stricken, smitten of God, and afflicted. But He was wounded for our transgressions, He was bruised for our iniquities: the chastisement of our peace was upon Him; and with His stripes we are healed. All we like sheep have gone astray; we have turned every one to his own way; and the LORD hath laid on Him the iniquity of us all. He was oppressed, and He was afflicted, yet he opened not His mouth: He is brought as a lamb to the slaughter, and as a sheep before her shearers is dumb, so He opened not His mouth. He was taken from prison and from judgment: and who shall declare His generation? for He was cut off out of the land of the living: for the transgression of My people was He stricken. And He made His grave with the wicked, and with the rich in His death; because He had done no violence, neither was any deceit in His mouth. Yet it pleased the LORD to bruise Him; He has put Him to grief: when You shall make His soul an offering for sin, He shall see His seed, He shall prolong His days, and the pleasure of the LORD shall prosper in His hand. He shall see of the travail of His soul, and shall be satisfied: by His knowledge shall My righteous Servant justify many; for He shall bear their iniquities. Therefore will I divide Him a portion with the great, and He shall divide the spoil with the strong; because He has poured out His soul unto death: and He was numbered with the transgressors; and He bore the sin of many, and made intercession for the transgressors."

- Isaiah 52:13-53:12

Some Jewish commentators believe that the Servant mentioned in this passage refers to the nation of Israel. They say that the Jewish people are being punished for their sins and that they are to atone for them by suffering affliction and persecution. The problem with this theory is that God required an unblemished creature to be an atoning sacrifice to Him. If the Jewish nation were in sin then it would be blemished. Therefore, the nation of Israel would not be an acceptable sacrifice to the Lord and could not be this suffering Servant.

The New Testament shows that Isaiah's prophetic description of the suffering Servant-Messiah is realized in Jesus Christ.

Fulfillment by Jesus Christ:

> *"Behold, My Servant shall deal prudently, He shall be exalted and extolled, and be very high. As many were astonished at you; His visage was so marred more than any man, and His form more than the sons of men: So shall He sprinkle many nations; the kings shall shut their mouths at Him: for that which had not been told them shall they see; and that which they had not heard shall they consider. Who has believed our report? and to whom is the arm of the LORD revealed? For He shall grow up before Him as a tender plant, and as a root out of a dry ground: He has no form nor comeliness; and when we shall see Him, there is no beauty that we should desire Him.*
>
> *- Isaiah 52:13-53:2*

Through the last two millennia Jesus has been exalted and extolled and kings and rulers have been in awe of Him. The French emperor Napoleon reportedly said, "I know men and I tell you that Jesus Christ is no mere man. Between him and every other person in the world, there is no possible term of comparison. Alexander, Caesar, Charlemagne, and I founded empires. But on what did we rest the creations of our genius? Upon force. Jesus Christ founded His Empire upon love; and at this hour millions of people would die for Him."[1] The Fourth Century Roman emperor Constantine changed the course of the Roman Empire and the world when he became a follower of Jesus Christ.

This prophecy goes on to say that the Messiah's appearance would be horribly disfigured: *"His visage was so marred more than any man."* A controversial movie came out in 2004 called "The Passion of the Christ". It portrays Jesus' body as it probably looked after the Romans had finished with Him during His arrest, scourging, and crucifixion. Some of the movie's critical "experts" said that the

Gospels were not explicit in their description of scourging. Therefore, the film's graphic depiction of that flogging may be historically inaccurate. I would like to counter this criticism with the words of the Jewish historian Josephus who lived from 37 A.D. to 100 A.D. He had participated in the Jewish revolt against Rome that started in 66 A.D. After that war ended he wrote a history of it. In that history he described what happened to a Jewish man who had prophesied of the Jewish Temple's destruction a few years before that war began. This man's prophecy had angered the Jewish rulers so they took him to the Romans to be punished:

"Hereupon our rulers, supposing, as the case proved to be, that this was a sort of divine fury in the man, brought him to the Roman procurator, *where he was whipped till his bones were laid bare*; yet he did not make any supplication for himself, nor shed any tears, but turning his voice to the most lamentable tone possible, at every stroke of the whip his answer was, 'Woe, woe to Jerusalem!'"[2]

Therefore, the depiction of the scourging of Jesus (which occurred some thirty years before the Jewish revolt) in this movie was probably a fair portrayal of the viciousness of it. I am sure that Jesus' appearance was grotesque after such a physical ordeal as the New Testament would indicate:

> *"Then Pilate therefore took Jesus, and scourged Him. And the soldiers platted a crown of thorns, and put it on His head, and they put on Him a purple robe, And said, Hail, King of the Jews! and they smote Him with their hands."*[3]

> *"He is despised and rejected of men; a Man of sorrows, and acquainted with grief: and we hid as it were our faces from Him; He was despised, and we esteemed Him not."*
>
> *- Isaiah 53:3*

Jesus is still despised by some people in this day and age. I believe the primary cause of this is because His life and death reminds them of their sinfulness. At the time of His crucifixion, the people mocked Him while He was dying on the cross for the sins of humanity (which included the sins of those who were mocking Him):

"Pilate said unto them, What shall I do then with Jesus which is called Christ? They all said unto him, Let Him be crucified."[4]

"And they that passed by reviled Him, wagging their heads, And saying, You that destroys the temple, and builds it in three days, save Thyself. If You be the Son of God, come down from the cross. Likewise also the chief priests mocking Him, with the scribes and elders, said, He saved others; Himself He cannot save. If He be the King of Israel, let Him now come down from the cross, and we will believe Him. He trusted in God; let Him deliver Him now, if He will have Him: for He said, I am the Son of God."[5]

"Surely He has borne our griefs, and carried our sorrows: yet we did esteem Him stricken, smitten of God, and afflicted. But He was wounded for our transgressions, He was bruised for our iniquities: the chastisement of our peace was upon Him; and with His stripes we are healed. All we like sheep have gone astray; we have turned every one to his own way; and the LORD has laid on Him the iniquity of us all."

- Isaiah 53:4-6

The New Testament states that Jesus died for the sins of the world. He was smitten by God to be acceptable sacrifice on behalf of humanity's sins:

"The next day John [the Baptist] saw Jesus coming unto him, and said, Behold the Lamb of God, which takes away the sin of the world."[6]

"Grace be to you and peace from God the Father, and from our Lord Jesus Christ, Who gave Himself for our sins, that

He might deliver us from this present evil world, according to the will of God and our Father."[7]

"For then must He often have suffered since the foundation of the world: but now once in the end of the world has He appeared to put away sin by the sacrifice of Himself. And as it is appointed unto men once to die, but after this the judgment: So Christ was once offered to bear the sins of many; and unto them that look for Him shall He appear the second time without sin unto salvation."[8]

"He was oppressed, and He was afflicted, yet he opened not His mouth: He is brought as a lamb to the slaughter, and as a sheep before her shearers is dumb, so He opened not His mouth. He was taken from prison and from judgment: And who shall declare His generation?"

- Isaiah 53:7-8a

How many people, falsely accused of breaking the law, would stand quietly by while their enemies prosecuted them? Jesus did exactly that. It was not only because it fulfilled this prophecy but also because it was God's will for Jesus to die a sacrificial death:

"And the high priest arose, and said unto Him, Answerest thou nothing? What is it which these witness against Thee? But Jesus held His peace."[9]

"And when He was accused of the chief priests and elders, He answered nothing. Then said Pilate unto Him, Hearest thou not how many things they witness against Thee? And He answered him to never a word; insomuch that the governor marveled greatly."[10]

"And when Herod saw Jesus, he was exceeding glad: for he was desirous to see Him of a long season, because he had heard many things of Him; and He hoped to have seen some miracle done by Him. Then he questioned with Him

in many words; but He answered him nothing."[11]

"...for He was cut off out of the land of the living: for the transgression of My people was He stricken. And He made His grave with the wicked, and with the rich in His death; because He had done no violence, neither was any deceit in His mouth."

- Isaiah 53:8b-9

By His crucifixion, Jesus was cut off out of the land of the living because of the sins of the world. His death occurred because of the sins of the wicked yet Jesus was buried in the grave of a rich man who believed in Him. Through Jesus' sacrificial death, even the wicked can have their sins forgiven if they choose to repent of their deeds. Not only did Jesus not utter deceitful words, He *was* truth personified:

"And all things are of God, Who has reconciled us to Himself by Jesus Christ, and has given to us the ministry of reconciliation; To wit, that God was in Christ, reconciling the world unto Himself, not imputing their trespasses unto them; and has committed unto us the word of reconciliation."[12]

"Say unto them, As I live, saith the Lord GOD, I have no pleasure in the death of the wicked; but that the wicked turn from his way and live: turn ye, turn ye from your evil ways; for why will ye die, O house of Israel?"[13]

"When the even was come, there came a rich man of Arimathaea, named Joseph, who also himself was Jesus' disciple: He went to Pilate, and begged the body of Jesus. Then Pilate commanded the body to be delivered. And when Joseph had taken the body, he wrapped it in a clean linen cloth, And laid it in his own new tomb, which he had hewn out in the rock: and he rolled a great stone to the door of the sepulcher, and departed."[14]

"For I have not spoken of Myself; but the Father which sent Me, He gave Me a commandment, what I should say, and what I should speak."[15]

"Jesus said unto him, I am the way, the TRUTH, and the life: no man cometh unto the Father, but by Me."[16]

"Yet it pleased the LORD to bruise Him; He has put Him to grief: when you shall make His soul an offering for sin, He shall see His seed, He shall prolong His days, and the pleasure of the LORD shall prosper in His hand. He shall see of the travail of His soul, and shall be satisfied: by His knowledge shall My righteous Servant justify many; for He shall bear their iniquities."

- Isaiah 53:10-11

It was the Lord's will to offer up His Son as a sacrifice for the sins of the world so that He could reconcile the world to Himself. The travail or anguish of Jesus' soul was exhibited in the Garden of Gethsemane. Yet He obeyed willingly His Father's plans because He loved humankind:

"So Christ was once offered to bear the sins of many; and unto them that look for Him shall He appear the second time without sin unto salvation."[17]

"For He has made Him to be sin for us, Who knew no sin; that we might be made the righteousness of God in Him."[18]

"Then came Jesus with them unto a place called Gethsemane, and said unto the disciples, Sit ye here, while I go and pray yonder...Then said He unto them, My soul is exceeding sorrowful, even unto death: tarry ye here, and watch with Me. And He went a little further, and fell on His face, and prayed, saying, O My Father, if it be possible, let this cup pass from Me: nevertheless not as I will, but as You will."[19]

"For God so loved the world, that He gave His only begotten Son, that whosoever believeth in Him should not perish, but have everlasting life. For God sent not His Son into the world to condemn the world; but that the world through Him might be saved."[20]

"Therefore will I divide Him a portion with the great, and He shall divide the spoil with the strong; because He has poured out His soul unto death: and He was numbered with the transgressors; and He bore the sin of many, and made intercession for the transgressors."

- Isaiah 53:12

Jesus did finish the mission His Father had sent Him to do. He was among transgressors when He died and He did make intercession for them *on the cross*:

"When Jesus therefore had received the vinegar, He said, It is finished: and He bowed His head, and gave up the spirit."[21]

"For I say unto you, that this that is written must yet be accomplished in Me, And He was reckoned among the transgressors: for the things concerning Me have an end."[22]

"And there were also two other, malefactors, led with Him to be put to death. And when they were come to the place, which is called Calvary, there they crucified Him, and the malefactors, one on the right hand, and the other on the left. Then said Jesus, Father, forgive them; for they know not what they do." [23]

This entire passage in Isaiah is clearly speaking of a personal Messiah. A Messiah that was not triumphant over the armies of men but a Messiah that was triumphant over the forces of sin by being *"cut off out of the land of the living"*.

There is another prophecy in the Book of Isaiah that has similarities in the description of the suffering Messiah with the passage we just looked at. There are also some added depictions in this prophecy concerning the activities and nature of the Messiah. As will be seen below, this passage is an accurate description of Jesus Christ and His ministry on earth:

> *"Behold My Servant, whom I uphold; mine Elect, in whom My soul delights; I have put My Spirit upon Him: He shall bring forth judgment to the Gentiles. He shall not cry, nor lift up, nor cause His voice to be heard in the street. A bruised reed shall He not break, and the smoking flax shall He not quench: He shall bring forth judgment unto truth. He shall not fail nor be discouraged, till He have set judgment in the earth: and the isles shall wait for His law. Thus saith God the LORD, He that created the heavens, and stretched them out; He that spread forth the earth, and that which cometh out of it; He that gives breath unto the people upon it, and spirit to them that walk therein: I the LORD have called Thee in righteousness, and will hold Your hand, and will keep You, and give You for a covenant of the people, for a light of the Gentiles; To open the blind eyes, to bring out the prisoners from the prison, and them that sit in darkness out of the prison house."*
>
> \- *Isaiah 42:1-7*

Fulfillment by Jesus Christ:

> *"Behold My Servant, whom I uphold; mine Elect, in whom My soul delights; I have put My Spirit upon Him: He shall bring forth judgment to the Gentiles."*
>
> \- *Isaiah 42:1*

Here again, this Servant of God is to have God's Spirit upon Him and God will delight in Him:

"And Jesus, when He was baptized, went up straightway out of the water: and, lo, the heavens were opened unto Him, and he saw the Spirit of God descending like a dove, and lighting upon Him: And lo a voice from heaven, saying, This is My beloved Son, in Whom I am well pleased."[24]

"He shall not cry, nor lift up, nor cause His voice to be heard in the street. A bruised reed shall He not break, and the smoking flax shall He not quench: He shall bring forth judgment unto truth. He shall not fail nor be discouraged, till He have set judgment in the earth: and the isles shall wait for His law."
- Isaiah 42:2-4

We have already seen how Jesus did not cry out before His accusers. It is noteworthy that in this prophecy God calls His Servant-Messiah a "*bruised reed*". This hearkens back to the first Messianic prophecy in the Bible:

"And I will put enmity between you [i.e., the Devil] *and the woman, and between your seed and her seed; it shall bruise your head, and you shall bruise His heel."*[25]

As mentioned earlier in this book, the "bruise" was the crucifixion of Jesus.

Jesus did bring forth the truth of God during His ministry. God will judge humanity against the standard of His perfection through Jesus Christ. This perfection is only attainable through a person accepting the sacrificial death of Jesus as atonement for their sins. Jesus will set His judgment upon the earth and issue His laws to *"the isles"* at His second coming.

"Thus saith God the LORD, He that created the heavens, and stretched them out; He that spread forth the earth, and that which cometh out of it; He that gives breath unto the people upon it, and spirit to them that walk therein: I the LORD have called Thee in righteousness, and will hold

Your hand, and will keep You, and give You for a covenant of the people, for a light of the Gentiles;"

- Isaiah 42:5-6

God declared that He was going to give His Servant *"for a covenant of the people*" and *"for a light of the Gentiles"*. I find it interesting that here in the Old Testament, which is written primarily about God's relationship with the Jewish people, He includes the Gentiles in this Messianic covenant. The Jewish prophet Jeremiah speaks of this same covenant in his prophetic book:

"Behold, the days come, saith the LORD, that I will make a new covenant with the house of Israel, and with the house of Judah: Not according to the covenant that I made with their fathers in the day that I took them by the hand to bring them out of the land of Egypt; which My covenant they broke, although I was an husband unto them, saith the LORD: But this shall be the covenant that I will make with the house of Israel; After those days, saith the LORD, I will put My law in their inward parts, and write it in their hearts; and will be their God, and they shall be My people."[26]

The Old Testament teaches that the first covenant between God and the Jewish people required the Jews to keep and obey the Laws of God. The Jews were required to circumcise their males eight days after they were born as a sign that their children would be under this covenant. Jeremiah prophesied here that a *new* covenant between God and His people would require, not an outward keeping of God's Laws, but that they would allow the "spirit" of His Law to be written upon their hearts. This new "circumcision of their hearts" would be the basis of a relationship between God and all humans.

The New Testament declares that Jesus is this new covenant that God promised to both the Jews and the Gentiles:

"And as they were eating, Jesus took bread, and blessed it, and broke it, and gave it to the disciples, and said, Take, eat; this is My body. And He took the cup, and gave thanks,

> *and gave it to them, saying, Drink ye all of it; For this is My blood of the new covenant, which is shed for many for the remission of sins."*[27]

> *"And to Jesus the mediator of the new covenant, and to the blood of sprinkling, that speaks better things than that of Abel."*[28]

> *"Now the God of peace, which brought again from the dead our Lord Jesus, that great Shepherd of the sheep, through the blood of the everlasting covenant"*[29]

> *"Wherefore remember, that you being in time past Gentiles in the flesh, who are called Uncircumcision by that which is called the Circumcision in the flesh made by hands; That at that time you were without Christ, being aliens from the commonwealth of Israel, and strangers from the covenants of promise, having no hope, and without God in the world: But now in Christ Jesus you who sometimes were far off are made near by the blood of Christ."*[30]

> *"To open the blind eyes, to bring out the prisoners from the prison, and them that sit in darkness out of the prison house."*
>
> *- Isaiah 42:7*

Lastly, according to this prophecy of Isaiah's the Messiah would open the eyes of the blind. The New Testament Gospels relate several miracles where Jesus healed blind people:

> *"And, behold, two blind men sitting by the way side, when they heard that Jesus passed by, cried out, saying, Have mercy on us, O Lord, thou Son of David...And Jesus stood still, and called them, and said, What will ye that I shall do unto you? They said unto Him, Lord, that our eyes may be opened. So Jesus had compassion on them, and touched their eyes: and immediately their eyes received sight, and they followed Him."*[31]

> *"Then was brought unto Him one possessed with a devil, blind, and dumb: and He healed him, insomuch that the blind and dumb both spoke and saw."*[32]

Jesus used these prophetic passages in Isaiah chapters 52-53 and 42 to identify Himself as the Messiah to John the Baptist. John had been thrown into prison by King Herod Antipas.[33] While he was lying in prison John began to question whether Jesus was indeed the Messiah. It seems that he, like so many other Jews, was expecting a triumphant Messiah to come in order to overthrow the Roman government:

> *"Now when John had heard in the prison the works of Christ, he sent two of his disciples, And said unto Him, Are you He* [i.e., the Messiah] *that should come, or do we look for another? Jesus answered and said unto them, Go and show John again those things which you do hear and see: The blind receive their sight, and the lame walk, the lepers are cleansed, and the deaf hear, the dead are raised up, and the poor have the gospel preached to them. And blessed is he, whosoever shall not be offended in Me."*[34]

When Isaiah uttered these prophecies, it was as though He was describing Jesus' life as if he had personally witnessed it taking place. The amazing part of this is that Isaiah spoke these prophecies *seven hundred years before* Jesus came to earth.

Crucifixion and the Messiah

God chose King David to be the ruler over the nation of Israel because he was a *"man after [My] own heart."*[35] God gave David many gifts of talent, one of which was the gift of prophetic utterance. There are several psalms written by him that pertain to the Messiah. I want to focus on one of them. As you read this psalm, you will see that he is plainly describing a crucifixion, a form of capital punishment that would not be invented until three hundred years after the death of King David:

> *"My God, my God, why have You forsaken me? Why are You so far from helping me, and from the words of my roaring? O my God, I cry in the daytime, but You hear not; and in the night season, and am not silent. But You are holy, O You that inhabits the praises of Israel. Our fathers trusted in You: they trusted, and You did deliver them. They cried unto You, and were delivered: they trusted in You, and were not confounded. But I am a worm, and no man; a reproach of men, and despised of the people. All they that see me laugh me to scorn: they shoot out the lip, they shake the head, saying, He trusted on the LORD that He would deliver him: let Him deliver him, seeing He delighted in him. But You are He that took me out of the womb: You did make me hope when I was upon my mother's breasts. I was cast upon thee from the womb: You are my God from my mother's womb. Be not far from me; for trouble is near; for there is none to help. Many bulls have compassed me: strong bulls of Bashan have beset me round. They gaped upon me with their mouths, as a ravening and a roaring lion. I am poured out like water, and all my bones are out of joint: my heart is like wax; it is melted in the midst of my bowels. My strength is dried up like a potsherd; and my tongue cleaves to my jaws; and You have brought me into the dust of death. For dogs have compassed me: the assembly of the wicked has enclosed me: they pierced my hands and my feet. I may tell all my bones: they look and stare upon me. They part my garments among them, and cast lots upon my vesture. But be not You far from me, O LORD: O my strength, haste You to help me. Deliver my soul from the sword; my darling from the power of the dog. Save me from the lion's mouth:* for *You have heard me from the horns of the wild oxen. I will declare Your name unto my brethren: in the midst of the congregation will I praise You. You that fear the LORD, praise Him; all you the seed of Jacob, glorify Him; and*

fear Him, all you the seed of Israel. For He has not despised nor abhorred the affliction of the afflicted; neither has He hid His face from him; but when he cried unto Him, He heard. My praise shall be of You in the great congregation: I will pay my vows before them that fear Him. The meek shall eat and be satisfied: they shall praise the LORD that seek Him: your heart shall live for ever. All the ends of the world shall remember and turn unto the LORD: and all the kindreds of the nations shall worship before You. For the kingdom is the LORD's: and He is the Governor among the nations. All they that are fat upon earth shall eat and worship: all they that go down to the dust shall bow before Him: and none can keep alive his own soul. A seed shall serve Him; it shall be accounted to the Lord for a generation. They shall come, and shall declare His righteousness unto a people that shall be born, that He has done this."

- *Psalm 22:1-31*

Fulfillment by Jesus Christ:

I will not take the time to discuss each of these verses as they pertain to Jesus. I do want to highlight the prophetic references in this passage as they relate to the crucifixion of Jesus Christ.

The most obvious allusion to crucifixion is the phrase, *"they pierced my hands and my feet"*. The act of crucifying a man involved driving spikes through the hands (or wrists) and feet of a person. The crucifixion of Jesus is a central theme in the New Testament:

"And they crucified [Jesus]."[36]

"But Thomas, one of the twelve, called Didymus, was not with them when Jesus came. The other disciples therefore said unto him, We have seen the Lord. But he said unto them, Except I shall see in His hands the print of the nails, and put my finger into the print of the nails, and thrust my hand into His side, I will not believe. And after eight days again His disciples were within, and Thomas with them:

> *then came Jesus, the doors being shut, and stood in the midst, and said, Peace be unto you. Then said He to Thomas, Reach here your finger, and behold My hands; and reach here your hand, and thrust it into My side: and be not faithless, but believing."*[37]

There is another crucifixion reference in the Old Testament that refers to the second coming of the Messiah. It describes what the world will see when Jesus comes as the triumphant Messiah: *"And I will pour upon the house of David, and upon the inhabitants of Jerusalem, the spirit of grace and of supplications: and they shall look upon Me whom they have pierced, and they shall mourn for Him, as one mourns for his only son, and shall be in bitterness for Him, as one that is in bitterness for his firstborn."*[38] The mourning in this verse refers to when the world will finally understand at Jesus' second coming that they crucified God's Son.

David in this psalm quotes this crucified man saying, *"All they that see me laugh me to scorn: they shoot out the lip, they shake the head, saying, He trusted on the LORD that He would deliver him: let Him deliver him, seeing He delighted in him."* The Gospel writers testified that this is exactly what happened while Jesus was hanging on the cross:

> *"And they that passed by railed on Him, shaking their heads, and saying, Ah, You that destroys the temple, and builds it in three days, Save Yourself, and come down from the cross. Likewise also the chief priests mocking said among themselves with the scribes, He saved others; Himself He cannot save. Let Christ the King of Israel descend now from the cross that we may see and believe. And they that were crucified with Him reviled him."*[39]

This prophetic psalm of a crucified man elaborates on the physical condition he would be in during this execution: *"I am poured out like water, and all My bones are out of joint: My heart is like wax; it is melted in the midst of My bowels. My strength is dried up like a potsherd; and My tongue cleaves to my jaws."*

The weight of a man's body while hanging on a cross could dislocate his bones during the crucifixion process. Though this happened to Jesus, none of His bones was broken:

> *"The Jews therefore, because it was the preparation, that the bodies should not remain upon the cross on the Sabbath day, (for that Sabbath day was an high day,) asked Pilate that their legs might be broken, and that they might Be taken away. Then came the soldiers, and broke the legs Of the first, and of the other which was crucified with him. But when they came to Jesus, and saw that He was dead already, they broke not His legs."*[40]

The psalmist prophesies that this man's tormenters would *"part My garments among them, and cast lots upon my vesture."* This is precisely what the Roman soldiers did to Jesus' clothes while they were crucifying Him:

> *"Then the soldiers, when they had crucified Jesus, took His garments, and made four parts, to every soldier a part; and also His coat: now the coat was without seam, woven from the top throughout. They said therefore among themselves, Let us not rend it, but cast lots for it, whose it shall be: that the scripture might be fulfilled, which said, They parted my raiment among them, and for my vesture they did cast lots. These things therefore the soldiers did."*[41]

Lastly and most importantly, I want to point out that Jesus understood this psalm of David as referring to the death of Messiah. The first line of Psalm 22 says: *"My God, My God, why have You forsaken Me?"* Jesus cried out these exact words while hanging on the cross:

> *"And at the ninth hour Jesus cried with a loud voice, saying, Eloi, Eloi, lama sabachthani? which is, being interpreted, My God, My God, why have You forsaken Me?"*[42]

As written here in the Gospel of Mark, Jesus actually spoke these words in the Aramaic language. This was clearly a fulfillment by Jesus of the Messianic prophecy concerning His crucifixion.

There is one other aspect concerning Jesus' utterance of these words that I wish to discuss. Why did Jesus feel forsaken by God on the cross?

The New Testament states that when Jesus was on the cross, God laid the sins of the world upon Him.[43] The apostle Paul declares that not only did Jesus have the world's sins upon Him at His crucifixion but that Jesus actually *became* sin.[44] This means that when the Father looked at Jesus on the cross He saw a murderer, a thief, a rapist, a child molester, a drunkard, a liar, a blasphemer, an idolater, a sexually immoral person, and every other sin that humans have ever committed.

As a human being, I know the guilt feelings that I have had when I committed a sin. I cannot imagine what Jesus felt when God laid every sin that humanity has committed or will commit upon Him while He was hanging on the cross. Since Jesus had never committed a sin, this feeling was something He had never experienced before. Just as the Bible declares that our sins separate us from God,[45] our sins separated Jesus from His Father.

In the garden of Gethsemane, did Jesus dread the physical suffering He knew that He was about to endure or was there more to it than that? While Jesus was totally God, He was also totally a human being and therefore suffered physical pain.[46] However, I believe the reason Jesus asked His Heavenly Father to use His will to find another way to save mankind was not because Jesus was afraid of the flogging and the excruciating pain of the crucifixion that He was about to experience. Rather it was because Jesus knew that for the first time in eternity He would not feel the Father's presence. What I really find amazing about this is that Jesus knew after three days the presence of His Father would be restored to Him. Yet He did not want to be away from His Father's presence for even that short period of time. But we know that on the cross Jesus could not sense the presence of His Father because He said, *"My God, my God, why have you forsaken Me?"*

There is one last prophecy that I want to mention now although it really has a connection to the prophecy that I will be discussing in the next chapter. It is an obvious prophetic reference to the Messiah given by the prophet Zechariah:

> *"Rejoice greatly, O daughter of Zion; shout, O daughter of Jerusalem: behold, your King comes unto you: He is just, and having salvation; lowly, and riding upon an donkey, and upon a colt the foal of an donkey".*
>
> *- Zechariah 9:9*

Kings and rulers at that time did not ride donkeys. They rode horses as a sign of their power. Yet in this prophecy we see that the Messiah rides a donkey. This would be the equivalent of the President of the United States arriving at a meeting of the world's leaders in a Volkswagen Beetle automobile. The dignity of his office demands that he arrive in a Limousine.

This is another sign that at a certain time, the Messiah would come, not in glorious triumph, but rather in a lowly and humble manner.

Fulfillment by Jesus Christ:

> *"And when they drew nigh unto Jerusalem, and were come to Bethphage, unto the mount of Olives, then sent Jesus two disciples, Saying unto them, Go into the village over against you, and straightway you shall find a donkey tied, and a colt with her: loose them, and bring them to Me ... And the disciples went, and did as Jesus commanded them, And brought the donkey, and the colt, and put on them their clothes, and they set Him thereon. And a very great multitude spread their garments in the way; others cut down branches from the trees, and spread them in the way. And the multitudes that went before, and that followed, cried, saying, Hosanna to the Son of David: Blessed is He that comes in the name of the Lord; Hosanna in the highest."*[47]

There are many other prophecies written in the Old Testament that Jesus fulfilled with His first coming. However, the ones that I have listed in the first few chapters of this book illustrate that a humble, suffering Messiah was going to come to the earth at some point in time. These prophecies have answered *what* the Messiah would be like and what He would do when He did come.

In the next chapter, I am going to discuss the most precise prophecy given in the entire Old Testament. Unlike Jesus' second coming of which *"that day and hour knows no man, no, not the angels of heaven, but my Father only"*, [48] God did tell the Jews the *exact* day that the Messiah would appear at His first coming.

---

[1] Napoleon Bonaparte, quoted in Bertrand's Memoirs (Paris, 1844).
[2] ["Wars of the Jews", Book VI, Ch. V, Sec. 3].
[3] *John 19:1-3*
[4] *Matthew 27:22*
[5] *Matthew 27:39-43*
[6] *John 1:29*
[7] *Galatians 1:3-4*
[8] *Hebrews 9:26-28*
[9] *Matthew 27:62-63*
[10] *Matthew 27:12-14*
[11] *Luke 23:8-9*
[12] *2 Corinthians 5:18-19*
[13] *Ezekiel 33:11*
[14] *Matthew 27:57-60*
[15] *John 12:49*
[16] *John 14:6*
[17] *Hebrews 9:28*
[18] *2 Corinthians 5:21*
[19] *Matthew 26:36, 38-39*
[20] *John 3:16-17*
[21] *John 19:30*
[22] *Luke 22:37*
[23] *Luke 23:32-34*
[24] *Matthew3:16-17*
[25] *Genesis 3:15*
[26] *Jeremiah 31:31-33*
[27] *Matthew 26:26-28*
[28] *Hebrews 12:24*
[29] *Hebrews 13:20*
[30] *Ephesians 2:11-13*
[31] *Matthew 20:30, 32-34*

[32] *Matthew 12:22*
[33] *Matthew 14:1-12*
[34] *Matthew 11:2-6*
[35] *1 Samuel 13:14*
[36] *Matthew 27:35*
[37] *John 20:24-27*
[38] *Zechariah 12:10*
[39] *Mark 15:29-32*
[40] *John 19:31-33*
[41] *John 19:23-24*
[42] *Mark 15:34*
[43] *John 1:29*
[44] *II Corinthians 5:14-21*
[45] *Isaiah 59:2*
[46] *John 1:1-3, 14*
[47] *Matthew 21:1-2, 6-9*
[48] *Matthew 24:36*

5 - 70 Weeks = 490 Years?

The prophetic Book of Daniel contains some of the most precise prophecies written in the Old Testament. Because this book contains such specific predictions, a controversy has swirled around it since the first centuries of Christianity.

The critics maintain that this book had to be written long after the prophet Daniel lived (ca. Sixth Century B.C.), most likely during the Maccabean period (ca. Second Century B.C.). Their reasoning for this conclusion lies in the fact that the events that Daniel foretold did come true in the interim time between his death and the arrival of the Jesus Christ. Liberal scholars and theologians late date his book because they cannot accept the fact that God would give such accurate prophecies to human beings. This attitude of course denies that God is omniscient. God, through the prophet Isaiah, differed with their conclusion saying: *"Remember the former things of old: for I am God, and there is none else; I am God, and there is none like Me, Declaring the end from the beginning, and from ancient times the things that are not yet done, saying, My counsel shall stand, and I will do all My pleasure."*[1]

In recent years, the discovery of the Dead Sea Scrolls has caused the dating issue of the Book of Daniel to be revisited. Among the many scrolls found was Daniel's book. Since it is determined that the Dead Sea Scrolls were written between the Third Century B.C. and the First Century A.D. this has led some scholars to assign an earlier date to the Book of Daniel.[2]

However, from my perspective, one overriding factor supports the accuracy and authorship of the Book of Daniel. Jesus Christ spoke of Daniel when He described to His disciples the signs of His second coming on the Mount of Olives. He said, *"When you therefore shall see the abomination of desolation, spoken of by Daniel the prophet, stand in the holy place...".*[3] With this statement, Jesus declared that the Book of Daniel was authentic prophetic writing.

Nevertheless, even those who refuse to accept this premise and continue to maintain that this book was written around 165 B.C. cannot sidestep the accuracy of the prophecy I will be discussing in this chapter. A prophecy that was written well before the birth of Jesus yet had its fulfillment in His lifetime.

The importance of the prophecy that I am going to be covering here *cannot* be overstated. It was one of the leading factors that caused the late Orthodox Jewish Talmudic scholar, Rachmiel Frydland, to accept Jesus as the Messiah.[4] Rabbi Leopold Cohn had read this prophecy and also came to the realization that only Jesus Christ could fulfill it. He became a believer in Jesus as the Messiah and started the organization called the "American Board of Missions to the Jews".[5] That other Jews like them have also come to the same conclusion based primarily on this prophetic scripture passage illustrates an important truth. The Jews in Jesus' day had the same opportunity as modern Jews to accept that Jesus was the fulfillment of this prophecy. As will be shown, this is exactly what Jesus told the religious leaders of His day.

In the year 1895, Sir Robert Anderson wrote a book called "The Coming Prince" in which he wrote about the prophecies in the Book of Daniel. He is generally credited with bringing the interpretation of the prophecy found in chapter 9 of Daniel to the modern era. There have been many other biblical scholars since who have agreed with his interpretation.

King Nebuchadnezzar had taken the prophet Daniel as a captive along with the rest of the Jews back to the land of Babylon. While he was there he continued to serve God faithfully even at the risk to his own life.

Daniel not only had a heart toward God but he also was concerned about his people and desperately wanted to know what God's plan was for their future. He had been reading the Old Testament Book of

Jeremiah when he came across a passage that caught his attention: *"In the first year of his reign* [i.e., King Darius - 538/537 B.C.] *I Daniel understood by books the number of the years, whereof the word of the LORD came to Jeremiah the prophet, that He would accomplish seventy years in the desolations of Jerusalem."*[6] The scripture passage Daniel had read is found in the Book of Jeremiah: *"Therefore thus saith the LORD of hosts; Because you have not heard My words, Behold, I will send and take all the families of the north, saith the LORD, and Nebuchadnezzar the king of Babylon, My servant, and will bring them against this land, and against the inhabitants thereof, and against all these nations round about, and will utterly destroy them, and make them an astonishment, and an hissing, and perpetual desolations...And this whole land shall be a desolation, and an astonishment; and these nations shall serve the king of Babylon seventy years...For thus saith the LORD, That after seventy years be accomplished at Babylon I will visit you, and perform my good word toward you, in causing you to return to this place."*[7]

The reason God gives for this punishment is because the Jews had transgressed against His laws. One of the many laws that they had broken helped determine the length of time of their punishment, in this case 70 years.

When God gave His laws to the Jews He told them that they could plant and harvest the land of Israel for six consecutive years. However, on the seventh year they had to give the land a rest and thus they could not plant anything in the ground. God said that He would provide a bountiful harvest in the sixth year that would carry them through the seventh or Sabbath year.[8]

But the Jews did not obey this law of God's as He makes clear: *"And those that had escaped from the sword carried he* [i.e., Nebuchadnezzar] *away to Babylon; where they were servants to him and his sons until the reign of the kingdom of Persia: To fulfill the word of the LORD by the mouth of Jeremiah, until the land had enjoyed her Sabbaths: for as long as she lay desolate she kept Sabbath, to fulfill threescore and ten years."*[9]

Therefore, God based the length of the punishment for the Jews upon how many Sabbath years they had ignored. The resulting punishment of seventy "Sabbath" years means that for 490 years the

Jews did not give the land a rest. To make up for each of those seventh or Sabbath years they had not observed God added one year of captivity to their sentence.

With this understanding, Daniel then spoke one of the most heartfelt prayers of repentance and supplication in the entire Bible.[10] While he was praying the angel Gabriel appeared to him and gave to him a prophetic message that would declare the future of the Jewish people:

> *"Seventy weeks are determined upon your people and upon your holy city, to finish the transgression, and to make an end of sins, and to make reconciliation for iniquity, and to bring in everlasting righteousness, and to seal up the vision and prophecy, and to anoint the most Holy. Know therefore and understand, that from the going forth of the commandment to restore and to build Jerusalem unto the Messiah the Prince shall be seven weeks, and threescore and two weeks: the street shall be built again, and the wall, even in troublous times. And after threescore and two weeks shall Messiah be cut off, but not for Himself: and the people of the prince that shall come shall destroy the city and the sanctuary; and the end thereof shall be with a flood, and unto the end of the war desolations are determined. And he shall confirm the covenant with many for one week: and in the midst of the week he shall cause the sacrifice and the oblation to cease, and for the overspreading of abominations he shall make it desolate, even until the consummation, and that determined shall be poured upon the desolate."*
>
> \- *Daniel 9:24-27*

The word *"weeks"* in this passage is translated from the Hebrew word "shabuwa" which literally means "sevens". Therefore, this prophecy gives a time frame for the Jewish nation that would span "seventy sevens". The question is, What time period does these "sevens" encompass? Since the context of this prophecy was the seventy Sabbath years of punishment given to the Jews these "sevens" are actually years.[11] Thus, "seventy sevens of years" or 490 years are determined for the time frame of this prophecy.

This scripture passage concerns only the Jewish people since the people of Daniel were Jews. The holy city can only refer to Jerusalem since this is the only city in the world that is holy to Jews. At the end of this 490-year period God would put an end to the transgressions and sins of the Jewish people. Then He would bring in everlasting righteousness and anoint the most holy [i.e., the Jewish Temple].

According to this prophecy, the 490-year period would commence with the issuing of a commandment or decree to rebuild Jerusalem and restore its streets and walls that the Babylonian invasion had destroyed. There are two major decrees given in the Old Testament that concern the restoration of Jerusalem. The first is found in the Book of Ezra where King Cyrus of Persia proclaimed that the house [i.e., Temple] of God was to be rebuilt in Jerusalem.[12] This decree was issued in the year 539 B.C. However, it cannot be the commandment referred to in this prophecy of Daniel's because it does not speak to the rebuilding of the streets and walls of Jerusalem.

The second decree is found in the Book of Nehemiah. King Artaxerxes issued it in the Jewish month of Nisan in the twentieth year of his reign[13] (many biblical passages give the specific numerical day when it lists a Jewish month. In this case, no specific day is mentioned so by default the first day of Nisan is probably what is meant here). This decree specifically mentions that Nehemiah was to receive *"timber to make beams for the gates of the palace which appertained to the house, and for the wall of the city, and for the house that I shall enter into. And the king granted me, according to the good hand of my God upon me."*[14] Unlike the Ezra decree, this one fulfills precisely the prophecy of Daniel to *"restore and to build Jerusalem...the street shall be built again, and the wall"*. This decree then starts the "seventy weeks" prophecy on March 5, 444 B.C.[15]

Thus, from the date that the decree was issued, Daniel states that it will be 69 "sevens of years" or 483 years until the time the Messiah comes to His Jewish people.

The Bible gives the length of a year as consisting of 360 days.[16] This biblical year was based upon the lunar phases which comprised 30-day time periods. In modern times, our calendar is based upon the solar year which lasts 365 days with an extra "leap" day being added every fourth year. This of course keeps the days of each year occurring at the same time during the seasons. The Jews adjusted their lunar-year calendar by adding an extra month every few years by which to keep their seasons consistent.

To calculate the "69 weeks" until the Messiah came, you multiply the 483 years by 360 days. The result is that the Messiah would appear 173,880 days from March 5, 444 B.C. By converting these days, using the precise length of our solar year, the day the Messiah would appear is the 10th of Nisan or March 30, 33 A.D. That the Messiah would appear on the 10th of Nisan has a tremendous significance that I will disclose shortly. This means that according to Daniel's prophecy, any person not proclaimed the Messiah on March 30, 33 A.D. could not in fact be the Messiah.

The final part of this prophecy addressed in this section concerns the prophetic phrase that states the *"Messiah [shall] be cut off, but not for Himself"*. This of course pertains to the earlier prophecy of Isaiah in which he said: *"for He* [i.e., the Messiah] *was cut off out of the land of the living: for the transgression of My people was He stricken".*[17] Therefore, after the Messiah appeared He would be killed according to this prophecy of Daniel's and the prophecy of Isaiah.

The New Testament illustrates how perfectly Jesus Christ fulfilled this prophecy.

Fulfillment by Jesus Christ:

The biblical writer Luke gives timing of the beginning of Jesus' ministry on earth in his Gospel:

> *"and Jesus increased in wisdom and stature, and in favor with God and man. Now in the fifteenth year of the reign of Tiberius Caesar, Pontius Pilate being governor of Judea, and Herod being tetrarch of Galilee, and his brother Philip tetrarch of Ituraea and of the region of Trachonitis, and Lysanias the tetrarch of Abilene...Now when all the people were baptized, it came to pass, that Jesus also being baptized, and praying, the heaven was opened, And the*

Holy Ghost descended in a bodily shape like a dove upon Him, and a voice came from heaven, which said, You are My beloved Son; in You I am well pleased. And Jesus Himself began to be about thirty years of age..."[18]

Biblical scholars recognize the Gospel writer Luke as a historian of the first degree. His book illustrates thoroughly the attention he gives to historical detail. In this passage, he makes it clear that Jesus was baptized and began His ministry in the 15th year of the reign of the Roman emperor Tiberius Caesar. Since historians state that the Roman emperor Augustus died on August 19, 14 A.D., this means that Tiberius became sole emperor that same year. Thus, Jesus began His ministry in 29 A.D., which was the 15th year of Tiberius' reign.

Most biblical scholars have concluded that Jesus' earthly ministry lasted three and one-half years. They base this belief on the listing of the various Jewish feasts in the Gospels that occurred during His ministry. Since His ministry started in the latter half of 29 A.D., He would have finished it in the spring of 33 A.D.

The final feast mentioned in the Gospels is the feast of Passover, which begins on the 14th of the Jewish month Nisan. According to our modern Gregorian calendar, this converts to Friday, April 3, 33 A.D. It was during this final feast that the Romans crucified Jesus.

At the risk of offending centuries of Christian tradition, I will point out that the 10th of Nisan, 33 A.D. actually occurred on a Monday. This would have been the exact date of Jesus' "triumphal entry" into Jerusalem when the multitudes of Jewish people proclaimed Him the Messiah. The tradition that refers to this day as "Palm Sunday" has its basis in a certain reading of a passage in the Gospel of John:

"Then Jesus six days before the Passover came to Bethany, where Lazarus was which had been dead, whom He raised from the dead...On the next day much people that were come to the feast, when they heard that Jesus was coming to Jerusalem, Took branches of palm trees, and went forth to meet Him, and cried, Hosanna: Blessed is the King of Israel that comes in the name of the Lord. And Jesus, when He had found a young donkey, sat thereon; as it is written,

> *Fear not, daughter of Zion: behold, your King cometh, sitting on a donkey's colt."*[19]

The dilemma here is based on how you count the days before the Passover feast mentioned by John. If the Passover was on Friday, then counting backwards five days from that day takes you to Monday, which actually started Sunday evening according to the way the Jews count their days *(Genesis 1:5 - "And the evening and the morning were the first day").*

So according to this prophecy of Daniel, the Messiah would appear on the 10th of Nisan, 33 A.D. or using our calendar, March 30, 33 A.D. Jesus fulfilled it to the exact day. The fact that Jesus was sitting on a donkey, just as the prophet Zechariah had foretold about the Messiah with the people proclaiming Him "King" or "Messiah", confirms that He alone fulfilled this prophecy. *JESUS CHRIST IS THE MESSIAH.*

It is significant that several times during Jesus' ministry the people wanted to publicly proclaim Him the Messiah. Each of these times Jesus refused to allow them to perform this coronation.[20] However, on the 10th of Nisan, 33 A.D. Jesus not only welcomed the praises and proclamations of the people declaring Him the Messiah, He stated that it had to happen on this very day.

The religious leaders approached Jesus during this public homage to Him. They were angry that He was accepting this Messianic declaration of the people and said to Him, *"Master, rebuke thy disciples."* Jesus responded to them and said, *"I tell you that, if these [people] should hold their peace, the stones would immediately cry out."*[21] Jesus was saying that it was so important that He be proclaimed Messiah on this very day that if the people wouldn't do it the rocks on the ground would. That is because God's prophecies and His will *always* come to pass and He will use whatever means available to accomplish them. The psalmist also refers to this specific day when he wrote: *"This is the day which the LORD has made; we will rejoice and be glad in it. Save now, I beseech You, O LORD: O LORD, I beseech You, send now prosperity. Blessed be He that comes in the name of the LORD: we have blessed You out of the house of the LORD."*[22] Thus, in order to fulfill this prophecy of

Daniel, Jesus was going to be proclaimed the Messiah on this specific day one way or another.

As Jesus approached the city of Jerusalem on the donkey, He stopped and wept saying:

> *"Saying, If you had known, even you, at least in this your day, the things which belong unto your peace! But now they are hid from your eyes. For the days shall come upon you, that your enemies shall cast a trench about you, and encircle you, and keep you in on every side, And shall lay you even with the ground, and your children within you; and they shall not leave in you one stone upon another; because you knew not the time of your visitation."*[23]

This saying of Jesus is of the utmost importance because it shows that according to Jesus, the Jews should have *known* that this was the exact day that the Messiah would visit His people. How could they have known? By correctly interpreting Daniel's prophecy, along with those prophecies of Isaiah and Zechariah, that foretold not only that the Messiah would be a humble, suffering servant but also the precise day of His arrival. However, the Jewish leaders did not want a suffering Messiah so they only focused on the royal Messiah prophecies.

I believe this is an important biblical principle that Jesus has put forth to God's people. We are to study the Bible to ascertain the plans of God for mankind and the timing of those plans. Jesus rebuked the Jews for not knowing when the Messiah would first appear because they didn't properly study the Old Testament. As Christians we should not miss the timing (although not the specific day) of Jesus' second coming because He has revealed to us through the prophetic passages of the Bible when that event would occur. The apostle Paul wrote: *"But of the times and the seasons, brethren, you have no need that I write unto you. For yourselves know perfectly that the day of the Lord so comes as a thief in the night...But you, brethren, are not in darkness, that that day should overtake you as a thief."*[24] This principle is the crux of this book I have written so that Jesus will not rebuke His followers for not knowing the times of His second visitation.

Finally, we come to the death of Messiah to which Daniel's prophecy speaks. It states that after the Messiah comes, He will be *"cut off"* or killed. As both Daniel and Isaiah state, the reason for His death will be for the sins of mankind.

Jesus was crucified on Friday the 14th of Nisan, 33 A.D. He died at 3pm[25] that day. The New Testament makes it clear that the next day was a Saturday or the Sabbath as the Jews called it: *"And now when the even was come, because it was the preparation, that is, the day before the Sabbath, Joseph of Arimathaea, an honorable counselor, which also waited for the kingdom of God, came, and went in boldly unto Pilate, and desired to take the body of Jesus."*[26]

These two dates, the 10th and 14th of Nisan, have tremendous significance concerning the proclamation of Jesus as the Messiah and in the date of His death.

In the Law that God gave to the Jewish people He ordained them to keep a feast called the Passover. It had its origins in the Jewish nation's escape from the bondage of Egyptian slavery. God culminated the deliverance of the Jews on the night that He killed all the firstborn male children of the Egyptians. His purpose in this was to show the rebellious Egyptians that He was God and to cause them to free the Jews. On that night, God commanded the Jews living in Egypt to sacrifice an unblemished lamb and spread its blood on the doorposts of their homes. When the Angel of Death came to kill all the firstborn male children in Egypt, he would pass over any homes that had the lamb's blood on it. Indeed, the Jewish homes that had this blood-covering had their firstborn males spared from death.[27]

God ordained that the Jews keep the feast of Passover as a remembrance of the night of their deliverance:

> *"And the LORD spoke unto Moses and Aaron in the land of Egypt, saying, This month* [i.e., Nisan] *shall be unto you The beginning of months: it shall be the first month of the Year to you. Speak you unto all the congregation of Israel, saying, In the tenth day of this month they shall take to them every man a lamb, according to the house of their fathers, a lamb for an house...Your lamb shall be without blemish, a male of the first year: you shall take it out from the sheep, or from the goats: And you shall keep it up until*

> *the fourteenth day of the same month: and the whole assembly of the congregation of Israel shall kill it in the evening. And they shall take of the blood, and strike it on the two side posts and on the upper door post of the houses, wherein they shall eat it...For I will pass through the land of Egypt this night, and will smite all the firstborn in the land of Egypt, both man and beast; and against all the gods of Egypt I will execute judgment: I am the LORD. And the blood shall be to you for a token upon the houses where you are: and when I see the blood, I will pass over you, and the plague shall not be upon you to destroy you, when I smite the land of Egypt. And this day shall be unto you for a memorial; and you shall keep it a feast to the LORD throughout your generations; you shall keep it a feast by an ordinance for ever."*[28]

The Jews were to examine their flocks and choose one unblemished lamb on the 10th day of Nisan and kill it on the 14th day of Nisan. The fact that this lamb was to be unblemished meant that it was to have no imperfections.

Jesus fulfilled the purpose of this feast on those exact days. During His "triumphal entry" on the 10th of Nisan, 33 A.D., the people *chose* Jesus as their Messiah. It is significant that after Jesus came to Jerusalem He went to the Jewish Temple. There He was questioned and examined by the religious leaders to see if they could find any fault *or blemish* in Him.[29] No fault was found in Him and so, like the unblemished lamb, Jesus was sacrificed on the 14th day of Nisan fulfilling the true role of the Passover lamb.

John the Baptist recognized this sacrificial role of Jesus: *"John saw Jesus coming to him, and said, Behold the Lamb of God, which takes away the sin of the world."*[30]

The apostle Paul also saw this biblical truth fulfilled in Jesus when he declared, *"For even Christ our Passover is sacrificed for us."*[31]

It was during the Passover meal on Thursday night the 13th of Nisan, 33 A.D. when Jesus instituted a new memorial in which His shed blood would replace the Passover lamb's blood as atonement for the sins of mankind:

> *"And as they were eating, Jesus took bread, and blessed it, and broke it, and gave it to the disciples, and said, Take, eat; this is My body. And He took the cup, and gave thanks, and gave it to them, saying, Drink you all of it; For this is My blood of the new testament, which is shed for many for the remission of sins."*[32]

When Christians receive communion they are taking part in the Passover meal by eating the bread and drinking the wine that memorializes Jesus Christ as the true Passover Lamb of God who takes away their sins.

After reading through this prophecy of Daniel, I hope you understand why this is such an important Messianic prophecy. It answers the final question of our original six as to *when* would the Messiah come. This means that no one else can be the Messiah except Jesus Christ because He is the only one who came on the dates specified as necessary by God.

I would like to point out that the last part of this "seventy weeks" prophecy pertains to a yet future time of fulfillment that I will be discussing in the second part of this book.

Before we look at the timing of the second coming of Jesus Christ there is one more chapter in which I would like to cover two more vital aspects to the first coming of the Messiah.

---

1 *Isaiah 46:9-10*

2 "Secrets of the Dead Sea Scrolls", Dr. Randall Price, p. 80-81; 157-163; (Harvest House Publishers, 1996)

3 *Matthew 24:15*

4 "What the Rabbis Know About the Messiah", Rachmiel Frydland, p. 73-77; (Messianic Publishing Company, 1991, 1993)

5 "The Handwriting on the Wall", David Jeremiah, ch. 15, p. 185; (Word Publishing, 1992). See also Jews for Jesus website.

6 *Daniel 9:2*

7 *Jeremiah 25:8-9, 11; 29:10*

8 *Leviticus 25:1-22*

9 *II Chronicles 36:20-21*

10 *Daniel 9:3-20*

11 Even the Jewish Publication Society (a non-Christian organization) has in their Hebrew-English Tanakh (i.e., Old Testament in the Christian Bible)

a footnote to Daniel 9:24 which states that the word sevens here means sevens "of years". [JPS Hebrew-English Tanakh; p.1828, footnote "a" (The Jewish Publication Society, 2000)]

12 *Ezra 1:1-2*

13 *Nehemiah 2:1-8*

14 *Nehemiah 2:8*

15 Sir Robert Anderson states that the year was actually 445 B.C. but other scholars have concluded that the 20th year Artaxerxes reign took place in 444 BC.

16 Both the first and last books of the Bible, Genesis and Revelation (when compared with *Daniel 7:24-25*), give the specific number of days which when calculated define the biblical year as consisting of 360 days. See *Genesis 7:11, 24; 8:3-4 and Revelation 13:4-7; 12:13-14*

17 *Isaiah 53:8b*

18 *Luke 2:52-3:1; 3:21-23a*

19 *John 12:1, 12-15*

20 *Matthew16:13-20; John 6:14-15; etc*

21 *Luke 19:39-40*

22 *Psalm 118:24-26*

23 *Luke 19:41-44*

24 *I Thessalonians 5:1-2, 4*

25 The Gospel of Matthew states that "*about the ninth hour...Jesus yielded up His spirit*". The daylight hours were counted from 6am and therefore Jesus died at 3pm. (*Matthew 27:45-50)*

26 *Mark 15:42-43*

27 *Exodus 12:1-39*

28 *Exodus 12:1-3, 5-7, 12-14*

29 *Matthew 21:1-24:1*

30 *John 1:29*

31 *I Corinthians 5:7*

32 *Matthew 26:26-28*

6 - The Deity of Messiah

After this chapter, I will be moving on to the prophecies that foretold of a royal Messiah and His coming to earth. Here though, I want to discuss two Messianic prophetic issues that are at the heart of the Christian faith and Jesus' claim to be the Messiah. The first is the resurrection of Jesus Christ from the dead.

As we read previously, the Old Testament prophesied that the Messiah would die. However, it also makes clear that God would not leave Him in that state.

We have already seen that God gave the gift of prophetic utterance to King David. It was one such prophecy in which he states that God would not allow death to permanently affect His Messiah:

> *"For You will not leave My soul in hell; neither will You allow your Holy One to see corruption."*
>
> \- *Psalm 16:10*

This passage speaks to the resurrection of the Holy One of God, the Messiah. The word "hell" in this verse is translated from the Hebrew word "sheol" which means "the grave". Therefore, this prophecy is stating that God would not allow His Messiah to remain in His grave after He was *"cut off out of the land of the living"*. God would not allow His body to become corrupted or decayed.

Fulfillment by Jesus Christ:

The New Testament references this particular verse as pertaining to Jesus Christ. Fifty days after the resurrection of Jesus, on the Day of Pentecost, the apostle Peter delivered a sermon in which he spoke of this prophecy of David's:

> *"You men of Israel, hear these words; Jesus of Nazareth, a Man approved of God among you by miracles and wonders and signs, which God did by Him in the midst of you, as you yourselves also know: Him, being delivered by the determinate counsel and foreknowledge of God, you have taken, and by wicked hands have crucified and slain: Whom God has raised up, having loosed the pains of death: because it was not possible that He should be held by it. For David speaks concerning Him, I foresaw the Lord always before my face, for He is on my right hand, that I should not be moved: Therefore did my heart rejoice, and my tongue was glad; moreover also my flesh shall rest in hope: Because You will not leave My soul in hell, neither will You suffer your Holy One to see corruption...Men and brethren, let me freely speak unto you of the patriarch David, that he is both dead and buried, and his sepulcher is with us unto this day. Therefore being a prophet, and knowing that God had sworn with an oath to him, that of the fruit of his loins, according to the flesh, He would raise up Christ to sit on His throne; he seeing this before spoke of the resurrection of Christ, that His soul was not left in hell, neither His flesh did see corruption. This Jesus has God raised up, whereof we all are witnesses."*[1]

One interesting thing about this sermon is that the night before Jesus' crucifixion, the apostle Peter had denied Jesus Christ three times. He was afraid of being arrested and crucified along with Jesus. After his denial he ran away and wept bitterly.[2] Here, Peter is publicly speaking by the Temple about Jesus Christ without fear for his life. What happened to turn a cowering, fearful man into a confident, unwavering public speaker?

The answer lies in two events. The first is that Peter had seen the resurrected Jesus as he says in this sermon, *"This Jesus has God raised up, whereof we all are witnesses."* The second is that the Holy

Spirit had come upon him earlier that day which then prompted him to go out and boldly proclaim this message.[3]

All the Gospels in the New Testament clearly state that Jesus' grave was empty because He had risen from the dead. The Gospel of Mark says that when some of the women disciples of Jesus went to the tomb on the Sunday after the crucifixion an angel said to them:

> *"Be not afraid: You seek Jesus of Nazareth, which was crucified: He is risen; He is not here: behold the place where they laid Him."*[4]

The resurrection of Jesus Christ is crucial to those of the Christian faith who believe that Jesus was the fulfillment of God's Messianic prophecies. The apostle Paul said as much when he declared:

> *"And if Christ be not risen, then is our preaching vain, and your faith is also vain."*[5]

The day that Jesus was buried on and the day of His resurrection also have significance because of two other feast days that God ordained the Jews to keep *immediately* following the Passover.

In the Book of Leviticus, God gave to the Jews the dates of the seven feasts that He would require them to keep. As I mentioned, the Passover was to occur on the 14th of Nisan. On the 15th of Nisan, the Jews were to observe the week-long feast of Unleavened Bread.[6] They were to eat bread that contained no leaven in it. The Bible records that leaven represents sin in a spiritual sense: *"Your glorying is not good. Know you not that a little leaven leavens the whole lump? Purge out therefore the old leaven that you may be a new lump, as ye are unleavened. For even Christ our Passover is sacrificed for us: Therefore let us keep the feast, not with old leaven, neither with the leaven of malice and wickedness; but with the unleavened bread of sincerity and truth."*[7] Jesus had taken the world's sins upon Himself and died. He was buried, and our sins with Him, on the 15th of Nisan, 33 A.D. In doing so Jesus fulfilled the second of the seven Jewish feasts.

The third feast ordained by God was the feast of Firstfruits by which the Jews were to honor God with the first or spring harvest of the year.[8] They were to observe it on the Sunday after the first Sabbath day after Passover. In 33 A.D. the feast of Firstfruits occurred on Sunday the 16th of Nisan. Jesus Christ rose from the dead on that Sunday of Firstfruits. The apostle Paul recognized Jesus' fulfillment of this feast day by declaring: *"But now is Christ risen from the dead, and become the firstfruits of them that slept."*[9]

There are four more feasts ordained by God for the Jewish people. I will note one later in this chapter and the other three in Part Two of this book.

As I mentioned in Chapter 3, the disciples willingly died for their belief that Jesus Christ was God's Messiah. They based this belief on the *fact* that they had seen Jesus alive after His death and burial. They *knew* that God had raised Him from the dead.

God the Son

The second and final Messianic issue that I want to cover in Part One of this book has been a source of controversy among some persons and groups in history. It is the historically orthodox doctrine concerning the deity of Jesus Christ. That the infinite God became a man is a difficult concept for a finite human being to grasp. However, just because we humans are unable to understand the vastness of who God is does not make such a doctrine erroneous.

The Old Testament does have a Messianic prophecy that speaks to this issue:

> *"For unto us a Child is born, unto us a Son is given: and the government shall be upon His shoulder: and His name shall be called Wonderful, Counselor, The mighty God, The everlasting Father, The Prince of Peace. Of the increase of His government and peace there shall be no end, upon the throne of David, and upon His kingdom, to order it, and to establish it with judgment and with justice from henceforth even for ever. The zeal of the LORD of hosts will perform this."*
>
> *- Isaiah 9:6-7*

Thirty-nine verses earlier Isaiah speaks of this child, *"Therefore the Lord Himself shall give you a sign; Behold, a virgin shall conceive, and bear a Son, and shall call His name Immanuel."*[10] I explained in Chapter 2 that this was a prophecy concerning the virgin birth of Jesus Christ and His name Immanuel, which means: "God with us" or "God is with us".

The appellations that were given to this Child in chapter 9 of Isaiah refer to the nature of the Messiah. Though two of these names could be attributed to any human being (i.e., Wonderful and Counselor) the others could not. In history, there have been some individuals who have claimed to be divine such as the Roman emperors yet they were usually anything but a "prince of peace".

The two most conclusive names listed here which reveal that the Messiah would be divine are *"The mighty God"* and *"The everlasting Father"*. The New Testament is clear in assigning these divine attributes to Jesus Christ. The early church recognized that Jesus was "Immanuel" and that He, as God, was with them.

Fulfillment by Jesus Christ:

The clearest example in the New Testament that illustrates that Jesus was God, come in the form of a man, is found in the Gospel of John:

> *"In the beginning was the Word, and the Word was with God, and the Word was God. The same was in the beginning with God. All things were made by Him; and without Him was not any thing made that was made...And the Word was made flesh, and dwelt among us, (and we beheld His glory, the glory as of the only begotten of the Father,) full of grace and truth."*[11]

The writer of this passage was a disciple of Jesus named John. For three and one-half years he walked with Jesus and saw Him work miracles and speak the words of God. In these verses John states that the "Word" was God and that the "Word" became flesh or a human being. Since his Gospel focuses explicitly on Jesus it is clear that he is speaking of Jesus Christ as God incarnate.

John points out that Jesus created the universe and everything in it. The first book of the Bible is definitive about the fact that God is the creator of everything:

"In the beginning God created the heaven and the earth."[12]

There was no doubt in John's mind that Jesus was God in the flesh. The fact that he starts out his Gospel with the same phrase as the one used in Genesis is illustrative of this belief.

The apostle Paul was even more elaborate in equating Jesus with God the Creator when he wrote to the Christians in the Colossian Church:

> *"[God] has delivered us from the power of darkness, and has translated us into the kingdom of His dear Son: In Whom we have redemption through His blood, even the forgiveness of sins: Who is the image of the invisible God, the firstborn of every creature: For by Him were all things created, that are in heaven, and that are in earth, visible and invisible, whether they be thrones, or dominions, or principalities, or powers: all things were created by Him, and for Him: And He is before all things, and by Him all things consist. And He is the head of the body, the church: Who is the beginning, the firstborn from the dead; that in all things He might have the preeminence. For it pleased the Father that in Him should all fullness dwell...For in Him dwells all the fullness of the Godhead bodily."*[13]

Paul was unambiguous in his belief that Jesus was God in the flesh. Like John, he recognized that Jesus created all things whether in heaven or on earth. He also made mention of this in his letter to the Church of Ephesus:

> *"And to make all men see what is the fellowship of the mystery, which from the beginning of the world has been hid in God, Who created all things by Jesus Christ."*[14]

The writer of the Book of Hebrews is equally emphatic in his belief that Jesus is God:

> *"God, Who at sundry times and in various manners spoke in time past unto the fathers by the prophets, Has in these last days spoken unto us by His Son, Whom He has appointed heir of all things, by Whom also He made the worlds; Who being the brightness of His glory, and the express image of His person, and upholding all things by the word of His power, when He had by Himself purged our sins, sat down on the right hand of the Majesty on high."*[15]

The author refers to Jesus as the *"express image"* of God and *"His glory"*. In Chapter 4 of this book I quoted a Messianic prophecy found in the first seven verses of chapter 42 of Isaiah. God, continuing this prophecy in verse eight of that passage, states:

> *"I am the LORD: that is My name: and My glory will I not give to another, neither My praise to graven images."*[16]

God says that He will not give His glory to another being yet the writer of Hebrews states that Jesus was the glory of God. Jesus was therefore God because God the Father gave His glory to His Son, the Messiah.

What claims did Jesus make concerning Himself? There was no doubt in His enemies' minds (as I illustrate below) that Jesus claimed to be God in the flesh:

> *"Then answered Jesus and said unto them, Truly, truly, I say unto you, The Son can do nothing of Himself, but what He sees the Father do: for whatsoever things He does, these also do the Son likewise. For the Father loves the Son, and shows Him all things that He Himself does: and He will show Him greater works than these, that you may marvel. For as the Father raises up the dead, and makes them alive; even so the Son makes alive whom He will. For the Father judges no man, but has committed all judgment*

> *unto the Son: That all men should honor the Son, even as they honor the Father. He that honors not the Son honors not the Father which has sent Him."*[17]

Jesus states that He should receive the same honor as that of the Father God. As we read in the verse above this passage God will not give His glory to anyone else. Yet here we see that Jesus is equal to the Father in the power to resurrect men, to judge men, and to receive God's honor for Himself.

While Jesus was teaching in the Temple, the Jewish religious leaders were questioning Him:

> *"Are You greater than our father Abraham, who is dead? and the prophets are dead: whom do You make Yourself to be? Jesus answered, If I honor Myself, My honor is nothing: it is My Father that honors Me; of Whom you say, that He is your God: Yet you have not known Him; but I know Him: and if I should say, I know Him not, I shall be a liar like you: but I know Him, and keep His saying. Your father Abraham rejoiced to see My day: and he saw it, and was glad. Then said the Jews unto Him, You are not yet fifty years old, and have You seen Abraham? Jesus said unto them, Truly, truly, I say unto you, Before Abraham was, I AM. Then took they up stones to cast at Him: but Jesus hid Himself, and went out of the Temple, going through the midst of them, and so passed by."*[18]

What did Jesus say here that made the Jewish leaders want to stone Him to death? Jesus stated that Abraham rejoiced to see Jesus come to earth. Since Abraham had lived two thousand years before Jesus was born, the Jews wanted to know how that was possible. The answer Jesus gave was the reason they wanted to stone Him. He said before Abraham lived *"I AM"*.

To a Gentile this phrase would have meant nothing. However, the Jews understood perfectly what Jesus was saying.

When God called Moses to be the deliverer of the children of Israel from their bondage in Egypt, he asked God a question:

> *"And Moses said unto God, Behold, when I come unto the children of Israel, and shall say unto them, The God of your fathers has sent me unto you; and they shall say to me, What is His name? What shall I say unto them?"*

God's reply was enigmatic but straightforward:

> *"And God said unto Moses, I AM THAT I AM: and He said, Thus shall you say unto the children of Israel, I AM has sent me unto you."*[19]

Therefore, these Jewish religious leaders knew that Jesus was claiming to be God. Thus, they were going to stone Him to death for blasphemy.

However, it seems that during Jesus' ministry, His disciples were not so clear in their understanding of His claim to be divine:

> *"Thomas said unto Him, Lord, we know not where You are going; and how can we know the way? Jesus said unto him, I am the way, the truth, and the life: no man comes to the Father, but by Me. If you had known Me, you should have known My Father also: and from henceforth you know Him, and have seen Him. Philip said to Him, Lord, show us the Father, and it is sufficient for us. Jesus said to him, Have I been so long time with you, and yet have you not known Me, Philip? He that has seen Me has seen the Father; and how say you then, Show us the Father? Do you not believe that I am in the Father, and the Father in Me? The words that I speak unto you I speak not of Myself: but the Father that dwells in Me, He does the works."*[20]

Again though, the enemies of Jesus had no illusions that He was claiming to be God:

> *"And therefore did the Jews persecute Jesus, and sought to slay Him, because He had done these things* [i.e., healed a man] *on the Sabbath day. But Jesus answered them, My Father works until now, and I work. Therefore the Jews*

sought the more to kill Him, because He not only had broken the Sabbath, but said also that God was His Father, making Himself equal with God."[21]

"I and My Father are one. Then the Jews took up stones again to stone Him. Jesus answered them, Many good works have I shown you from My Father; for which of those works do you stone Me? The Jews answered Him, saying, For a good work we stone you not; but for blasphemy; and because that you, being a man, make yourself God."[22]

The Jewish religious leaders may not have understood the spirit of the laws that God had given to them but they clearly understood blasphemy (according to their standards) when they heard it. They *knew* that Jesus was claiming to be God by the words that He spoke. In this second passage Jesus stated that He and His Father were *one*.

The New Testament mentions a few times when persons had witnessed the power of God working through Jesus' disciples at which they fell at their feet and worshiped them. However, the disciples quickly told them that they were not to be worshiped:

"And as Peter was coming in, Cornelius met him, and fell down at his feet, and worshipped him. But Peter took him up, saying, Stand up; I myself also am a man."[23]

Sometimes men fell before angels to worship them because of their glory yet they too, being creatures of God, refused to allow such worship take place:

"And I John saw these things, and heard them. And when I had heard and seen, I fell down to worship before the feet of the angel which showed me these things. Then said he unto me, See you do it not: for I am thy fellow servant, and of your brethren the prophets and of them which keep the sayings of this book: worship God."[24]

During His temptation by Satan, Jesus told the devil that God alone was to be worshiped:

> *"Then said Jesus unto him, Get you behind Me, Satan: for it is written, You shall worship the Lord your God, and Him only shall you serve."*[25]

Jesus knew that the Law of God only allowed the worship of God. Yet many times during Jesus' ministry, people who had witnessed His miraculous powers fell down at His feet and worshiped Him. Not one of these times did Jesus ever tell them not to worship Him:

> *"And, behold, there came a leper and worshipped Him, saying, Lord, if You will, You can make me clean. And Jesus put forth His hand, and touched Him, saying, I will; be you clean. And immediately his leprosy was cleansed."*[26]

> *"And as they went to tell His disciples, behold, Jesus met them, saying, All hail. And they came and held Him by the feet, and worshipped Him. Then said Jesus unto them, Be not afraid: go tell My brethren that they go into Galilee, and there shall they see Me."*[27]

> *"Jesus heard that they had cast him out; and when He had found him, He said unto him, Do you believe on the Son of God? He answered and said, Who is He, Lord, that I might believe on Him? And Jesus said unto him, You have both seen Him, and it is He that talks with you. And he said, Lord, I believe. And he worshipped Him."*[28]

The New Testament is explicit in its claims that Jesus Christ fulfilled the prophecy of Isaiah which stated that the Messiah would be a divine being.

It is revealing that this prophecy which spoke to the deity of Messiah is linked with the prophecy that foretold that the Messiah would also be a human being. This prophecy of Isaiah's, which I mentioned earlier, stated that the Messiah would be born of human virgin female. This is an important and crucial aspect in that it assigns to the Messiah the ability to save humans from their sins since He would also be a human being.

The Bible states that animals were not a permanent solution that was accepted by God as atonement for the sins of mankind. Though God accepted the sacrifice of animals as a covering for human sin,[29] they did not completely remove sin from humans' spirits:

> *"For the law having a shadow of good things to come, and not the very image of the things, can never with those sacrifices which they offered year by year continually make the ones who drew near perfect. For then would they not have ceased to be offered? Because that the worshippers once purged should have had no more conscience of sins. But in those sacrifices there is a remembrance again made of sins every year. For it is not possible that the blood of bulls and of goats should take away sins."*[30]

The Book of Hebrews says that if the sacrifices of animals were enough to purge sin completely from humans then it should not have been necessary for the high priests to offer those sacrifices every year on behalf of the people. Yet because they were not efficacious in removing the sins of the Jews they had to be offered yearly.

The writer of Hebrews goes on to declare that Jesus Christ's death on the cross was an acceptable sacrificial offering and that no more offerings would be required or accepted by God:

> *"By which we are sanctified through the offering of the body of Jesus Christ once for all. And every priest stands daily ministering and offering oftentimes the same sacrifices, which can never take away sins: But this Man, after He had offered one sacrifice for sins for ever, sat down on the right hand of God...For by one offering He has perfected for ever them that are sanctified. Whereof the Holy Ghost also is a witness to us: for after that God had said before, This is the covenant that I will make with them after those days, saith the Lord, I will put My laws into their hearts, and in their minds will I write them; And their*

> *sins and iniquities will I remember no more. Now where remission of these is, there is no more offering for sin."*[31]

Therefore, the only way God would accept the permanent absolution of mankind's sins was to have a sinless man die as an atoning sacrifice for them. The New Testament states that Jesus was a sinless human:

> *"Seeing then that we have a great High Priest, that is passed into the heavens, Jesus the Son of God, let us hold fast our profession. For we have not an High Priest which cannot be touched with the feeling of our infirmities; but was in all points tempted like as we are, yet without sin."*[32]

According to the New Testament scriptures that I listed here, Jesus Christ was God come in human flesh.

The Trinity

The New Testament also equates the Holy Spirit as equal with God.[33] This belief by Christians that God is one and yet consists of the Father, the Son, and the Holy Spirit is known as the Trinitarian doctrine. They refer to God as a "Trinity" which means that there are not three "Gods" but one God who has three personages who are co-equal and co-eternal. Man, whom God created in His image, is a kind of trinity by the fact that he is body, soul, and spirit.[34]

Orthodox historical Christianity declares that Jesus Christ is the promised Messiah and by His fulfillment of Messianic prophecy is completely God *and* completely human. Some religious people deny the deity of Jesus Christ yet in doing so they are denying the plain teachings of the Bible and the beliefs of historical Christianity.

Early in Church history, there were several ecumenical councils of Christian leaders in order to bring Christianity to a common understanding of the biblical truths of God. These councils determined such issues as the nature of God and the nature of Jesus Christ. They also decided which of the numerous beliefs that had become part of Christendom since the First Century were orthodox and which were heretical.

The Nicene Creed, which the leaders agreed upon at the councils of Nicaea (325 A.D.) and Constantinople (381 A.D.), is a clear and absolute statement of the orthodox Christian faith. This creed speaks to the belief that God is a triune yet unified being and that He became a human being in order to save us:

The Nicene Creed

I believe in one God,
the Father Almighty,
maker of heaven and earth,
and of all things visible and invisible;

And in one Lord Jesus Christ,
the only begotten Son of God,
begotten of his Father before all worlds,
God of God, Light of Light,
very God of very God,
begotten, not made,
being of one substance with the Father;
by whom all things were made;
who for us men and for our salvation
came down from heaven,
and was incarnate by the Holy Ghost
of the Virgin Mary,
and was made man;
and was crucified also for us under Pontius Pilate;
he suffered and was buried;
and the third day he rose again
according to the Scriptures,
and ascended into heaven,
and sitteth on the right hand of the Father;
and he shall come again, with glory,
to judge both the quick and the dead;
whose kingdom shall have no end.
And I believe in the Holy Ghost the Lord, and Giver of Life,
who proceedeth from the Father;
who with the Father and the Son together

is worshipped and glorified;
who spake by the Prophets.
And I believe one holy Catholic and Apostolic Church;
I acknowledge one baptism for the remission of sins;
and I look for the resurrection of the dead,
and the life of the world to come. Amen.

There is one final and very important question concerning the first coming of the Messiah that must be addressed: Why didn't Jesus set up His Messianic kingdom on earth immediately after His resurrection?

A Psalm of David contains a prophetic clue as to why this did not occur:

> *"You have ascended on high, You have led captivity captive: You have received gifts for men; yea, for the rebellious also, that the LORD God might dwell among them."*
> *-Psalm 68:18*

According to this verse, the Messiah would ascend on high [i.e., heaven] to where He would lead those who had been held captive by sin and death. The Messiah would receive gifts to give to His followers left on the earth. Then the Lord will set up His Kingdom on earth and dwell among men.

Fulfillment by Jesus Christ:

Jesus Christ did ascend to heaven forty days after His resurrection:

> *"And [Jesus] led them out as far as to Bethany, and He lifted up His hands, and blessed them. And it came to pass, while He blessed them, He was parted from them, and carried up into heaven. And they worshipped Him, and returned to Jerusalem with great joy."*[35]

During those forty days, He would appear and disappear from the midst of His disciples and then reappear to them.[36] I believe there were two main reasons why Jesus did this.

The first and most important is that He had to show the disciples that He had indeed been resurrected from death, *"Until the day in which He was taken up, after that He through the Holy Ghost had given commandments unto the apostles whom He had chosen: To whom also He showed Himself alive after His passion by many infallible proofs, being seen of them forty days, and speaking of the things pertaining to the kingdom of God."*[37]

The other reason is that the disciples had physically seen Jesus walking and talking with them for three and one-half years. He knew that He would be leaving them shortly. I believe Jesus wanted them to know that even though they could not see Him anymore, He was still present with them: *"And Jesus came and spoke unto them, saying, All power is given unto Me in heaven and in earth. Go you therefore, and teach all nations, baptizing them in the name of the Father, and of the Son, and of the Holy Ghost: Teaching them to observe all things whatsoever I have commanded you: and, lo, I am with you always, even unto the end of the world. Amen."*[38]

Even though the disciples didn't understand at the time, Jesus did tell them He would be leaving them one day:

> *"But these things have I told you, that when the time shall come, you may remember that I told you of them. And these things I said not unto you at the beginning, because I was with you. But now I go My way to Him that sent Me; and none of you asks Me, Where are you going? But because I have said these things unto you, sorrow has filled your heart. Nevertheless I tell you the truth; It is expedient for you that I go away: for if I go not away, the Comforter* [i.e., the Holy Spirit] *will not come unto you; but if I depart, I will send Him unto you...Howbeit when He, the Spirit of truth, is come, He will guide you into all truth: for He shall not speak of Himself; but whatsoever He shall hear, that shall He speak: and He will show you things to come."*[39]

Jesus told the disciples the reason He was ascending back to heaven was so that He could send the Holy Spirit to come upon them. As we read earlier in this chapter, the Holy Spirit did come upon them ten days after Jesus' ascension and the apostle Peter went out and boldly preached his sermon to the multitudes.

The Holy Spirit descended upon the disciples on the day of Pentecost, which occurred fifty days after Firstfruits Sunday. This fulfilled, to the exact day, the fourth feast of the year that God had ordained the Jews to keep.[40]

The apostle Paul quoted this passage written in the Psalm 68 in a letter he wrote to the Christians in Ephesus:

> *"But unto every one of us is given grace according to the measure of the gift of Christ. Wherefore He said, When He ascended up on high, He led captivity captive, and gave gifts unto men...And He gave some, apostles; and some, prophets; and some, evangelists; and some, pastors and teachers; For the perfecting of the saints, for the work of the ministry, for the edifying of the body of Christ: Till we all come in the unity of the faith, and of the knowledge of the Son of God, unto a perfect man, unto the measure of the stature of the fullness of Christ."*[41]

Paul is stating that when Jesus ascended into heaven He was going to give gifts to His followers so that they would be able to fulfill the mission that He gave to them. The gifts that Jesus gave to them were the gifts of the Holy Spirit.

Jesus had given the reason for the delay between His first coming and second coming was so that the gospel could be preached to the whole world:

> *"And this gospel of the kingdom shall be preached in all the world for a witness unto all nations; and then shall the end come."*[42]

God wanted not only the Jews to be reconciled to Him but also the Gentiles. The New Testament states: *"The Lord is not slack concerning His promise, as some men count slackness; but is longsuffering toward us, not willing that any should perish, but that all should come to repentance."*[43] It is God's desire that every person accept the sacrificial death of His Son so that their sins will be removed forever. The following verse shows how much God desires this:

> *"For God so loved the world, that He gave His only begotten Son, that whosoever believeth in Him should not perish, but have everlasting life."*
>
> \- *John 3:16*

Jesus will set up His Messianic Kingdom after the gospel has been preached to the entire world.

This concludes Part One of my book. I believe it is clear beyond a doubt that Jesus did fulfill all of the prophecies that were given by God concerning the coming of the suffering Messiah.

In Part Two, I hope that it will be just as evident that Jesus will soon fulfill the prophecies of the coming of the royal Messiah.

Though nearly two millennia have passed since Jesus ascended into heaven, He did make a promise to His followers:

"I go and prepare a place for you, I will come again, and receive you unto Myself; that where I am there you may be also."

\- *John 14:3*

[1] *Acts 2:21-32*
[2] *Matthew 26:69-75*
[3] *Acts 2:1-41*
[4] *Mark 16:1-6*
[5] *I Corinthians 15:14*
[6] *Leviticus 23:6-8*
[7] *I Corinthians 5:6-8*
[8] *Leviticus 23:9-14*
[9] *I Corinthians 15:20*
[10] *Isaiah 7:14*
[11] *John 1:1-3, 14*
[12] *Genesis 1:1*
[13] *Colossians 1:13-19; 2:9*
[14] *Ephesians 3:9*
[15] *Hebrews 1:1-3*
[16] *Isaiah 42:8*
[17] *John 5:19-23*
[18] *John 8:53-59*
[19] *Exodus 3:13-14*
[20] *John 14:5-10*
[21] *John 5:16-18*
[22] *John 10:30-33*
[23] *Acts 10:25-26*
[24] *Revelation 22:8-9*
[25] *Matthew 4:10*
[26] *Matthew 8:2-3*
[27] *Matthew 28:9-10*
[28] *John 9:35-38*
[29] *Leviticus 16:1-30*
[30] *Hebrews 10:1-4*
[31] *Hebrews 10:10-12, 14-18*
[32] *Hebrews 4:14-15*
[33] *John 4:24; Acts 5:1-4* Peter says in verse 3 they lied to the Holy Spirit and in verse 4 they lied to God; *Matthew1:18,20; 10:20*
[34] *Hebrews 4:12*
[35] *Luke 24:50-52*
[36] *John 20:19-29*
[37] *Acts 1:2-3*
[38] *Matthew 28:18-20*
[39] *John 16:4-7, 13*
[40] *Leviticus 23:15-22*
[41] *Ephesians 4:7-8, 11-13*
[42] *Matthew 24:14*
[43] *II Peter 3:9*

Part Two

The Second Coming Of The Messiah

7 - The End-Times Royal Messiah

In Part One of this book I have shown clearly that Jesus fulfilled those Messianic prophecies in the Old Testament that spoke of a suffering Messiah. This means that Jesus is the one and only Messiah.

Thus, in Part Two it will be my intention, not to prove that Jesus will also fulfill the prophecies in the Old Testament of the royal Messiah, but to show how and when He will fulfill them.

However, in this chapter I will simply list those prophecies written in the Old Testament which show that God will establish a kingdom on earth with the Messiah as the reigning King.

In the following chapters, I will illustrate how Jesus will accomplish the fulfillment of the prophecies listed here. I will also be including New Testament prophecies that concern His second coming, the events surrounding it, and His reign as the King.

With that understanding, let us turn again to the Book of Daniel to get the foundational prophecies of the Messiah and the kingdom He will rule over:

> *"And in the days of these kings shall the God of heaven set up a kingdom, which shall never be destroyed: and the kingdom shall not be left to other people, but it shall break in pieces and consume all these kingdoms, and it shall stand for ever."*
>
> *- Daniel 2:44*

The Messiah's kingdom will take precedence over all kingdoms that have come before it. It will be ruled over, not by other people, but by God's Messiah alone.

> *"I saw in the night visions, and, behold, one like the Son of man came with the clouds of heaven, and came to the Ancient of days, and they brought Him near before Him. And there was given Him dominion, and glory, and a kingdom, that all people, nations, and languages, should serve Him: His dominion is an everlasting dominion, which shall not pass away, and His kingdom that which shall not be destroyed."*
>
> *- Daniel 7:13-14*

The Messiah's kingdom will be ruled by one like the "Son of man". Jesus identified with this phrase and frequently used it to refer to Himself:

> *"But that you may know that the Son of man has power on earth to forgive sins, (then said He to the sick of the palsy,) Arise, take up thy bed, and go unto your house."*[1]

> *"But when they persecute you in this city, flee you into another: for truly I say to you, You shall not have gone over the cities of Israel, till the Son of man be come."*[2]

> *"For the Son of man is Lord even of the Sabbath day."*[3]

> *"And whosoever speaks a word against the Son of man, it shall be forgiven him: but whosoever speaks against the Holy Spirit, it shall not be forgiven him, neither in this world, neither in the world to come."*[4]

> *"The Son of man shall send forth His angels, and they shall gather out of His kingdom all things that offend, and they which do iniquity."*[5]

> *"When Jesus came into the coasts of Caesarea Philippi, He asked His disciples, saying, Whom do men say that I the Son of man am? ...And Simon Peter answered and said, You are the Messiah* [lit. Christ], *the Son of the living God."*[6]

> *"And Jesus said unto them, Truly I say to you, That you which have followed Me, in the regeneration when the Son of man shall sit in the throne of His glory, you also shall sit upon twelve thrones, judging the twelve tribes of Israel."*[7]

God will give the Son of man, the Messiah, the kingdom of the world to rule over. He will be sitting upon a throne ordained for Him by God, the Ancient of Days, which will last for eternity. He will receive glory and obeisance from all people forever.

The psalmist, King David, also prophesied of this Messianic kingdom:

> *"Why do the heathen rage, and the people imagine a vain thing? The kings of the earth set themselves, and the rulers take counsel together, against the LORD, and against His Anointed* [lit. in Hebrew mashiach which is Messiah], *saying, Let us break their bands asunder, and cast away their cords from us. He that sits in the heavens shall laugh: the Lord shall have them in derision. Then shall He speak to them in His wrath, and vex them in His sore displeasure. Yet have I set My King upon My holy hill of Zion. I will declare the decree: the LORD has said unto Me, You are My Son; this day have I begotten You. Ask of Me, and I shall give You the heathen for your inheritance, and the uttermost parts of the earth for your possession. You shall break them with a rod of iron; You shall dash them in pieces like a potter's vessel. Be wise now therefore, O you kings: be instructed, you judges of the earth. Serve the LORD with fear, and rejoice with trembling. Kiss the Son, lest He be angry, and you perish from the way, when His wrath is kindled but a little. Blessed are all they that put their trust in Him."*
>
> *- Psalm 2:1-12*

David prophesies that before the Messiah begins His reign, He will execute judgment upon the kingdoms of the earth who have opposed God. He will break them and rule His kingdom with a *"rod of iron"*.

The prophet Jeremiah also mentions the manner in which the Messiah will reign over the world:

> *"Behold, the days come, saith the LORD, that I will raise unto David a righteous Branch, and a King shall reign and prosper, and shall execute judgment and justice in the earth. In His days Judah shall be saved, and Israel shall dwell safely: and this is His name whereby He shall be called, THE LORD OUR RIGHTEOUSNESS."*[8]

As you read in Chapter 3, the "Branch" is another name for the Messiah. Jeremiah confirms the execution of righteous judgment by the Messiah in another passage:

> *"Behold, the days come, saith the LORD, that I will perform that good thing which I have promised unto the house of Israel and to the house of Judah. In those days, and at that time, will I cause the Branch of righteousness to grow up unto David; and He shall execute judgment and righteousness in the land. In those days shall Judah be saved, and Jerusalem shall dwell safely: and this is the name wherewith she shall be called, The LORD our righteousness."*[9]

During the Messiah's reign, lawlessness will no longer go unpunished. However, unlike human judges who rule with a sinful human nature, the Messiah's judgments will be righteous and fair.

I have already referenced the following prophecy in this work as pertaining to two different aspects of the Messiah's coming to earth. The first was to show His humanity and the second His deity. A third component to this prophecy, which is appropriate for the subject under discussion, concerns the reign of the Messiah-King:

> *"For unto us a Child is born, unto us a Son is given: and the government shall be upon His shoulder: and His name shall be called Wonderful, Counselor, The mighty God,*

> *The everlasting Father, The Prince of Peace. Of the increase of His government and peace there shall be no end, upon the throne of David, and upon his kingdom, to order it, and to establish it with judgment and with justice from henceforth even for ever. The zeal of the LORD of hosts will perform this."*[10]

The Messiah's kingdom will be unlike any other kingdom that mankind has experienced. There will be justice and fairness among the people. In response the people will love, serve, and glorify the Messiah King. There will finally be *true* peace on earth.

Lastly, the Old Testament states that the Messiah will rule from Jerusalem where He will rebuild the Temple of God:

> *"And speak unto him, saying, Thus speaks the LORD of hosts, saying, Behold the Man whose name is the BRANCH; and He shall grow up out of His place, and He shall build the Temple of the LORD. Even He shall build the Temple of the LORD; and He shall bear the glory, and shall sit and rule upon His throne; and He shall be a Priest upon His throne: and the counsel of peace shall be between them both."*[11]

> *"And it shall come to pass in the last days, that the mountain of the LORD'S house* [i.e., Temple] *shall be established in the top of the mountains, and shall be exalted above the hills; and all nations shall flow unto it. And many people shall go and say, Come you, and let us go up to the mountain of the LORD, to the house of the God of Jacob; and He will teach us of His ways, and we will walk in His paths: for out of Zion shall go forth the law, and the word of the LORD from Jerusalem. And He shall judge among the nations, and shall rebuke many people: and they shall beat their swords into plowshares, and their spears into pruning hooks: nation shall not lift up sword against nation, neither shall they learn war any more."*[12]

There is a desire on the part of some Jews in modern Israel to rebuild the Jewish Temple. However, there is some disagreement between them and other Jews over this issue. Because of the above verses some Orthodox Jews believe that only the Messiah should rebuild the Temple. Nevertheless, in recent history there have been some very controversial attempts to lay the cornerstone for the building of the Jewish Temple. I do believe (because of New Testament prophecy) that a Temple will be rebuilt in Jerusalem before the Messiah comes to build His Temple. I will discuss this in a later chapter.

The Old Testament prophesies not only of a royal Messiah but also where and how He will establish His kingdom. It will be a kingdom of righteousness, fairness, justice, and above all a kingdom of peace.

As I mentioned at the beginning of this chapter, from this point on I will be interspersing both Old and New Testament prophecies that concern the "end-times".

The approach that I have chosen is to write the next several chapters in the order by which the end-time events will occur. Though there is some disagreement among Christians as to the exact time and placement of these events, I will list them in the order that I believe many Christians accept.

---

[1] *Matthew 9:6*
[2] *Matthew 10:23*
[3] *Matthew 12:8*
[4] *Matthew 12:32*
[5] *Matthew 13:41*
[6] *Matthew 16:13, 16*
[7] *Matthew 19:28*
[8] *Jeremiah 23:5-6*
[9] *Jeremiah 33:14-16*
[10] *Isaiah 9:6-7*
[11] *Zechariah 6:12-13*
[12] *Isaiah 2:2-4*

8 - The Rapture Mystery

The event I will be discussing in this chapter is probably the most controversial of all the end-time prophecies. The controversy lies not in the fact that this event will take place but rather the dispute arises as to when this event will occur.

The New Testament declares that close to the end of the current age we live in, Jesus Christ will appear in the sky and remove His followers from the earth. Christians call this event "the Rapture".

The Christians in the Church of Thessalonica in Greece were concerned that they had missed the second coming of Jesus Christ.[1] The apostle Paul tried to assuage their fears by telling them in a letter exactly what would happen toward the end:

> *"But I would not have you to be ignorant, brethren, concerning those which are asleep, that you sorrow not, even as others which have no hope. For if we believe that Jesus died and rose again, even so those also which sleep* [i.e., are dead] *in Jesus will God bring with Him. For this we say unto you by the word of the Lord, that we which are alive and remain unto the coming of the Lord shall not prevent those which are asleep. For the Lord Himself shall descend from heaven with a shout, with the voice of the archangel, and with the trump of God: and the dead in Christ shall rise first: Then we which are alive and remain shall be caught up together with them in the clouds, to meet the Lord in the air: and so shall we ever be with the Lord."*
>
> \- *I Thessalonians 4:13-17*

Paul states that Jesus *will* appear in the sky and that at His command Christians "*shall be caught up*" to meet Him in the air. We get the term "rapture" from the last two words of this phrase.

The New Testament was originally written in the Greek language of that era. The words "caught up" are the English translation of the Greek word "harpazo". It means to "seize suddenly" or to "snatch away". When the Fourth Century scholar Jerome translated the New Testament into Latin he rendered the Greek word "harpazo" as the Latin word "rapiemur". It is from this Latin word that the event, described by Paul in the passage above, came to be known as "the Rapture".

The apostle Paul, in his letter to the Corinthian Church, describes what the Rapture will be like:

> "*Behold, I show you a mystery; We shall not all sleep* [i.e., die], *but we shall all be changed, In a moment, in the twinkling of an eye, at the last trump: for the trumpet shall sound, and the dead shall be raised incorruptible, and we shall be changed. For this corruptible must put on incorruption, and this mortal must put on immortality. So when this corruptible shall have put on incorruption, and this mortal shall have put on immortality, then shall be brought to pass the saying that is written, Death is swallowed up in victory.*"[2]

Paul writes that God will transform the physical bodies of the believers in Christ Jesus in an instant from a mortal body into an immortal body. At that point Christians will have entered into a new dimension, the eternal dimension.

Earlier in this same letter Paul had explained his theological position to the Corinthian Church concerning what happens to Christians when they die:

> "*Therefore we are always confident, knowing that, while we are at home in the body, we are absent from the Lord...We are confident, I say, and willing rather to be absent from the body, and to be present with the Lord.*"[3]

According to Paul the spirits of Christians who die go immediately to be with the Lord. When Jesus comes to rapture His followers He will appear in the sky, an archangel will shout, and a trumpet will sound. This trumpet is probably a shofar (made out of either a ram's or an ibex's horn) which was blown for assembling the Jewish people and for other important events. The spirits of those Christians who are already dead will come down with Jesus and will be reunited with their bodies (albeit different from the fleshly bodies we have currently) which will be resurrected from the earth. These bodies will be in a glorified or eternal state so that they can function in eternal dimensions. Paul mentioned this in the passage above where he says, *"For this corruptible [body] must put on incorruption, and this mortal [body] must put on immortality"*.

It is interesting that after Jesus' resurrection He told the disciples to touch His resurrected body which still bore the marks of His crucifixion.[4] He said to them: *"Behold My hands and My feet, that it is I Myself: handle Me, and see; for a spirit has not flesh and bones, as you see Me have."*[5] As we read earlier in this book, God stated that the life of flesh is in the blood.[6] Here, Jesus states that His body was flesh and bone. After we die blood will no longer be the sustainer of life. Although our resurrected bodies will be of a physical nature and will have substance, it is the spirit and power of God that will sustain them. The disciple John wrote: *"Jesus said unto her, I am the resurrection, and the life: he that believes in Me, though he were dead, yet shall he live: And whosoever lives and believes in Me shall never die."*[7]

Therefore, born-again Christians who are living on the earth at the time of the Rapture will immediately have their mortal bodies changed into immortal or eternal bodies. They will be snatched off the earth to meet the Lord *"in the air"* and will be with Jesus forevermore.

The theological position that one holds concerning the timing of Rapture determines whether it will be a "mysterious or secret" event or whether the world will recognize it as part of God's end-times plans once it takes place.

If the Rapture takes place at the beginning of the end-times events then it will catch the world by surprise. People's friends, relatives, and acquaintances will suddenly disappear from the earth. A shocked world will be looking for explanations as to what exactly took place. Chaos will ensue after this disappearance of millions of persons because of all the accidents that occur from those who were driving cars, flying airplanes or performing other types of human activities. One would not be amiss in stating such a scenario as bizarre at the least and too fantastic to believe at the most. Yet the Bible records that the Rapture is going to take place in the future.

However, if the Rapture occurs after God begins the end-times events then the world may have a better grasp as to what happened. This would be due to the fact that the people on earth would have already witnessed other supernatural events that had occurred.

The Timing of the Rapture

When might the Rapture take place? Both the Old and New Testaments speak of a time of trouble coming upon the whole world at the end of this age. The Bible uses different expressions to describe this period but most Christians refer to it as the "Tribulation Period". I will be examining this time of trouble in the next chapter but for now I will mention that it will last seven years according to the Bible. The timing of the Rapture revolves around this seven-year Tribulation Period.

There are three major theological positions that most Christians adhere to as concerning when the timing of the Rapture will take place. They are that the Rapture will take place before the Tribulation Period starts, in the middle of it, or at the end of it. Christian terminology refers to these positions as the Pre-Tribulation Rapture, the Mid-Tribulation Rapture, and the Post-Tribulation Rapture

There is a fourth position that an individual suggested in a book[8] but it has not gained a foothold in Christian circles. This theory states that the Rapture will take place between the middle and the end of the Tribulation Period. That author refers to it as the Pre-Wrath Rapture.

The Pre-Tribulation Rapture

Let us look first at the Pre-Tribulation doctrine. This teaching had its beginnings early in the Nineteenth Century though there may have been some allusions to it before that in other Christian writings.

The basis for this belief is rooted in several Old and New Testament passages. The primary reason for believing in the Pre-Tribulation Rapture is that if God is going to judge the world because of its rebellion and opposition toward Him then He would spare His faithful followers this judgment.

The apostle Paul wrote in the same letter to the Thessalonians that they were *"to wait for His Son from heaven, Whom He raised from the dead, even Jesus, Who delivered us from the wrath to come."*[9] There are two ways to interpret this verse. Either the wrath to come refers to the Tribulation Period when God pours out His wrath on the earth or it refers to the very end of time when God will judge those opposed to Him by casting them into Hell. Later in this letter, Paul writes, *"For God has not appointed us to wrath, but to obtain salvation by our Lord Jesus Christ, Who died for us, that, whether we wake or sleep, we should live together with Him."*[10] This verse seems to associate salvation with being spared from God's wrath that will come upon unbelievers when He casts them into Hell. Those who believe in a Pre-Tribulation Rapture believe the wrath spoken of in these verses refers to God's wrathful judgments that occur during the Tribulation Period. Consequently, God will remove His people before He begins His judgment of the earth and its inhabitants.

Another reason that Pre-Tribulationists believe that Christians are going to be raptured before the Tribulation stems from a curious statement that Paul wrote in his second letter to the Thessalonians, *"Let no man deceive you by any means: for that day shall not come, except there come a falling away first, and that man of sin be revealed, the son of perdition; Who opposes and exalts himself above all that is called God, or that is worshipped; so that he as God sits in the Temple of God, showing himself that he is God. Remember you not, that, when I was yet with you, I told you these things? And now you know what withholds that he might be revealed in his time. For the mystery of iniquity does already work: only he who now restrains will restrain, until he be taken out of the way. And then shall that*

Wicked be revealed, whom the Lord shall consume with the spirit of His mouth, and shall destroy with the brightness of His coming."[11] Pretribulationism teaches that *"he who restrains"* refers to the Holy Spirit. Thus, before the wicked Antichrist can be revealed the Holy Spirit has to be removed from the earth. Since the Holy Spirit resides in the followers of Jesus Christ, they too must be removed by the Rapture from the earth. Then the Tribulation Period can start and the Antichrist can come to power.

There are a couple of Old Testament stories that indicate God may indeed act in this manner. The first is the story of Noah's flood.[12] In that event God declared that the world had become irrevocably wicked. He determined that He would judge the whole world for its evil by bringing a flood against it and thereby cleanse the earth. However, there were a few righteous followers of God whom He did not want to destroy. Thus, He had Noah build an ark or ship by which he would be safe from God's judgment. Indeed, God did flood the earth after *He*[13] closed the door of the ark behind Noah and his family. God protected His followers by putting them in a place of refuge where His wrath would not harm them.

The other story involves God's servant Abraham and his nephew Lot.[14] In the towns of Sodom and Gomorrah wickedness reigned supreme. God was determined to destroy those cities because of their evil. Abraham was concerned for his nephew Lot who lived in Sodom. He pleaded with the Lord not to destroy Sodom if He could find fifty righteous men living there. Eventually Abraham reduced the number of righteous men down to ten. Sadly, not even ten righteous persons lived in Sodom. Thus, God declared that He would destroy both cities but before He did this He would remove Lot and his family from its midst. God held back His judgment until Lot and his family were safely out of the city and then the He destroyed Sodom and Gomorrah. However, His people were saved from His wrath.

Both of these stories indicate that it may very well be God's plan to remove His followers from the earth before He judges it one final time. If this is the case then Jesus will come down to earth, seven years after the Rapture, to judge the nations of the world and set up His kingdom on earth.

Pre-Tribulation Christians make a distinction between Jesus' appearance in the sky to rapture His followers and His second coming to earth when He will begin His reign as the King-Messiah.

Pre-Tribulationists believe that there are no more prophetic signs that must be fulfilled before Jesus comes to rapture the Church. They refer to the belief that Jesus could return at any moment like a *"thief in the night"* as the doctrine of Imminency.

I want to mention one further note concerning the biblical end-time events. Both the Old and New Testaments frequently use the phrase "the Day of the Lord". There is a disagreement among some Christians as to what time frame constitutes "the Day of the Lord". Pre-Tribulation and Mid-Tribulation Christians believe it starts with the Rapture of the Church. Others hold to a different view that I will point out in the following sections.

The Mid-Tribulation Rapture

Those who believe in a Mid-Tribulation Rapture do so because of whose wrath will be involved during the Tribulation Period. As I show in the next chapter, a wicked *human* world ruler will dominate the first part of that seven-year period. He will eventually persecute and destroy many people by his own personal wrath. According to this belief, it will then be during the second half of the Tribulation Period that God will supernaturally bring His wrath down on the world.

Mid-Tribulation Christians make a distinction between God's wrath and man's wrath. They believe that since Christians have always suffered persecution from mankind they would not be experiencing anything different under the reign of an evil world leader. However, they also believe that God would not pour down His wrath on His people so He will remove them before the second half of the Tribulation Period begins.

This removal or Rapture would take place at the sounding of the seventh-trumpet judgment listed in the Book of Revelation. Mid-Tribulationists base this belief on the fact that Paul said the Rapture would take place at the *"last trump"*.[15]

This teaching came into prominence around the middle of the twentieth Century.

The Pre-Wrath Rapture

The teaching of the Pre-Wrath Rapture came to the fore in the early 1990s. The basis of this theory is rooted in the Book of Revelation. In the next chapter I will be discussing this prophetic book in more detail though at this time I need to allude to it here in order to discuss this theory.

Revelation uses descriptive language in laying out God's entire plans for the end-times. It lists three sets of judgments that are going to take place during the seven-year Tribulation Period. Respectively these judgments are referred to as the "seven seals", "seven trumpets", and "seven bowls". Each of these events unleashes a different type of calamity that is going to happen to the earth and its inhabitants.

According to the Pre-Wrath Rapture teaching, the "Day of the Lord" begins after the opening of the sixth seal. It is at that time when God pours out His wrath on the earth. The scriptural basis for this belief is found in the prophetic Book of Joel where the prophet speaks about the Tribulation Period: *"I will show wonders in the heavens and in the earth, blood, and fire, and pillars of smoke. The sun shall be turned into darkness, and the moon into blood, before the great and the terrible Day of the LORD come."*[16] The first five seals seem to indicate that the earth will suffer as a result of human causes. However, when the opening of the sixth seal takes place, cosmic judgments come upon the earth that only God could implement.

The opening of the seventh seal puts into motion the seven trumpet judgments which in turn start the final seven bowl judgments. Therefore, the Pre-Wrath Rapture will take place at the opening of the seventh seal. According to this belief the opening of the sixth and seventh seals does not take place until some time during the second half of the seven-year Tribulation Period. If this doctrine is correct then the time frames listed in the Book of Revelation indicate that the period of time between the Rapture and Jesus' second coming to earth could be anywhere from six months to one and one half years.

The Post-Tribulation Rapture

The last doctrine concerning the timing of the Rapture appears to be the historical position held by the early Church (although this teaching has been refined in recent years).

This belief states that the Rapture will take place in conjunction with the second coming of Christ, which occurs at the very end of the Tribulation Period. This doctrine is referred to as the Post-Tribulation Rapture.

This teaching is based on several issues. One is that Jesus' disciples asked Him to tell them what the signs would be leading up to His second coming.[17] Jesus explained to them that several events would take place before He came again. This raises the question that if the disciples or future Christians were going to be raptured before the Tribulation Period why would Jesus give them signs to watch for if they weren't going to be around to see them?

Another basis for Posttribulationism is the fact that persecution of Christians has been going on since Jesus Christ ascended into heaven. Therefore, it will be no different during the Tribulation Period since it will be a continuation of the suffering that has been going on for two millennia.

The apostle Paul in a second letter that he wrote to the Thessalonian Church also seemed to say that there are some signs that would take place before the Rapture: *"Now we beseech you, brethren, by the coming of our Lord Jesus Christ, and by our gathering together unto Him, That you be not soon shaken in mind, or be troubled, neither by spirit, nor by word, nor by letter as from us, as that the day of Christ is at hand. Let no man deceive you by any means: for that day shall not come, except there come a falling away first, and that man of sin be revealed, the son of perdition; Who opposes and exalts himself above all that is called God, or that is worshipped; so that he as God sits in the Temple of God, showing himself that he is God. Remember you not, that, when I was yet with you, I told you these things?"*[18] Here Paul uses the personal pronoun indicating that he and other Christians would not be raptured until after the wicked world ruler appeared on the scene. I will be speaking to the issue of this world leader and the timing of his appearance on earth in the next chapter. Suffice it to say now though that it seems as if Paul is saying that the Rapture would take place toward the end of the Tribulation Period and therefore would occur at Jesus' second coming to earth.

Lastly, those who adhere to the Post-Tribulation position believe that the "Day of the Lord" cannot start until Jesus destroys the nations of the world at the battle of Armageddon and sets up His Messianic Kingdom. They quote from the Book of Isaiah, which says, *"The lofty looks of man shall be humbled, and the haughtiness of men shall be bowed down, and the LORD alone shall be exalted in that day. For the Day of the LORD of hosts shall be upon every one that is proud and lofty, and upon every one that is lifted up; and he shall be brought low."*[19] This is the first mention in the Bible of the "Day of the Lord". Isaiah states that only the Lord will be exalted in that day. Since the wicked world ruler is to be exalted by humankind before the Messiah comes, the "Day of the Lord" has to be reserved for Him until the end of the Tribulation Period. Therefore, those Christians who say the "Day of the Lord" begins with the Rapture or at the beginning of the Tribulation would be in error according to this teaching.

Post-Tribulationists also reference other scripture verses in which the "Day of the Lord" revolves around the battle of Armageddon, which occurs at the very end of the Tribulation Period.[20]

Though there are many other reasons why Post-Tribulationists believe that the Rapture will take place at Jesus' second coming to earth I will not take the time to list them here.

Each of these teachings does have some problems associated with their particular stance on the timing of the Rapture.

For example, Pre-Tribulationism has to deal with a prophecy given in the Book of Malachi: *"Behold, I will send you Elijah the prophet before the coming of the great and dreadful Day of the Lord."*[21] The dilemma here is that if the "Day of the Lord" starts with the Rapture then the doctrine of the imminent return of Jesus is untenable. The prophet Malachi states that the prophet Elijah must appear before the Day of the Lord takes place. So there would be a prophetic sign that would have to occur before the Rapture takes place.

The Mid-Tribulation Rapture belief has a problem in its assumption that the seventh trumpet judgment is the "last trump" spoken of by Paul. The seven trumpet judgments are not blown for the believers' sake but to announce various judgments upon the unbelieving world.

The Pre-Wrath view declares that the wrath of God does not start until after the opening of the seventh seal. However, the Book of Revelation states that none of the "seal" judgments starts until Jesus Christ opens them. If the opening of the first five seals unleashes the wrath of man upon the world, it only happens because Jesus unseals the judgments. Therefore, it is God through His Son who initiates these judgments.[22]

Post-Tribulation has to account for the verse that the apostle Paul wrote to the Thessalonian Christians in which they are *"to wait for His Son from heaven, Whom He raised from the dead, even Jesus, which delivered us from the wrath to come."*[23] If this verse is referring to the wrath that God is going to pour out on the earth during the Tribulation Period then Christians will not have to go through the entire seven years of judgment.

Since the prophecies of the Old Testament do not mention the Church Age, there does not seem to be any reference to the Rapture taking place before, during, or after God judges the earth. However, the Old Testament does illustrate truths about God that indicate the principles by which He abides. A passage in the prophetic Book of Isaiah expresses the principle of God's protection of His people from His wrath:

> *"Come, My people, enter you into your chambers, and shut your doors about you: hide yourself as it were for a little moment, until the indignation be passed over. For, behold, the LORD comes out of His place to punish the inhabitants of the earth for their iniquity: the earth also shall disclose her blood, and shall no more cover her slain. In that day the LORD with His sore and great and strong sword shall punish leviathan the piercing serpent, even leviathan that*

crooked serpent; and He shall slay the dragon that is in the sea."[24]

There is one final aspect concerning the Rapture and the timing of it that I wish to point out. In Chapter 6, I mentioned that God ordained the Jewish people to observe seven feasts on specific days of the Jewish calendar. These seven feasts were divided into two seasonal periods of the years. The first four feasts were to take place in spring/early summer and the final three feasts would take place in the autumn or fall. These fall feasts were the "Feast of Trumpets", the "Day of Atonement", and the "Feast of Tabernacles". I want to discuss the Feast of Trumpets at this time.

In the Book of Leviticus God issued His ordinances for the seven Jewish feasts. Concerning the feast of Trumpets He said:

> *"Speak unto the children of Israel, saying, In the seventh month, in the first day of the month, shall you have a Sabbath, a memorial of blowing of trumpets, an holy convocation. You shall do no servile work therein: but you shall offer an offering made by fire unto the LORD."*[25]

This observance was to take place on the first day of the Jewish month Tishri. In modern times, the Jews celebrate Tishri as the first month in their calendar. The first day of Tishri is now called "Rosh haShanah" which means "head of the year". Hence, the Jews celebrate it as their New Years Day. In biblical times though, they called it "Yom Teruah" which means "the day of the sounding of the shofar [i.e., trumpet]".

Jews actually celebrate the Feast of Trumpets on the first and second days of Tishri. This is because the Jewish calendar is based on the lunar cycles. Each month begins on the new moon. In times past the Jews declared the new moon by observation. When the Sanhedrin (i.e., the Jewish ruling council) saw the new moon they declared that a new month had started. They then sent out messengers to tell people when the month began. However, they could not always notify those Jews who lived in distant communities in time to tell them that the new month had started. Since sending out messengers took some time these distant Jewish communities might not hear the announcement until the second day of the month. Therefore, the Jews celebrated the holidays on both days so that they would be faithful in obeying God's Law.

All God says about the Feast of Trumpets is that it is to be celebrated as a memorial by the blowing of trumpets. The Bible gives no other reason as to why God told the Jews they *must* observe this holy day. I believe the answer could lie in prophecy.

As we saw in Chapter 6, Jesus fulfilled each of the spring feasts on the specific days that God had ordained. He was crucified on Passover, buried on Unleavened Bread, resurrected on Firstfruits Sunday, and poured out the Holy Spirit upon the disciples on the Day of Pentecost. Since God was so meticulous in fulfilling the spring feasts with the Messiah's first coming, I believe it is entirely possible that the Jesus Christ will fulfill the fall feasts with His second coming.

Why then did God order the blowing of trumpets on the first (and now second) day of Tishri for a memorial? I believe it was foretelling of the day that the Messiah would appear in the sky and sound the trumpet to rapture His followers. If this is so then the Rapture may take place on the first or second day of Tishri, which is in the autumn. For two reasons however, this does not violate Jesus' statement that *"...of that day and that hour knows no man, no, not the angels which are in heaven, neither the Son, but the Father."*[26] The first is that we still don't know the year in which the Rapture will take place and therefore wouldn't know the date. The second is that the Feast of Trumpets is celebrated on two successive days of Tishri. Thus, we would not know which of these days the Rapture would occur.

I am not dogmatic about this theory but it would seem consistent with God's plans for the Messiah and His fulfillment of the spring feasts. The apostle Paul seems to allude to the idea that the holy or feast days had a deeper meaning than revealed in the Old Testament:

> *"Let no man therefore judge you in meat, or in drink, or in respect of an holyday, or of the new moon, or of the sabbath days: Which are a shadow of things to come; but the body is of Christ."*[27]

In conclusion, I will point out that as with many doctrines of the Christian faith, the Rapture teaching has resulted in some serious disputes among Christians. There are many books and web sites that discuss, defend, and examine at length each of these positions on the timing of the Rapture

The only thing that I am adamant about concerning this issue is that one day (or night) Jesus Christ *is* going to appear in the sky and rapture His followers off the earth. The Bible states that this event *is* going to happen in the future.

---

[1] *II Thessalonians 2:1-3*

[2] *I Corinthians 15:51-54*

[3] *I Corinthians 5:6, 8*

[4] *John 20:26-29*

[5] *Luke 24:39*

[6] *Leviticus 17:11, 14* - In these verses the Jews were not to eat any blood from the sacrificial animals that they killed. Therefore, the blood from the sacrificed animal had to be completely drained before the Jews could eat that animal. Since Jesus was the sacrificial offering for the sins of mankind, all of His blood would also have been removed. Not necessarily at the cross but at the time of God's acceptance of His sacrifice on behalf of humans. The Book of Hebrews states that Jesus entered into the heavenly Temple and offered His blood in the Holy Place as a sacrificial offering for the sins of humankind: "*...by His own blood He entered in once into the holy place, having obtained eternal redemption for us"(Hebrews 9:12).* Paul, in speaking of the change of our mortal bodies into immortal bodies, states clearly that blood cannot be a part of our eternal bodies: *"Now this I say, brethren, that [human] flesh and blood cannot inherit the kingdom of God; neither doth corruption inherit incorruption."(I Corinthians 15:50)*

[7] *John 11:25-26*

[8] "The Pre-Wrath Rapture of the Church"; by Marvin J. Rosenthal; (Thomas Nelson Publishers, 1990)

[9] *I Thessalonians 1:10*

[10] *I Thessalonians 5:9-10*

[11] *II Thessalonians 2:3-8*

[12] *Genesis 6:1-8:22*

[13] *Genesis 7:16*

[14] *Genesis 18:16-19:28*

[15] *Revelation 11:15-19*

[16] *Joel 2:30-31*

[17] *Matthew 24:1-51*

[18] *II Thessalonians 2:1-5*

[19] *Isaiah 2:11-12*

[20] *Isaiah 13:9; Joel 2:1-11; Zechariah 14:1-9*
[21] *Malachi 4:5*
[22] *Revelation 5:1-8:1*
[23] *I Thessalonians 1:10*
[24] *Isaiah 26:20-27:1*
[25] *Leviticus 23:24-25*
[26] *Mark 13:32*
[27] *Colossians 2:16-17*

9 - Daniel's Seventieth Week: Jacob's Time of Trouble

There are two life issues that should concern non-Christians. The first has been around for nearly two millennia. It is the matter of a person dying before they accept Jesus Christ as their Lord and Savior by receiving His sacrificial death as atonement for or cleansing from their sins. The second is the subject of this chapter.

In Chapter 5 of this book, I discussed the "seventy weeks" prophecy of Daniel. We learned that God had decreed 490 years for the fulfillment of the Messianic prophecies. This prophecy also determined the time frames for the Jewish people's future. We saw how Jesus accomplished the fulfillment of the first 483 years of this prophecy with His first coming. Now we will revisit that prophetic passage and study the final seven years of the "seventy weeks":

> *"Seventy weeks are determined upon your people and upon your holy city, to finish the transgression, and to make an end of sins, and to make reconciliation for iniquity, and to bring in everlasting righteousness, and to seal up the vision and prophecy, and to anoint the most Holy. Know therefore and understand, that from the going forth of the commandment to restore and to build Jerusalem unto the Messiah the Prince shall be seven weeks, and threescore and two weeks: the street shall be built again, and the wall, even in troublous times. And after threescore and two weeks shall Messiah be cut off, but not for Himself: and the people of the prince that shall come shall destroy the city and the sanctuary; and the end thereof shall be with a*

flood, and unto the end of the war desolations are determined. And he shall confirm the covenant with many for one week: and in the midst of the week he shall cause the sacrifice and the oblation to cease, and for the overspreading of abominations he shall make it desolate, even until the consummation, and that determined shall be poured upon the desolate."

- *Daniel 9:24-27*

The first thing to note in this passage is that this prophecy is for the Jews and not the Gentiles (although as we will see the Gentiles will also suffer greatly during this time). Daniel says that these seventy "sevens" of years will affect his people, the Jews, and the holy city of Jerusalem.

By the end of the fulfillment of this passage, the Jews will have obtained an end of their transgressions and sins through their reconciliation to God. They will also have acquired everlasting righteousness. Though Jesus did make a way for the Jews to have forgiveness of their sins (and many Jews did accept Him), they as a nation rejected Him and He was *"cut off"* or killed. So the time of everlasting righteousness has not taken place yet. The fulfillment of this part of the prophecy will take place at the end of this final week or seven-year period of the seventy weeks.

During this final period the people of a ruler will come and destroy Jerusalem and the Temple therein. There was a foreshadow of this future event in 70 A.D. Jesus, when discussing the signs of the end-times while He was on the Mount of Olives with His disciples, said that the Temple standing before them would be destroyed:

"And Jesus went out, and departed from the Temple: and His disciples came to Him for to show Him the buildings of The Temple. And Jesus said unto them, See you not all These things? Truly I say unto you, There shall not be left Here one stone upon another, that shall not be thrown down."[1]

Less than forty years later, in 70 A.D., the Roman army under General (and later emperor) Titus did invade Jerusalem and destroy the Temple. The Jewish historian Josephus describes how during this war the Jews were tortured, persecuted, and killed.[2] As you will see, this was not a fulfillment of seventieth week of Daniel but rather a prophetic *type* of what will occur.

Christians refer to this future ruler as the "Antichrist" or the "Beast". I will elaborate on who he is and what he will do more fully later. For now though we will look at what the Book of Daniel has to say about him in reference to the seventieth week.

In the last verse of this passage in chapter 9 of Daniel, it states that this ruler or prince will confirm a covenant with many for one week of seven years. Many believe this covenant will be a peace treaty of some kind. Daniel speaks of this ruler or Antichrist and what he will do during this period:

> *"And in the latter time of their kingdom, when the transgressors are come to the full, a king of fierce countenance, and understanding dark sentences, shall stand up. And his power shall be mighty, but not by his own power: and he shall destroy wonderfully, and shall prosper, and practice, and shall destroy the mighty and the holy people. And through his policy also he shall cause craft to prosper in his hand; and he shall magnify himself in his heart, and by peace shall destroy many: he shall also stand up against the Prince of princes; but he shall be broken without hand."*[3]

It states here that this ruler will destroy many through his policy of peace, which I will discuss in a moment. The apostle Paul agrees with Daniel where he says that the Antichrist will magnify himself and stand up against the Prince of princes:

> *"Let no man deceive you by any means: for that day shall not come, except there come a falling away first, and that man of sin be revealed, the son of perdition; Who opposes and exalts himself above all that is called God, or that is worshipped; so that he as God sits in the Temple of God,*

showing himself that he is God."[4]

On the Mount of Olives Jesus too made mention of the Antichrist entering the Temple when He said:

> *"When you therefore shall see the abomination of desolation, spoken of by Daniel the prophet, stand in the holy place, (whoso reads, let him understand:) Then let them which be in Judea flee into the mountains."*[5]

It appears this future leader will either author or at least support a peace treaty that lasts seven years. Part of this agreement will probably include the rebuilding of the Jewish Temple since the last verse of Daniel chapter 9 states that in the middle of this seven-year period the Antichrist will cause the Temple sacrifices to cease. This cessation of sacrificial offerings will come about when the Antichrist enters the Temple to declare himself God. Daniel writes that this will lead to the desolation or desecration of the Temple. Paul seems to be speaking about the results of this peace treaty in his first letter to the Thessalonians:

> *"For yourselves know perfectly that the day of the Lord so comes as a thief in the night. For when they shall say, Peace and safety; then sudden destruction comes upon them, as travail upon a woman with child; and they shall not escape."*[6]

At the current time it is hard to see how such a scenario could come about. The Jews do want to rebuild their Temple so that they can start offering sacrifices again. The problem is that at present the religion of Islam has their shrine called "The Dome of the Rock" located on the mount where the Jews must build their Temple. This of course provides quite a dilemma for the Jews and their desires. Many believe that the Antichrist, who will possess great might, deception, and charisma, will provide a solution to this problem through this peace treaty spoken of by Daniel. It is possible that because of the wisdom he shows in resolving this issue, both the Gentiles and the Jews will accept him as the Messiah. As we read earlier in Chapter 7, the Messiah is supposed to rebuild the Temple. If the Antichrist were able to accomplish this then the world would indeed accept him as the Messiah. The Book of Revelation states that the whole world, excepting the followers of Jesus, will worship him: *"And all that dwell upon the earth shall worship him, whose names are not written in the book of life of the Lamb slain from the foundation of the world."*[7]

When I was a new Christian I talked to a friend about Jesus Christ. He said that he would believe what the Bible said about Jesus' second coming when he saw the Temple rebuilt in Jerusalem. Having recently been saved I had no idea what he was referring to. Since then I have studied the end-times prophecies and came to understand what my friend was alluding to back then. The problem with waiting for this event to occur is that by then, it may be too late for my friend or others to open their hearts to the truths of God.

There has indeed been a recent movement in Israel to rebuild the Temple. Every year this Jewish organization[8] tries to lay a cornerstone for the Temple in Jerusalem. If they were ever successful this would be the third Jewish Temple to stand on the Temple Mount in history. The first one was Solomon's Temple, which King Nebuchadnezzar destroyed when he invaded Israel in the sixth century before Jesus Christ was born. The second one was Zerubabbel's Temple, which the Israelites built eighty years after the destruction of Solomon's Temple. In 19 B.C., King Herod decided to renovate Zerubabbel's Temple. This project was completed in 63 A.D. but the Romans destroyed this Temple of Herod's in 70 A.D.

The effort to rebuild the third Temple has not stopped at the attempt of the laying of a cornerstone. There is also another Jewish group[9] in Israel who has remade all of the sacred utensils and vessels that the priests will need to use in the Temple services according to the Bible. However, they have not remade the Ark of the Covenant because they believe they know where it has been hidden all these centuries. When they build the Temple, they will then put everything into place including the Ark.

Therefore, from Daniel's seventy-weeks prophecy, we know that a wicked ruler will arise on the scene toward the end of the current age. He will make a peace treaty that will last for seven years and will include the rebuilding of the Jewish Temple. In the middle of that seven-year treaty he will proclaim himself God, desecrate the Jewish Temple, and proceed to persecute the Jews. This last event will happen in the middle of the seven-year Tribulation Period.

The prophet Jeremiah confirms that this period will last seven years and that it will pertain primarily to the Jews:

> *"The word that came to Jeremiah from the LORD, saying, Thus speaks the LORD God of Israel, saying, Write you all the words that I have spoken unto you in a book. For, lo, the days come, says the LORD, that I will bring again the captivity of My people Israel and Judah, says the LORD: and I will cause them to return to the land that I gave to their fathers, and they shall possess it. And these are the words that the LORD spoke concerning Israel and concerning Judah. For thus says the LORD; We have heard a voice of trembling, of fear, and not of peace. Ask you now, and see whether a man does travail with child? Wherefore do I see every man with his hands on his loins, as a woman in travail, and all faces are turned into paleness? Alas! For that day is great, so that none is like it: it is even the time of Jacob's trouble; but he shall be saved out of it."*[10]

God states that He will return the Jews to the land of Israel in the last days. He refers to this period as the *"time of Jacob's trouble"*. This time will be unlike any other in history. The Jews will experience great times of travail or anguish yet at the end God will save them out of it. They will hear a *"voice of trembling, of fear, and not of peace"* which is an allusion to the false peace that the *"king of fierce countenance"* will bring upon the earth.

The phrase *"the time of Jacob's trouble"* refers to an earlier period in the life of the Jewish patriarch Jacob. Jacob had returned to the native land of his grandfather, Abraham. While there, he fell in love with a daughter of his uncle whose name was Rachel. Jacob promised to work seven years for his Uncle Laban if he would allow Jacob to marry Rachel. Laban agreed but he deceived Jacob by putting a veil on his eldest daughter Leah and passing her off as Rachel on the wedding day. Jacob was angry when he found out he had been deceived but agreed to work another seven years for Laban in order to marry Rachel.[11] So Jacob's time of trouble lasted seven years, the same amount of time that Daniel's seventieth week will last.

Christians refer to this seven-year time span as the Tribulation Period. The prophet Daniel in writing of this time said:

> *"And at that time shall Michael [the archangel] stand up, the great prince which stands for the children of your people: and there shall be a time of trouble, such as never was since there was a nation even to that same time: and at that time your people shall be delivered, every one that shall be found written in the book."*[12]

When Jesus told the disciples what the signs of the end of the age will be He said:

> *"For then shall be great tribulation, such as was not since the beginning of the world to this time, no, nor ever shall be...Immediately after the tribulation of those days shall the sun be darkened, and the moon shall not give her light, and the stars shall fall from heaven, and the powers of the heavens shall be shaken."*[13]

It is from this saying of Jesus that we get the appellation: "The Tribulation Period". Please note that both Daniel and Jesus state that there never has been nor will ever be again such a time of trouble on the earth as that which will occur during the Tribulation Period. This time of tribulation will affect both Jews and Gentiles who are on the earth during that time.

The Tribulation Period

The Bible speaks of this period in many places. However, the primary source for our study of the Tribulation Period will be the Book of Revelation.

Many believe that the apostle John, one of Jesus' twelve disciples, wrote this prophetic Book.[14] Revelation states that he was banished to the island of Patmos off the coast of Greece.[15] While he was there an angel of the Lord visited him and showed him all the things that were going to happen in the future. John also saw the glorified Jesus Christ who said to him:

> *"Write the things which thou hast seen, and the things which are, and the things which shall be hereafter."*[16]

Accordingly, John wrote down everything he saw and heard in the Book of Revelation.

Some end-times scholars believe that the themes of each of the twenty-two chapters of Revelation speak of the progression of world history since the time of Jesus. The first chapter represents the time that John was alive in the First Century A.D. In chapters 2 and 3, Jesus told John to write letters to seven churches. Some think that each of these letters parallel the history of the Christian Church from the First Century to the end-times. In chapter 4 John hears a voice that sounds like a trumpet say, *"Come up here, and I will show you things which must be hereafter."*[17] John finds himself in the throne room of God. Pre-Tribulationists believe this represents the Rapture of the Church before the Tribulation Period starts. Chapter 5 declares that the Lamb of God, Jesus Christ, is the only one able to reveal the future of the world and its inhabitants. This future is written down in a scroll or book which has been sealed. Jesus Christ breaks open the seals in chapter 6. Chapters 6 through 18 reveal the events of the Tribulation Period with very descriptive language. As you read Revelation remember that John was looking at things that were at least two thousand years in the future. He was using First Century experiences and words to describe at least Twenty-first Century events. Chapter 19 tells of the second coming of Jesus Christ and the battle of Armageddon. Chapter 20 speaks of the Messianic Kingdom of Jesus Christ. Chapters 21 and 22 finish the Book of Revelation with a description of eternity.

I will begin with chapter 6 and the start of the Tribulation Period. I want to point out that the first series of events closely parallel what Jesus Christ said would be the signs of the end. Chapter 24 of the Gospel of Matthew lists these signs. Below each of the quoted scriptures from Revelation in this first section, I will write the corresponding signs given by Jesus in Matthew. Please note that I will maintain the order of these signs as given by Jesus as well as the order of the Book of Revelation.

"And I saw when the Lamb opened one of the seals, and I heard, as it were the noise of thunder, one of the four beasts saying, Come and see. And I saw, and behold a white horse: and he that sat on him had a bow; and a crown was given unto him: and he went forth conquering, and to conquer."

- Revelation 6:1-2

"And Jesus answered and said unto them, Take heed that no man deceive you. For many shall come in My name, saying, I am Christ; and shall deceive many."

- Matthew 24:4-5

Many scholars believe that this rider on the white horse is the Antichrist. Notice that even though he has a bow for a weapon he has no arrows to shoot. This could be a reference to the peace treaty that he will make with the Jews and Gentiles. No war will be involved in his conquering of the world. The world will receive him as the man with the answers to humanity's problems. This would fulfill Jesus' prophecy that false Christs or Messiahs will appear at the end.

How will it be possible for the Antichrist to come to such a position of power in the world without conquering it by force? I believe the Bible gives us two methods he will use to attain this power.

The Prophet Daniel mentions several times a descriptive phrase of the Antichrist (or "little horn" as he calls him): *"[The Antichrist has] a mouth speaking great things"; "I beheld then because of the voice of the great words which the horn spoke"; "and a mouth that spoke very great things"*[18] The Antichrist is going to be an orator the likes of which the world has never seen. Something similar has happened in our recent history.

In 1920, Adolph Hitler took over a political party that had around fifty members. By 1940 the membership of the Nazi Party numbered in the hundreds of thousands. Millions more in Germany and around the world believed in him. This was all do to the fact that Adolph Hitler was a mesmerizing orator. Because of this ability millions of people died during World War II.

The other method revolves around the Antichrist and his administration's ability to perform lying wonders and miracles. The apostle Paul said concerning the Antichrist: *"Even him, whose coming is after the working of Satan with all power and signs and lying wonders."*[19] Later in Revelation we will read of the Antichrist's right-hand man who also will have this ability: *"And he does great wonders, so that he makes fire come down from heaven on the earth in the sight of men, And deceives them that dwell on the earth by the means of those miracles which he had power to do in the sight of the beast* [i.e., Antichrist] *."*[20]

So the world will indeed be enchanted with this false messiah who will speak great words to their ears. When they see the lying wonders they will think that God Himself has come down to earth.

Second Seal

"And when He had opened the second seal, I heard the second beast say, Come and see. And there went out another horse that was red: and power was given to him that sat thereon to take peace from the earth, and that they should kill one another: and there was given unto him a great sword."

- Revelation 6:3-4

"And you shall hear of wars and rumors of wars: see that you be not troubled: for all these things must come to pass, but the end is not yet. For nation shall rise against nation and kingdom against kingdom..."

- Matthew 24:6-7a

As Daniel said, by peace he *"shall destroy many"*. After the Antichrist deceives the world, he will then raise an army with weapons and will cause a world war. The Book of Revelation states: *"And they worshipped the dragon* [i.e., Satan] *which gave power unto the beast: and they worshipped the beast* [i.e., Antichrist], *saying, Who is like unto the beast? Who is able to make war with him...And it was given unto him to make war with the saints, and to overcome them: and power was given him over all kindreds, and tongues, and nations."*[21]

Third Seal

"And when He had opened the third seal, I heard the third beast say, Come and see. And I beheld, and lo a black horse; and he that sat on him had a pair of balances in his hand. And I heard a voice in the midst of the four beasts say, A measure of wheat for a penny, and three measures of barley for a penny; and see thou hurt not the oil and the wine."

- Revelation 6:5-6

"...and there shall be famines..."

- Matthew 24:7b

This passage in Revelation is saying that people on the earth will spend great amounts of money to buy food (it lists a day's wages for the First Century here). In Germany after World War I, it took millions of German marks to buy a loaf of bread. In the future Tribulation Period famine from the war will be worldwide.

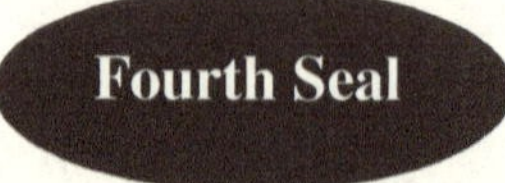

"And when He had opened the fourth seal, I heard the voice of the fourth beast say, Come and see. And I looked, and behold a pale horse: and his name that sat on him was Death, and Hell followed

with him. And power was given unto them over the fourth part of the earth, to kill with sword, and with hunger, and with death, and with the beasts of the earth."

- Revelation 6:7-8

"...and pestilences, and earthquakes, in various places. All these are the beginning of sorrows."

- Matthew 24:7c-8

The current population of the earth is around six billion people. If these events took place in the next few years, more than 1.5 billion people would be killed. The death and destruction from this war will result in the spread of diseases from all the dead bodies lying around. Animals will be running loose and will be so hungry they will start attacking human beings. If numerous nuclear weapons are involved in this war it could result in an increase in earthquake and volcanic activity.

Fifth Seal

"And when He had opened the fifth seal, I saw under the altar the souls of them that were slain for the word of God, and for the testimony which they held: And they cried with a loud voice, saying, How long, O Lord, holy and true, dost Thou not judge and avenge our blood on them that dwell on the earth? And white robes were given unto every one of them; and it was said unto them, that they should rest yet for a little season, until their fellowservants also and their brethren, that should be killed as they were, should be fulfilled."

- Revelation 6:9-11

"Then shall they deliver you up to be afflicted, and shall kill you: and you shall be hated of all nations for My name's sake. And then shall many be offended, and shall betray one another, and shall hate one another. And many false prophets shall rise, and shall deceive many. And because iniquity shall abound, the love of many shall wax cold.

But he that shall endure unto the end, the same shall be saved. And this gospel of the kingdom shall be preached in all the world for a witness unto all nations; and then shall the end come."

- Matthew 24:14

During this Tribulation Period, the Antichrist and his followers will persecute those who believe in Jesus Christ. He will kill many for their beliefs during this time as John saw in heaven. Jesus said that those who endure to the end will be saved.

Sixth Seal

"And I beheld when He had opened the sixth seal, and, lo, there was a great earthquake; and the sun became black as sackcloth of hair, and the moon became as blood; And the stars of heaven fell unto the earth, even as a fig tree casts her untimely figs, when she is shaken of a mighty wind. And the heaven departed as a scroll when it is rolled together; and every mountain and island were moved out of their places. And the kings of the earth, and the great men, and the rich men, and the chief captains, and the mighty men, and every bondman, and every free man, hid themselves in the dens and in the rocks of the mountains; And said to the mountains and rocks, Fall on us, and hide us from the face of Him that sits on the throne, and from the wrath of the Lamb: For the great day of His wrath is come; and who shall be able to stand?"

- Revelation 6:12-17

"Immediately after the tribulation of those days shall the sun be darkened, and the moon shall not give her light, and the stars shall fall from heaven, and the powers of the heavens shall be shaken."

- Matthew 24:29

Cosmic events will take place possibly as a result of a worldwide nuclear holocaust or by the hand of God. The world will finally know that they have worshiped a false god. But instead of turning to the true God they will try to hide from Him. The horrific part for the world is that this is just the *"beginning of sorrows"*.

The 144,000 Jewish Evangelists

In chapter 7 of the Book of Revelation, God stops the flow of events that John saw taking place during the Tribulation Period to show him two unique groups of His servants.

The first group consists of 144,000 Jews from the tribes of Israel who are living on the earth during the Tribulation Period. These cannot be Gentiles because John specifically mentions twelve Jewish tribes as the origin of these persons. Gentiles are not descended from the tribes of Israel.

God does something special with these Jewish servants of His. An angel of God tells four other angels who were carrying out the judgments on the earth during the Tribulation Period to stop until God can protect these Jews from harm:

"Hurt not the earth, neither the sea, nor the trees, till we have sealed the servants of our God in their foreheads. And I heard the number of them which were sealed: and there were sealed an hundred and forty and four thousand of all the tribes of the children of Israel."[22]

The angel is to put the seal of God on the 144,000 Jewish servants of the Lord, which will protect them from the judgments that are to come with the opening of the seventh seal. Later in Revelation we will see that the Antichrist also requires his followers to receive a mark on their foreheads or right hands. To be a servant of God after the first coming of Jesus Christ means that you believe in Jesus as the Messiah and that you live your life according to His will. During the Tribulation these Jewish servants will be fulfilling God's will by evangelizing the people who are living on the earth at that time. These servants may have accepted Jesus as their Savior after witnessing the first few seal judgments of God. The second unique group in chapter 7 of Revelation is the result of the preaching of these Jewish servants.

After witnessing this sealing of God's servants, John saw a much larger number of persons in heaven:

"After this I beheld, and, lo, a great multitude, which no man could number, of all nations, and kindreds, and people, and tongues, stood before the throne, and before the Lamb, clothed with white robes, and palms in their hands; And cried with a loud voice, saying, Salvation to our God who sits upon the throne, and unto the Lamb...And one of the elders answered, saying to me, Who are these which are arrayed in white robes? And from where came they? And I said unto him, Sir, you know. And he said to me, These are they which came out of great tribulation, and have washed their robes, and made them white in the blood of the Lamb."[23]

A heavenly elder told John that the blood of the Lamb had saved this multitude of people during the Great Tribulation Period. Since this episode occurred right after the sealing of the Jewish servants the logical conclusion is that it was their preaching that led to the salvation of many of this multitude. As mentioned earlier in this chapter, the Antichrist and his followers will persecute and kill the followers of Jesus Christ. They will be extremely successful in this persecution during the Tribulation Period as John states that those saved and killed were too many to count.

After this interlude in the future events that John was witnessing, he now starts again with the opening of the seventh seal.

Seventh Seal

"And when He had opened the seventh seal, there was silence in heaven about the space of half an hour. And I saw the seven angels which stood before God; and to them were given seven trumpets. And another angel came and stood at the altar, having a golden censer; and there was given unto him much incense, that he should offer it with the prayers of all saints upon the golden altar which was before the throne. And the smoke of the incense, which came with the prayers of the saints, ascended up before God out of the angel's hand. And the angel took the censer, and filled it with fire of the altar, and cast it into the earth: and there were voices, and

thunderings, and lightnings, and an earthquake. And the seven angels who had the seven trumpets prepared themselves to sound."
- Revelation 8:1-6

Pre-Wrath Tribulationists say that the Rapture takes place at this moment because they believe this is when God begins to pour out His full wrath upon the earth and its inhabitants. The fact that John mentions that there was silence for half an hour does indicate that something, the likes of which have never been seen on earth, is about to happen.

The seventh seal starts the upheaval in the earth's weather patterns. This is in response to the prayers of the saints of God in which His justice would finally come upon the earth: *"I saw under the altar the souls of them that were slain for the word of God, and for the testimony which they held: And they cried with a loud voice, saying, How long, O Lord, holy and true, do You not judge and avenge our blood on them that dwell on the earth?"*[24]

This also allows seven angels to prepare to blow their respective trumpets that will bring further judgments upon the earth.

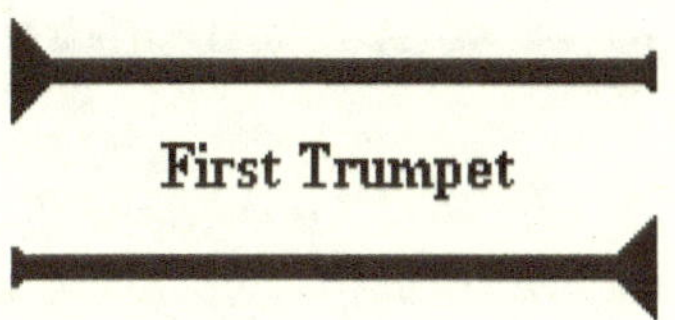

"The first angel sounded, and there followed hail and fire mingled with blood, and they were cast upon the earth: and the third part of trees was burnt up, and all green grass was burnt up."
- Revelation 8:7

Now that God has sealed His 144,000 Jewish servants for protection to preach the gospel, He allows the angels to bring down His judgments upon the earth. A strange hailstorm rains down from heaven that destroys one-third of the trees on the earth along with the grass. The earth will never have looked uglier then it will when this occurs.

"And the second angel sounded, and as it were a great mountain burning with fire was cast into the sea: and the third part of the sea became blood; And the third part of the creatures which were in the sea, and had life, died; and the third part of the ships were destroyed."

- *Revelation 8:8-9*

It is hard to know exactly what John saw here. Whatever this mountain is (possibly a meteor or asteroid etc), it poisons a third of the oceans and sea and kills the creatures therein. The stench from this event will be overwhelming.

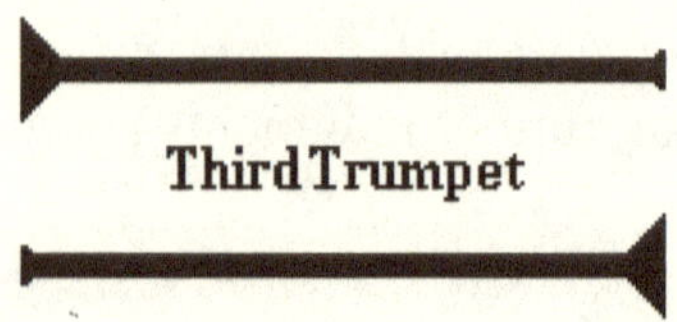

"And the third angel sounded, and there fell a great star from heaven, burning as it were a lamp, and it fell upon the third part of the rivers, and upon the fountains of waters; And the name of the star is called Wormwood: and the third part of the waters became wormwood; and many men died of the waters, because they were made bitter."

- *Revelation 8:10-11*

Whether what John sees here is a comet or meteor or something manmade is open for interpretation. He could be witnessing a nuclear intercontinental ballistic missile that poisons the water. The word "wormwood" is a translation of a Greek name of a plant that is bitter tasting. Many will drink this poisoned water because of an insatiable thirst that arises from the ecological devastations that have occurred.

"And the fourth angel sounded, and the third part of the sun was smitten, and the third part of the moon, and the third part of the stars; so as the third part of them was darkened, and the day shone not for a third part of it, and the night likewise."

- *Revelation 8:12*

Something was causing a partial darkness over the earth. Whether this occurred because of dust and smoke, which were the result of all the earthquakes and storms, is not clear. John might be witnessing and describing a nuclear winter.

Woe! Woe! Woe!

After the fourth trumpet sounded, John saw another angel issuing a warning:

"And I beheld, and heard an angel flying through the midst of heaven, saying with a loud voice, Woe, woe, woe, to the inhabiters of the earth by reason of the other voices of the trumpet of the three angels, which are yet to sound!"

- Revelation 8:13

As horrible as the Tribulation Period has been up to this point, *it is going to get much worse.*

"And the fifth angel sounded, and I saw a star fall from heaven unto the earth: and to him was given the key of the bottomless pit. And he opened the bottomless pit; and there arose a smoke out of the pit, as

the smoke of a great furnace; and the sun and the air were darkened by reason of the smoke of the pit. And there came out of the smoke locusts upon the earth: and unto them was given power, as the scorpions of the earth have power. And it was commanded them that they should not hurt the grass of the earth, neither any green thing, neither any tree; but only those men which have not the seal of God in their foreheads. And to them it was given that they should not kill them, but that they should be tormented five months: and their torment was as the torment of a scorpion, when he strikes a man. And in those days shall men seek death, and shall not find it; and shall desire to die, and death shall flee from them...And they had a king over them, which is the angel of the bottomless pit, whose name in the Hebrew tongue is Abaddon, but in the Greek tongue hath his name Apollyon. One woe is past; and, behold, there come two woes more hereafter."

- Revelation 9:1-6, 11-12

The sounding of the fifth trumpet begins the first "woe" that was spoken of by the angel. John sees a "star" that falls to the earth. This star is actually a living being of some sorts. He uses a masculine pronoun to describe this star that receives the key to the abyss. This creature unlocks this pit and great smoke rises out of it. Out of this smoke come loathsome looking locusts. These locust creatures are given the power to torment mankind for five months. Their power is restricted though, which prohibits them from killing or harming any human beings who have God's seal on their forehead. Those that are horribly tortured by these creatures will seek to die but will be unable to do so.

The name of the ruler of these locust creatures is "Apollyon" in the Greek language and "Abaddon" in the Hebrew. Both of these terms mean "destroyer".

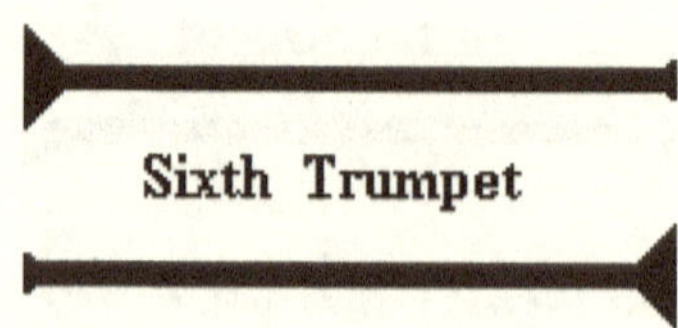

"And the sixth angel sounded, and I heard a voice from the four horns of the golden altar which is before God, Saying to the sixth angel which had the trumpet, Loose the four angels which are bound in the great river Euphrates. And the four angels were loosed, which were prepared for an hour, and a day, and a month, and a year, for to slay the third part of men. And the number of the army of the horsemen was two hundred thousand thousand: and I heard the number of them. And thus I saw the horses in the vision, and them that sat on them, having breastplates of fire, and of jacinth, and brimstone: and the heads of the horses were as the heads of lions; and out of their mouths issued fire and smoke and brimstone. By these three was the third part of men killed, by the fire, and by the smoke, and by the brimstone, which issued out of their mouths. For their power is in their mouth, and in their tails: for their tails were like unto serpents, and had heads, and with them they do hurt. And the rest of the men which were not killed by these plagues yet repented not of the works of their hands, that they should not worship devils, and idols of gold, and silver, and brass, and stone, and of wood: which neither can see, nor hear, nor walk: Neither repented they of their murders, nor of their sorceries, nor of their fornication, nor of their thefts."

- Revelation 9:13-21

The blowing of the sixth trumpet begins the second "woe" upon the inhabitants of the earth. Four angels receive their freedom from the spiritual chains that bound them to the River Euphrates. This river runs south from Turkey through Syria and through the middle of Iraq into the Persian Gulf. It appears as if these four angels will allow an army of 200 million horsemen to cross the Euphrates by drying up part of the river. Two issues militate against these 200 million men riding actual horses. The first is that there are probably less than half that many horses in the world today. The second is that John's description of what he saw is clearly not a horse in the sense that we know them. It is possible that since John is using First Century words to describe what he is seeing, they could be some type of modern mechanized military vehicles. However, the huge number of "horsemen" makes this scenario unlikely unless he saw them riding in vehicles of all kinds. Even then it would appear unfeasible simply because oil and gasoline supplies would probably be non-existent at this stage of the Tribulation Period.

In chapter 16 of Revelation, we find out that this massive army will be led by *"kings of the east"*.[25] These kings or leaders are probably from the Asian nation of China and some of the countries surrounding it. China currently has a population of 1.3 *billion* people. Even if half of their population were killed during the first half of the Tribulation Period they could still field an army of this size.

The result of this invasion will be the death of another third of mankind. Using current world population figures, this would mean that after this sixth trumpet judgment more than 3 *billion* persons would have died during the Tribulation Period. Now we know why the Bible states that this period of time will be unlike any other time in the earth's history.

The most unimaginable part of this entire scripture passage is that men's hearts have become so hardened that instead of repenting they continue in their hatred for God.

At this point (which is also the mid-point of the seven-year Tribulation Period) God again stops the revelation to John of the flow of Tribulation events that he has been witnessing. He now reveals to him another event that will occur during this period of time.

The Two Witnesses

In chapter 10 of Revelation an angel interacts with John. In the first section of this chapter he hears seven voices that sound like thunder. Mysteriously though a voice from heaven tells him not to write down what they said.[26] There has been much speculation as to what these voices uttered but no one knows what was spoken.

In the second part of this chapter the angel gives John a little book to swallow which tasted sweet but grew bitter in his stomach.[27] What the contents of this book were are not revealed. However, after eating this book the angel tells John that he must prophesy again to the inhabitants of the world. It is possible that this book is the Book of Revelation that John would write. Revelation is sweet in that John prophesies that Jesus Christ is coming again to set up His kingdom. It is also bitter in the fact that the world is going to suffer horribly before that event takes place.

In the first part of chapter 11, John is told to measure the Temple and the *people* that worship there.[28] This reveals that there will indeed be a third Jewish Temple rebuilt during the Tribulation Period This measuring might not refer so much to the physical dimensions of the Temple but as to how this Temple and the people who worship there "measure up" to the standards of God's righteousness. However, the angel tells John not to measure the outer court of the Temple since it belongs to the Gentiles for a period of 42 months or 1260 days. Some speculate this means that the Temple will be built beside the Islamic Dome of the Rock shrine, which currently is located on the Temple Mount. At the present time it is hard to imagine how either religion would allow the other to "desecrate" the Temple Mount with their religious building. Nevertheless, as we have seen so far, many supernatural events will have taken place during this time and so it is possible.

After this, John sees two powerful servants of God:

"And I will give power unto My two witnesses, and they shall prophesy a thousand two hundred and threescore days, clothed in sackcloth. These are the two olive trees, and the two candlesticks standing before the God of the earth. And if any man will hurt them, fire proceeds out of their mouth, and devours their enemies: and if any man will hurt them, he must in this manner be killed. These have power to shut heaven, that it rain not in the days of their prophecy: and have power over waters to turn them to blood, and to smite the earth with all plagues, as often as they will. And when they shall have finished their testimony, the beast that ascends out of the bottomless pit shall make war against them, and shall overcome them, and kill them. And their dead bodies shall lie in the street of the great city, which spiritually is called Sodom and Egypt, where also our Lord was crucified. And they of the people and kindreds and tongues and nations shall see their dead bodies three days and an half, and shall not suffer their dead bodies to be put in graves. And they that dwell upon the earth shall rejoice over them, and make merry, and shall send gifts one to another; because these two prophets tormented them that dwelt on the earth. And after three

days and an half the spirit of life from God entered into them, and they stood upon their feet; and great fear fell upon them which saw them. And they heard a great voice from heaven saying unto them, Come up here. And they ascended up to heaven in a cloud; and their enemies beheld them."

- *Revelation 11:3-12*

There has been much speculation as to whom these two witnesses are. The most common belief is that they are Elijah and Moses who represent the "prophets" and the "law" of the Old Testament. Elijah is prophesied to come before the *"great and dreadful Day of the Lord"*.[29] Also Elijah did cause the rain to stop during his prophetic ministry on earth[30] and Moses did invoke the plagues which included turning water into blood.[31]

Regardless of whom these two witnesses are they will be preaching salvation for forty-two months in the city of Jerusalem. If anyone tries to harm or stop them, the two witnesses will kill them with fire coming from their mouths. There is a disagreement as to when these two servants of God will start this ministry. Some scholars believe they will start it near the beginning of the Tribulation Period and others at the mid-point of the Tribulation Period.

At the end of their preaching ministry God allows the beast (probably the Antichrist[32]) to kill them. He will leave their bodies lying in the streets of Jerusalem for everyone to see. It is worth noting that only with the coming of television in the Twentieth Century is it now possible for everyone living on the earth to witness such an event. They will rejoice at the sight of God's prophets lying dead. However, after three and one-half days God will resurrect them and they will ascend to heaven with the entire world watching.

Immediately an earthquake destroys a tenth part of Jerusalem and kill seven thousand persons who live there. It is possible that this earthquake also destroys the third Temple. This event witnessed by John could take place after the Antichrist enters the Temple and declares himself God.[33] It is also possible that the Temple may be standing until near the end of the Tribulation Period since the Antichrist's desecration of it may take place after the seventh trumpet sounds. The fact that the third or Tribulation Temple will be destroyed at some point is based on Zechariah's prophecy that the Messiah will build the Temple when He comes to set up His kingdom.[34] Thus, the desecrated Tribulation Temple will not be standing when Jesus establishes His Messianic reign on earth.

"And the seventh angel sounded; and there were great voices in heaven, saying, The kingdoms of this world are become the kingdoms of our Lord, and of His Christ; and He shall reign for ever and ever. And the four and twenty elders, which sat before God on their seats, fell upon their faces, and worshipped God, Saying, We give You thanks, O LORD God Almighty, Which are, and were, and are to come; because You have taken to You Your great power, and have reigned. And the nations were angry, and Your wrath is come, and the time of the dead, that they should be judged, and that You should give reward unto Your servants the prophets, and to the saints, and them that fear Your name, small and great; and should destroy them which destroy the earth. And the Temple of God was opened in heaven, and there was seen in His temple the ark of His testament: and there were lightnings, and voices, and thunderings, and an earthquake, and great hail."

- Revelation 11:15-19

The seventh trumpet sounds and the final seven bowl judgments upon the earth and its inhabitants begin. It is at this point that Mid-Tribulationists believe that the Rapture will occur. This is the third "woe" of the three warnings that the angel gave earlier to the people dwelling on the earth.

The last verse of this passage is actually a forecast of the final seventh bowl judgment that will consummate the end of Tribulation Period judgments.[35] However, before John sees these final bowl judgments he is shown some events that occur at the mid-point of the Tribulation Period.

The Woman, The Dragon, The Heavenly War

In chapter 12 of Revelation, John sees a heavenly wonder in the form of a woman clothed with the sun, the moon under her feet, and a crown with twelve stars on it.[36] This vision is very similar to a dream that the Jewish patriarch Joseph had.

In that episode Joseph dreamed that he saw the sun and the moon and the eleven stars which did obeisance to him.[37] This was a prophetic dream that did come true. The sun was his father Jacob and the moon his mother Rachel. The eleven stars were his brothers who fathered the tribes of Israel. Joseph also was the father of the two of the twelve tribes of Israel through his two sons. Therefore, that dream represented the nation of Israel.

Here John sees twelve stars, which would include Joseph. Accordingly, this vision was also a picture of the nation of Israel.

Then John sees a great red dragon that stood before the woman to devour her child as soon as it was born. She gave birth to a male child who was to rule all nations with a rod of iron and He was caught up to God.[38] As we will see shortly, this dragon is the devil and the male child is Jesus Christ who came from a Jewish mother of the nation of Israel.

Then John writes:

"And the woman [i.e., Jews of Israel] *fled into the wilderness, where she hath a place prepared of God, that they should feed her there a thousand two hundred and sixty days."*

- Revelation 12:6

The Jews will flee into the wilderness to a place where God protects them because of what happens next:

"And there was war in heaven: Michael and his angels fought against the dragon; and the dragon fought and his angels, And prevailed not; neither was their place found any more in heaven. And the great dragon was cast out, that old serpent, called the Devil, and Satan, which deceives the whole world: he was cast out into the earth, and his angels were cast out with him. And I heard a loud voice saying in heaven, Now is come salvation, and strength, and the

kingdom of our God, and the power of His Christ: for the accuser of our brethren is cast down, which accused them before our God day and night. And they overcame him by the blood of the Lamb, and by the word of their testimony; and they loved not their lives unto the death. Therefore rejoice, you heavens, and you that dwell in them. Woe to the inhabiters of the earth and of the sea! for the devil is come down unto you, having great wrath, because he knows that he has but a short time."

- *Revelation 12 7-12*

During the mid-point of the Tribulation Period there is a war in heaven between Michael and his angels and Satan and his angels. Michael's forces prevail and they remove Satan from the heavenly realm forever. As the angel says though this is not good for those who dwell on earth because the Devil knows he has only a little time left before God judges him. Between the persecution of humanity by the Devil and the final judgments of God's wrath on them, this truly will be the time of Great Tribulation such as never was on earth nor ever will be again.

As we will see next, the Devil will possess the Antichrist and take his vengeance out on the rest of the world. This might be when the possessed Antichrist enters the Jewish Temple in Jerusalem and declares himself God. It will be at this moment that the Jewish nation as a whole will realize they have believed in the false Messiah. They will follow Jesus' warnings that He gave in chapter 24 of Matthew when they see the *"abomination of desolation"* [i.e., the possessed Antichrist] enter into the Temple:

"When you therefore shall see the abomination of desolation, spoken of by Daniel the prophet, stand in the holy place, then let them which be in Judea flee into the mountains: Let him which is on the housetop not come down to take any thing out of his house: Neither let him which is in the field return back to take his clothes. And woe unto them that are with child, and to them that give suck in those days! But pray you that your flight be not in the winter, neither on the Sabbath day: For then shall be great tribulation, such as was not since the beginning of the world to this time, no, nor ever shall be.

And except those days should be shortened, there should no flesh be saved: but for the elect's sake those days shall be shortened."

- Matthew 24:15-22

"And when the dragon saw that he was cast unto the earth, he persecuted the woman which brought forth the male child. And to the woman were given two wings of a great eagle, that she might fly into the wilderness, into her place, where she is nourished for a time, and times, and half a time, from the face of the serpent. And the serpent cast out of his mouth water as a flood after the woman, that he might cause her to be carried away of the flood. And the earth helped the woman, and the earth opened her mouth, and swallowed up the flood which the dragon cast out of his mouth. And the dragon was wroth with the woman, and went to make war with the remnant of her seed, which keep the commandments of God, and have the testimony of Jesus Christ."

- Revelation 12:13-17

The Jewish people who flee to God's protective place will be safe until Jesus Christ returns at His second coming. Some think that their destination will be the ancient rock fortress of Petra in Jordan (biblical Edom). This belief is based on a couple of references in the Book of Isaiah that associate the Jews in hiding with a place called Sela, which is also known as Petra. In any event those who remain outside of God's protection will suffer the most horrifying time the earth has ever seen.

The Antichrist

"And I stood upon the sand of the sea, and saw a beast rise up out of the sea, having seven heads and ten horns, and upon his horns ten crowns, and upon his heads the name of blasphemy. And the beast which I saw was like unto a leopard, and his feet were as the feet of a bear, and his mouth as the mouth of a lion: and the dragon gave him his power, and his seat, and great authority."

- Revelation 13:1-2

In this passage, John sees a beast who is the Antichrist and the epitome of blasphemy against God and who is possessed with all the authority and power of the Devil.

"And I saw one of his heads as it were wounded to death; and his deadly wound was healed: and all the world wondered after the beast. And they worshipped the dragon which gave power unto the beast: and they worshipped the beast, saying, Who is like unto the beast? Who is able to make war with him? And there was given unto him a mouth speaking great things and blasphemies; and power was given unto him to continue forty and two months. And he opened his mouth in blasphemy against God, to blaspheme his name, and his tabernacle, and them that dwell in heaven. And it was given unto him to make war with the saints, and to overcome them: and power was given him over all kindreds, and tongues, and nations. And all that dwell upon the earth shall worship him, whose names are not written in the book of life of the Lamb slain from the foundation of the world."

- *Revelation 13:3-8*

John sees the Antichrist mortally wounded. Whether someone assassinates him or he dies by some other cause is not clear. But he will be resurrected, which causes the whole world to worship him.

Up to this point in the Tribulation Period, the Antichrist was a wicked human being who deceived the world through great words and actions. Now he is the Devil-incarnate and will reign as such during the last three and one-half years of the Tribulation Period. He will openly oppose the God of heaven and the world will love him for it. They will follow him into war against the followers of God and will overcome them. As was mentioned earlier in this chapter, John saw the victims of this war:

"After this I beheld, and, lo, a great multitude, which no man could number, of all nations, and kindreds, and people, and tongues, stood before the throne, and before the Lamb, clothed with white robes...These are they which came out of great tribulation, and have washed their robes, and made them white in the blood of the Lamb."[39]

After this, John sees another "beast" whom Christians call the False Prophet:

"And I beheld another beast coming up out of the earth; and he had two horns like a lamb, and he spoke as a dragon. And he exercises all the power of the first beast before him, and causes the earth and them which dwell therein to worship the first beast, who's deadly wound was healed. And he does great wonders, so that he makes fire come down from heaven on the earth in the sight of men, And deceives them that dwell on the earth by the means of those miracles which he had power to do in the sight of the beast; saying to them that dwell on the earth, that they should make an image to the beast, which had the wound by a sword, and did live. And he had power to give life unto the image of the beast, that the image of the beast should both speak, and cause that as many as would not worship the image of the beast should be killed."

\- *Revelation 13:11-15*

The fact that he appeared as a lamb and causes the world to worship the Antichrist but speaks as a dragon alludes to his being a falsely religious person. He has the ability to perform miracles by which he deceives those who live on the earth. He has them create an image of the Antichrist and then he causes this image to come alive and forces the people to worship it. He does this to separate the true followers of Jesus from the followers of Satan and puts the former to death. In a later chapter of Revelation, we read that one method of the execution of these Christians is by beheading:

"and I saw the souls of them that were beheaded for the witness of Jesus, and for the word of God, and which had not worshipped the beast, neither his image..."[40]

Chapter 17 of Revelation speaks metaphorically of this worship of the Antichrist as a worldwide religion. The only holdouts from following this religion will be those who receive Jesus Christ as their Savior:

"Come here; I will show unto you the judgment of the great whore that sits upon many waters: With whom the kings of the earth have committed fornication, and the inhabitants of the earth have been made drunk with the wine of her fornication. So he carried me away in the spirit into the wilderness: and I saw a woman sit upon a scarlet colored beast, full of names of blasphemy, having seven heads and ten horns. And the woman was arrayed in purple and scarlet color, and decked with gold and precious stones and pearls, having a golden cup in her hand full of abominations and filthiness of her fornication: And upon her forehead was a name written, MYSTERY, BABYLON THE GREAT, THE MOTHER OF HARLOTS AND ABOMINATIONS OF THE EARTH. And I saw the woman drunken with the blood of the saints, and with the blood of the martyrs of Jesus: and when I saw her, I wondered with great admiration."

- *Revelation 17:1-6*

The fornication spoken of here refers to spiritual fornication or adultery. It speaks of that part of humanity who, instead of following the one and true God, deserts Him for the false god of this world. This woman represents a religious system that has been on the earth since the early days of human history.

In the ancient land of Shinar (i.e., Babylonia), the human race was united by one language. However, they became proud and decided they could become as God:

"And they said, Go to, let us build us a city and a tower, whose top may reach unto heaven; and let us make us a name, lest we be scattered abroad upon the face of the whole earth."[41]

The people did build the tower of Babel on what is considered to be the site of Babylon. God was displeased with their haughtiness and dispersed them by confusing their language. The problem is that this desire to become like God spread throughout the world after this and many false religions sprang up. The basis for most of these is the worship of idols, worship of humans, worship of animals, worship of nature, and worship of self. Therefore, the human race as a whole no longer worshiped the true and only God who had created them.

In the Tribulation Period all of these false religions culminate in one unified religion known as "spiritual Babylon" that worships the epitome of evil and the one opposed to God since the Garden of Eden: *Satan incarnate.*

"And he causes all, both small and great, rich and poor, free and bond, to receive a mark in their right hand, or in their foreheads: And that no man might buy or sell, except he that had the mark, or the name of the beast, or the number of his name. Here is wisdom. Let him that has understanding count the number of the beast: for it is the number of a man; and his number is Six hundred sixty and six."

- *Revelation 13:16-18*

The False Prophet will create an economic system, which, just like the religious system he sets up, will also separate the true followers of Jesus from the followers of Satan.

This is one area of end-times prophecy where speculation runs rampant. However, the plain reading of this text states that during the Tribulation Period only those people who have the mark of the Antichrist (whether his name or the number that represents him) will be able to engage in commerce. Those who refuse to receive his mark will probably need to have some type of barter system in place or grow their own food.

Many end-times scholars believe the basis for this system will be the use of digital money through worldwide computer systems. Some think that this may involve the implantation of some type of computer chip in a person's body. This would probably result in a "cashless" society, which would mean that no one would be able to buy or sell anything without the mark of the Antichrist.

I was talking to an agnostic friend of mine about just such a scenario occurring in our lifetime. He said that it would never happen because people wouldn't want to give up on cash. I asked him if he paid taxes to which he replied yes. I then asked him why he paid taxes. He said because the government forced him to. I made it clear that this future evil government would make it mandatory for people to give up their cash so that they could keep track of who was buying and selling.

I have heard of some people who are concerned that one day they may accidentally receive the Antichrist's mark. As I pointed out above, the False Prophet will institute both the religious and economic systems so that he can weed out the followers of God from the followers of the Antichrist. This leads me to believe that a person will have to openly acknowledge their allegiance to the Antichrist so that there is no mistake as to whose side they are on. Therefore, I do not think anyone is going to receive the mark of the Antichrist accidentally. John points out that the way the False Prophet will "*cause*" people to receive this mark is by threatening them economically. If he could force everyone to take the mark he wouldn't need to threaten them. This would mean that the Antichrist could compel even those who want to follow God during the Tribulation Period to receive the mark. Since there are going to be many who die because they refuse to worship the Antichrist or receive his mark we know that he won't have the power to make people take his mark.

Chapter 18 of Revelation speaks of this economic system as a type of "commercial Babylon":

"And after these things I saw another angel come down from heaven, having great power; and the earth was lightened with his glory. And he cried mightily with a strong voice, saying, Babylon the great is fallen, is fallen, and is become the habitation of devils, and the hold of every foul spirit, and a cage of every unclean and hateful bird. For all nations have drunk of the wine of the wrath of her fornication, and the kings of the earth have committed fornication with her, and the merchants of the earth are waxed rich through the abundance of her delicacies...How much she has glorified herself, and lived deliciously, so much torment and sorrow give her: for she says in her heart, I sit a queen, and am no widow, and shall see no sorrow. Therefore shall her plagues come in one day, death, and mourning, and famine; and she shall be utterly burned with fire: for strong is the Lord God who judges her. And the kings of the earth, who have committed fornication and lived deliciously with her, shall bewail her, and lament for her, when they shall see the smoke of her burning, Standing afar off for the fear of her torment, saying, Alas, alas that great city Babylon, that mighty city! for in one hour is thy

judgment come. And the merchants of the earth shall weep and mourn over her; for no man buys their merchandise any more: The merchandise of gold, and silver, and precious stones, and of pearls, and fine linen, and purple, and silk, and scarlet, and all thyine wood, and all manner vessels of ivory, and all manner vessels of most precious wood, and of brass, and iron, and marble, And cinnamon, and odors, and ointments, and frankincense, and wine, and oil, and fine flour, and wheat, and beasts, and sheep, and horses, and chariots, and slaves, and souls of men. And the fruits that thy soul lusted after are departed from you, and all things which were dainty and goodly are departed from you, and you shall find them no more at all. The merchants of these things, which were made rich by her, shall stand afar off for the fear of her torment, weeping and wailing, And saying, Alas, alas that great city, that was clothed in fine linen, and purple, and scarlet, and decked with gold, and precious stones, and pearls! For in one hour so great riches is come to nothing. And every shipmaster, and all the company in ships, and sailors, and as many as trade by sea, stood afar off, And cried when they saw the smoke of her burning, saying, What city is like unto this great city! And they cast dust on their heads, and cried, weeping and wailing, saying, Alas, alas that great city, wherein were made rich all that had ships in the sea by reason of her costliness! for in one hour is she made desolate. Rejoice over her, thou heaven, and ye holy apostles and prophets; for God has avenged you on her. And a mighty angel took up a stone like a great millstone, and cast it into the sea, saying, Thus with violence shall that great city Babylon be thrown down, and shall be found no more at all."

- *Revelation 18:1-3, 7-21*

There has been much debate concerning whether this financial capital of the world's commerce is the literal city of Babylon or some other city. Wherever it is, it is destroyed in one hour and the world will wail and weep over its demise. The Antichrist will no longer have control over the finances of the world.

Materialism and greed, which have destroyed men's souls throughout history, are themselves judged and destroyed by God.

The Final Preaching of Gospel

While still in this interlude from the events of the judgments of the Tribulation Period, John sees an angel flying through the sky above the earth:

"And I saw another angel fly in the midst of heaven, having the everlasting gospel to preach unto them that dwell on the earth, and to every nation, and kindred, and tongue, and people, Saying with a loud voice, Fear God, and give glory to Him; for the hour of His judgment is come: and worship Him that made heaven, and earth, and the sea, and the fountains of waters."

- *Revelation 14:6-7*

This correlates with what Jesus said would happen before the end of the Tribulation Period:

"And this gospel of the kingdom shall be preached in all the world for a witness unto all nations; and then shall the end come."

- *Matthew 24:14*

The inhabitants of the world who have not yet taken the mark of the Antichrist will have one last chance to repent of their sins and follow Jesus Christ.

Those who choose to follow the Antichrist will suffer the consequences of their decision:

"And the third angel followed them, saying with a loud voice, If any man worship the beast and his image, and receive his mark in his forehead, or in his hand, The same shall drink of the wine of the wrath of God, which is poured out without mixture into the cup of His indignation; and he shall be tormented with fire and brimstone in the presence of the holy angels, and in the presence of the Lamb: And the smoke of their torment ascends up for ever and ever: and they have no rest day nor night, who worship the beast and his image, and whosoever receives the mark of his name."

- *Revelation 14:9-11*

The language here is very clear. There is a real Hell and those that enter it will be there for eternity. To those who believe that a God of love would not perform such an act are not aware of the judgments of God that we are discussing in this chapter. God *is* loving but He is also just and therefore must punish sin. God sent His Son Jesus Christ to take the punishment for sin in man's place. All He asks is that we accept Jesus' sacrificial death as atonement for us. If we do then our sin's debt to God is paid. However, if a person refuses to receive Jesus Christ as their Savior from sin then God will punish that person. This is because it is intrinsic in God's nature that He must punish sin. I will discuss further the biblical concept of sin and punishment in Chapter 13.

With this we now come to the seven final judgments of God that are to come upon the earth and its inhabitants:

"And I saw another sign in heaven, great and marvelous, seven angels having the seven last plagues; for in them is filled up the wrath of God. And I saw as it were a sea of glass mingled with fire: and them that had gotten the victory over the beast, and over his image, and over his mark, and over the number of his name, stand on the sea of glass, having the harps of God...And after that I looked, and, behold, the Temple of the Tabernacle of the testimony in heaven was opened: And the seven angels came out of the temple, having the seven plagues, clothed in pure and white linen, and having their breasts girded with golden girdles. And one of the four beasts gave unto the seven angels seven golden bowls full of the wrath of God, Who lives for ever and ever. And the temple was filled with smoke from the glory of God, and from His power; and no man was able to enter into the temple, till the seven plagues of the seven angels were fulfilled."

- Revelation 15:1-2, 5-8

"And I heard a great voice out of the Temple saying to the seven angels, Go your ways, and pour out the bowls of the wrath of God

upon the earth. And the first went, and poured out his bowl upon the earth; and there fell a noisome and grievous sore upon the men which had the mark of the beast and upon them which worshipped his image."

- Revelation 16:1-2

Prior to the emptying of this bowl, the last physical judgment upon humanity was the fifth trumpet sounding which unleashed a horde of locust-type creatures. They had the power to torment humans for five months yet not kill them. Now the followers of the Antichrist will be afflicted with loathsome ulcers. Those still living who have not accepted the mark of the Antichrist nor worshipped him will be spared this judgment.

During some of the plagues that God sent upon a rebellious Egypt during the time of Moses, He supernaturally protected His people. The insects that came upon the Egyptians did not bother the Israelites. The cattle of the Egyptians were afflicted with disease while God spared the Israelites' cattle. When hail fell upon Egypt, it did not fall in the Land of Goshen where the children of Israel were living. When God brought a darkness, which the Egyptians could actually feel, over their entire countryside, the Israelites had light in their places of habitation. Finally, when the Angel of Death killed the firstborn of Egypt, he passed over those who had the blood of the lamb on their dwelling places.[42]

"And the second angel poured out his bowl upon the sea; and it became as the blood of a dead man: and every living soul died in the sea."

- Revelation 16:3

The oceans of the world turn into blood and every sea creature dies as a result. With the physical pain that rebellious humanity is suffering at this point they now have the added distress of an unimaginable stench from the bloody water and dead creatures of the sea.

"And the third angel poured out his bowl upon the rivers and fountains of waters; and they became blood. And I heard the angel of the waters say, You are righteous, O Lord, Which are, and was, and shall be, because You have judged thus. For they have shed the blood of saints and prophets, and You have given them blood to drink; for they are worthy. And I heard another out of the altar say, Even so, Lord God Almighty, true and righteous are your judgments."

- Revelation 16:4-7

Next, God pours out His wrath on the fresh water systems of the earth. Just as God used the false gods of Egypt to judge that nation so now He is turning man's drinking water into blood because they had slain millions of God's peoples. Before they were bloodthirsty in killing the followers of Jesus Christ, now they will have their fill of blood while they are thirsting for water.

Some people say that a God of love would not punish nor pour out His wrath upon humanity. By saying this they are actually sitting in judgment of God. If He does do what the Bible tells us He is going to do during the Tribulation Period then these people are saying that God is not a loving God. Yet after this third bowl judgment, heaven declares that God's judgments are "*true and righteous*".

"And the fourth angel poured out his bowl upon the sun; and power was given unto him to scorch men with fire. And men were scorched with great heat, and blasphemed the name of God, Who has power

over these plagues: and they repented not to give Him glory."

- Revelation 16:8-9

With no fresh water to drink and already in severe pain, God sends an unbearable heat upon mankind. The term "global warming" does not do justice to what the earth will experience with this judgment.

The hearts of men will be irrevocably hardened by this point that they will continue to blaspheme God rather than repent of their rebellion against Him.

"And the fifth angel poured out his bowl upon the seat of the beast; and his kingdom was full of darkness; and they gnawed their tongues for pain, And blasphemed the God of heaven because of their pains and their sores, and repented not of their deeds."

- Revelation 16:10-11

This judgment of darkness falling over the kingdom of the Antichrist is similar to the one that God poured out upon the Egyptians when they would not free His people. In that story God said to Moses, *"Stretch out your hand toward heaven, that there may be darkness over the land of Egypt, even darkness which may be felt."*[43] This darkness will not only keep people from seeing anything but they will also probably feel the oppressiveness of it.

The pain at this point is so excruciating that humans will chew on their tongues in response. Yet again they continue to blaspheme and hate God because of their sufferings and refuse to repent of their evil ways.

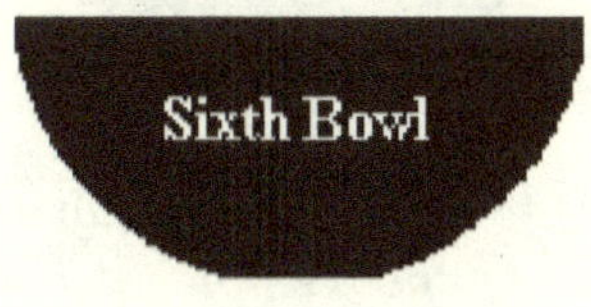

"And the sixth angel poured out his bowl upon the great river Euphrates; and the water thereof was dried up, that the way of the kings of the east might be prepared. And I saw three unclean spirits like frogs come out of the mouth of the dragon, and out of the mouth of the beast, and out of the mouth of the false prophet. For they are the spirits of devils, working miracles, which go forth unto the kings of the earth and of the whole world, to gather them to the battle of that great day of God Almighty. Behold, I come as a thief. Blessed is he that watches, and keeps his garments, lest he walk naked, and they see his shame. And He gathered them together into a place called in the Hebrew tongue Armageddon."

- Revelation 16:12-16

Earlier we read that the sixth trumpet judgment freed four angels who were bound to the Euphrates River. There John saw an army of 200 million men on the move. With this sixth bowl judgment we see a consummation of that earlier trumpet judgment.

The kings of the east and their massive army try a power move against the Antichrist. They cross the dried-up river (probably through Iraq) in order to attack him and his army. But this battle is not only going to be between the East and the West but also the North and the South.

The satanic "trinity" of the Devil, Antichrist, and False Prophet is going to send out demonic spirits to gather the rest of the world to the "*battle of that great Day of God Almighty*". The armies of the world converge on the plains of Esdraelon in the northern part of Israel in the valley of Megiddo (some believe that the name Armageddon is a reference to Megiddo). While this war is raging an angel pours out the seventh bowl judgment on the earth, which is also the final judgment that God brings during the Tribulation Period.

"And the seventh angel poured out his bowl into the air; and there came a great voice out of the Temple of heaven, from the throne, saying, It is done. And there were voices, and thunders, and

lightnings; and there was a great earthquake, such as was not since men were upon the earth, so mighty an earthquake, and so great. And the great city was divided into three parts, and the cities of the nations fell: and great Babylon came in remembrance before God, to give unto her the cup of the wine of the fierceness of His wrath. And every island fled away, and the mountains were not found. And there fell upon men a great hail out of heaven, every stone about the weight of a talent: and men blasphemed God because of the plague of the hail; for the plague thereof was exceeding great."

- Revelation 16:17-21

The historically unprecedented noise and light show of this final judgment will be unimaginable. Then a worldwide earthquake shakes the planet. The *"great earthquake"* that John sees here was spoken of by Isaiah:

"And it shall come to pass, that he who flees from the noise of the fear shall fall into the pit; and he that comes up out of the midst of the pit shall be taken in the snare: for the windows from on high are open, and the foundations of the earth do shake. The earth is utterly broken down, the earth is clean dissolved, the earth is moved exceedingly. The earth shall reel to and fro like a drunkard, and shall be removed like a cottage; and the transgression thereof shall be heavy upon it; and it shall fall, and not rise again. And it shall come to pass in that day, that the LORD shall punish the host of the high ones that are on high, and the kings of the earth upon the earth. And they shall be gathered together, as prisoners are gathered in the pit, and shall be shut up in the prison, and after many days shall they be visited. Then the moon shall be confounded, and the sun ashamed, when the LORD of hosts shall reign in mount Zion, and in Jerusalem, and before His ancients gloriously." [44]

This earthquake destroys the cities of the world including "Babylon". It appears that this shaking of the earth *"to and fro like a drunkard"* will level mountains and sink islands in the oceans.

Finally, hailstones weighing more than one-hundred pounds each, rain down on the earth and once again cause those still alive to blaspheme God.

This final, apocalyptic storm, which includes thunder, lightning, an earthquake, and hailstones will occur as the armies of the world are slaughtering each other in Israel. However, the second coming of the Lord Jesus Christ will terminate all these events.

A voice comes out of the Temple in Heaven and declares, *"It is done!"* The Tribulation Period judgments of the world for its rebellious rejection of God and His Son are over.

In chapter 19 of Revelation, John sees the second coming of Jesus Christ and His destruction of the armies of the world during the battle of Armageddon. In the next chapter I will examine this battle in detail as it is spoken of several times in both the Old and New Testaments. In Chapter 11 of this book, I will discuss the second coming of Jesus the Messiah.

Before leaving this extremely long chapter, I would like to reiterate what I said at the beginning of it: Two life issues should be of concern to non-Christians. The first has been around for nearly two millennia. It is the matter of the unsaved dying before they accept Jesus Christ as their Lord and Savior. The second is this future time of trouble that is coming upon the whole world.

I believe we can see this period of tribulation on the horizon as we head toward economic and governmental globalization. The horrific nightmare that John saw coming upon the earth is almost unfathomable to the modern hearer. Yet as we saw in Part One of this book, Jesus did fulfill the Messianic prophecies that spoke of a suffering Messiah. Just as assuredly, the biblical prophecies that speak of this future time of distress will also come to pass.

The question that each person on earth has to answer is, "Do I want to suffer the wrath of God either in this life or in the next or do I want to spend eternity with God in peace?" Jesus said, *"he that is not against us is for us."*[45] It is up to each individual to decide whether they are going to be on God's side or on the Devil's side.

---

[1] *Matthew 24:1-2*

[2] ["War of the Jews"; Josephus; Books IV-V]

[3] *Daniel 8:23-25*

[4] *II Thessalonians 2:3-4*
[5] *Matthew 24:15-16*
[6] *I Thessalonians 5:2-3*
[7] *Revelation 13:8*
[8] This organization is called the "Temple Mount and Land of Israel Faithful Movement". Immediately after the Six Day War in Israel was over, the Jews had regained control of the Temple Mount for the first time in 1900 Years. However, the Israeli Defense Minister Moshe Dayan shortly thereafter relinquished control back to the Muslims. So the Temple Mount Faithful group was organized with the hopes of one day regaining control of the Temple Mount and rebuilding the third Jewish Temple.
[9] This group is called "The Temple Institute"
[10] *Jeremiah 30:1-7*
[11] *Genesis 29:1-30*
[12] *Daniel 12:1*
[13] *Matthew 24:21, 29*
[14] *Revelation 1:1*
[15] *Revelation 1:9*
[16] *Revelation 1:19*
[17] *Revelation 4:1*
[18] *Daniel 7:8; 11; 20*
[19] *II Thessalonians 2:9*
[20] *Revelation 13:13-14*
[21] *Revelation 13:4, 7*
[22] *Revelation 7:3-4*
[23] *Revelation 7:9-10, 13-14*
[24] *Revelation 6:9-10*
[25] *Revelation 16:12*
[26] *Revelation 10:1-4*
[27] *Revelation 10:9-11*
[28] *Revelation 11:1-2*
[29] *Malachi 4:5*
[30] *I Kings 17:1*
[31] *Exodus 7:19*
[32] *Revelation 13:1-18*
[33] *I Thessalonians 2:1-4*
[34] *Zechariah 6:12-13*
[35] *Revelation 16:17-18*
[36] *Revelation 12:1-2*
[37] *Genesis 37:9*
[38] *Revelation 12:4-5*
[39] *Revelation 7:9, 14*
[40] *Revelation 20:4*
[41] *Genesis 11:4*
[42] *Exodus 8:22-24; 9:4-7; 9:22-25; 10:21-23; 12:1-30*
[43] *Exodus 10:21*

[44] *Isaiah 24:18-23*
[45] *Luke 9:50*

10 - Armageddon

One day soon, I believe an evil world ruler whom Christians call the Antichrist is going to rise on the world scene. The apostle Paul calls him the *"man of lawlessness"* and the *"son of perdition"*.[1] The first appellation refers to the fact that he will disregard God's laws. The prophet Daniel said: *"And he shall speak great words against the most High, and shall wear out the saints of the most High, and think to change times and laws: and they shall be given into his hand until a time and times and the dividing of time."*[2] The second term, "son of perdition", is literally "son of destruction". As we read in the last chapter, when he comes to power the world will essentially be destroyed.

The reign of Adolph Hitler, in which the people (and particularly the Jews) lived and suffered, will pale in comparison to what will happen under the reign of the Antichrist. Hitler came to power during the economic depression of the 1920s and 1930s. One tool that he found indispensable was to create a scapegoat for Germany's problems. He told the people that the Jews were the cause of their troubles. This allowed him to persecute them since the German people wanted their hard economic times to go away. Similarly, I believe that the Antichrist will rise to power during harsh economic conditions as described in the Third Seal judgment. He too will find a convenient scapegoat for all the woes of the world. As Daniel said above, he will blame the followers of God and wear them out through persecution.

Some people wonder if the Antichrist is alive on the earth at this time. If the events that I have spoken of are in the near future, then it is very possible that he is indeed living somewhere on the earth at this moment. However, I would like to submit another possibility.

In previous generations what I am about to say would have been unthinkable. However, with modern science it is not only possible but also feasible. This idea revolves around the cloning of human beings. Currently there is a theological debate concerning the ethics of cloning. One aspect dealing with this issue is whether a cloned human would have a soul. If human cloning ever does take place then I submit that it is possible that such a man would indeed be soulless. The Bible's description of the Antichrist would also indicate that such a possibility is tenable.

Satan is an imitator of God yet he perverts God's designs. Jesus Christ was born of a virgin woman without the occurrence of a sexual union between a man and a woman. A cloned human being would also be the result of a human life that did not occur from the natural human procreation process. This concept fits well the Devil's ways of fulfilling his plans. If a scientist did successfully clone a human in the very near future, the process would take several years for the cloned baby to reach adulthood. This of course would delay the end-time events for probably twenty years. Either way the Antichrist is going to come to power in God's timing.

He will begin the process of his ascendancy to world domination through some sort of agreement or peace treaty. He will seemingly have the answers to the world's economic and spiritual problems. Meanwhile, he will be raising an international army to suppress opposition, particularly those who are followers of God.

Some believe that the Antichrist will come to power in the continent of Europe. There are primarily two biblical reasons for this assertion. Both of them are in the Book of Daniel.

The first has to do with an interpretation that Daniel gave concerning a dream that King Nebuchadnezzar had. In that dream, Nebuchadnezzar saw a great or giant image, which may have been a statue. This statue had a head of gold, its chest and arms were made of silver, its stomach and thighs were brass, the legs were iron, and its feet and toes were part iron and part clay. Daniel stated that each of these sections of the image represented a world empire.[3]

Daniel said that the head was the Babylonian Empire of King Nebuchadnezzar. The chest and arms would be the Medo-Persian Empire, the stomach and thighs represented the Greek Empire under Alexander the Great, and the legs of iron were the Roman Empire which would trodden down the people. Daniel prophesied concerning this fourth or Roman Empire, *"And the fourth kingdom shall be strong as iron: forasmuch as iron breaks in pieces and subdues all things: and as iron that breaks all these, shall it break in pieces and bruise."*[4] This is an apt description of the Roman Empire which did conquer the known world with its mighty and disciplined armies. Daniel then states that the toes were made of iron and clay. This means that this final kingdom would be partly strong and partly broken or weak. These ten toes represented ten future kings. Daniel speaks of these kings in a later chapter.

In a vision that he himself had Daniel saw four beasts which represented the same four world empires of King Nebuchadnezzar's dream.[5] Concerning the fourth beast Daniel said:

> *"After this I saw in the night visions, and behold a fourth beast, dreadful and terrible, and strong exceedingly; and it had great iron teeth: it devoured and brake in pieces, and stamped the residue with the feet of it: and it was diverse from all the beasts that were before it; and it had ten horns. I considered the horns, and, behold, there came up among them another little horn, before whom there were three of the first horns plucked up by the roots: and, behold, in this horn were eyes like the eyes of man, and a mouth speaking great things."*[6]

This section again refers to the dreadful power of the Roman Empire. There are two things to notice in this passage. The first is that the beast had ten horns of which three fell. The second is the little horn was a man who spoke great things. An angel interprets this vision for Daniel:

> *"Thus he said, The fourth beast shall be the fourth kingdom upon earth, which shall be diverse from all kingdoms, and shall devour the whole earth, and shall tread it down, and break it in pieces. And the ten horns out of this kingdom are ten kings that shall arise: and another shall rise after them; and he shall be diverse from the first, and he shall subdue three kings. And he shall speak great words against*

the most High, and shall wear out the saints of the most High, and think to change times and laws: and they shall be given into his hand until a time and times and the dividing of time. But the judgment shall sit, and they shall take away his dominion, to consume and to destroy it unto the end."[7]

Both the dream of Nebuchadnezzar and the vision of Daniel spoke of the Roman Empire. The ten toes of the statue and the ten horns of the beast are ten kings. Then a great king comes along who will subdue three of the ten kings and will magnify himself against the most High God. This little horn or king will be the Antichrist.

The Book of Revelation also refers to these ten kings and the Antichrist who shall come from among them:

"And I stood upon the sand of the sea, and saw a beast rise up out of the sea, having seven heads and ten horns, and upon his horns ten crowns, and upon his heads the name of blasphemy. And the beast which I saw was like unto a leopard, and his feet were as the feet of a bear, and his mouth as the mouth of a lion: and the dragon [i.e., the Devil] *gave him his power, and his seat, and great authority."*[8]

Since the Roman Empire and its people gravitated to Europe, some believe that the descendants of the Romans comprise the majority of the Europeans. This leads to the belief that from them the Antichrist will rise to power.

The second passage in Daniel that seems to allude to the Antichrist coming out of the Roman Empire and therefore Europe states:

"And after threescore and two weeks shall Messiah be cut off, but not for Himself: and the people of the prince that shall come shall destroy the city and the sanctuary; and the end thereof shall be with a flood, and unto the end of the war desolations are determined."[9]

The "prince" who destroyed Herod's Temple in 70 A.D. was the Roman General Titus. Thus, the *"people of the prince"* were the Romans who made up his army. Since this was only a foreshadow of the final destruction of the third or Tribulation Period Temple, the fulfillment of this prophetic passage has yet to occur. However, this too appears to be a reference to the Roman Empire and a future "prince" who will arise out of it.

This has led some end-times scholars to believe that the Antichrist will rise to power through a confederation of European countries such as the European Union. He may indeed ascend to the leadership of the European Parliament since Europe has been historically anti-Semitic and he will be the greatest anti-Semite who ever lived. He will have the support of ten other leaders of whom three he will overcome. At some point early on, he will use his newfound power to insert himself into the politics of Israel and the Middle East. He will make a covenant or peace treaty with Israel (anti-Semitism notwithstanding in order to further his true agenda) and possibly the other nations of the world. Finally, he will oversee the rebuilding of the Temple in Jerusalem and will be proclaimed and worshiped by the world as the messiah.

After three and one-half years of his reign he will be possessed by the Devil and declare himself God while sitting in this newly rebuilt Jewish Temple in Jerusalem. Several things occur as soon as he commits this flagrant and nefarious act.

The Jews in Israel will realize they have followed a false Messiah and will flee to the wilderness (possibly Petra in Jordan) where God will supernaturally protect them. The other leaders in the world will determine that he is a megalomaniac and will send their armies toward Israel to make war against him. This will result in the final war of human history, which will take place in and around Israel and will end in the holy city of Jerusalem.

God foretold of this event in the Book of Zechariah:

> *"Behold, I will make Jerusalem a cup of trembling unto all the people round about, when they shall be in the siege both against Judah and against Jerusalem. And in that day will I make Jerusalem a burdensome stone for all people: all that burden themselves with it shall be cut in pieces,*

> *though all the people of the earth be gathered together against it. In that day, says the LORD, I will smite every horse with astonishment, and his rider with madness: and I will open Mine eyes upon the house of Judah, and will smite every horse of the people with blindness. And the governors of Judah shall say in their heart, The inhabitants of Jerusalem shall be my strength in the LORD of hosts their God. In that day will I make the governors of Judah like an hearth of fire among the wood, and like a torch of fire in a sheaf; and they shall devour all the people round about, on the right hand and on the left: and Jerusalem shall be inhabited again in her own place, even in Jerusalem...And it shall come to pass in that day, that I will seek to destroy all the nations that come against Jerusalem."*
>
> \- *Zechariah 12:2-6, 9*

The prophet Joel also prophesied concerning this final war that is to take place in Israel and Jerusalem:

> *"Blow ye the trumpet in Zion, and sound an alarm in My holy mountain: let all the inhabitants of the land tremble: for the day of the LORD cometh, for it is near at hand; A day of darkness and of gloominess, a day of clouds and of thick darkness, as the morning spread upon the mountains: a great people and a strong; there hath not been ever the like, neither shall be any more after it, even to the years of many generations. A fire devours before them; and behind them a flame burns: the land is as the garden of Eden before them, and behind them a desolate wilderness; yea, and nothing shall escape them. The appearance of them is as the appearance of horses; and as horsemen, so shall they run. Like the noise of chariots on the tops of mountains shall they leap, like the noise of a flame of fire that devours the stubble, as a strong people set in battle array. Before their face the people shall be much pained: all faces shall gather blackness. They shall run like mighty men; they shall climb the wall like men of war; and they*

shall march every one on his ways, and they shall not break their ranks: Neither shall one thrust another; they shall walk every one in his path: and when they fall upon the sword, they shall not be wounded. They shall run to and fro in the city; they shall run upon the wall, they shall climb up upon the houses; they shall enter in at the windows like a thief. The earth shall quake before them; the heavens shall tremble: the sun and the moon shall be dark, and the stars shall withdraw their shining: And the LORD shall utter His voice before His army: for His camp is very great: for He is strong that executes his word: for the day of the LORD is great and very terrible; and who can abide it?"

- *Joel 2:1-11*

You will notice that Joel mentions several of the final bowl judgments of Revelation as taking place just before and during this war. Darkness will come upon the earth, multitudes of horsemen (mechanized vehicles will probably be obsolete after the devastation of the Tribulation Period) will appear leaving destruction behind them and a great earthquake will shake the world.

This final war on earth will end with the coming of the army of the Lord. As we will see in the next chapter, this army consists of the saints of God who have been raptured or have died in Christ. Jesus Himself will lead them into battle.

The Eve of Destruction

In the popular culture of today, the word Armageddon refers to a catastrophic and devastating event that destroys the world. As we have read to this point, that is a reasonably accurate definition of what is going to take place at the end of the current age.

The act that sets in motion the events that culminate in the battle of Armageddon is the Antichrist's declaration that he is God. This causes the Jews in Israel to flee to Jordan, which is the biblical Edom. The Devil-possessed Antichrist will then go on the attack:

"And when the dragon [i.e., the Devil] *saw that he was cast*

> *unto the earth, he persecuted* [i.e., through the Antichrist] *the woman* [i.e., Israel] *which brought forth the man child. And to the woman were given two wings of a great eagle, that she might fly into the wilderness, into her place, where she is nourished for a time, and times, and half a time, from the face of the serpent. And the serpent cast out of his mouth water as a flood after the woman, that he might cause her to be carried away of the flood. And the earth helped the woman, and the earth opened her mouth, and swallowed up the flood which the dragon cast out of his mouth. And the dragon was wroth with the woman, and went to make war with the remnant of her seed, which keep the commandments of God, and have the testimony of Jesus Christ."*[10]

The Antichrist then sends a flood after the escaping Jews. This flood probably consists of parts of his army. God will supernaturally protect the Jews from the Devil and his Antichrist by opening crevasses in the earth's surface, which will swallow up his soldiers. After the Devil sees the impotency of his power against God he will then make war against God's people.

While this is going on the 200 million-man army is marching toward the Middle East in the hopes of stopping the Antichrist's war of aggression. If oil is still the mainstay of the world's economy at this time then the kings of the east may be concerned that the Antichrist is trying to monopolize those resources. Regardless of the reason the day of Armageddon is approaching rapidly during this time.

The prophet Daniel mentions other problems that the Antichrist will soon be facing as the final war looms before him:

> *"And the king* [i.e., Antichrist] *shall do according to his will; and he shall exalt himself, and magnify himself above every god, and shall speak marvelous things against the God of gods, and shall prosper till the indignation be accomplished: for that that is determined shall be done. Neither shall he regard the God of his fathers, nor the desire of women, nor regard any god: for he shall magnify*

> *himself above all. But in his estate shall he honor the god of forces: and a god whom his fathers knew not shall he honor with gold, and silver, and with precious stones, and pleasant things. Thus shall he do in the most strong holds with a strange god, whom he shall acknowledge and increase with glory: and he shall cause them to rule over many, and shall divide the land for gain. And at the time of the end shall the king of the south push at him: and the king of the north shall come against him like a whirlwind, with chariots, and with horsemen, and with many ships; and he shall enter into the countries, and shall overflow and pass over. He shall enter also into the glorious land, and many countries shall be overthrown: but these shall escape out of his hand, even Edom, and Moab, and the chief of the children of Ammon. He shall stretch forth his hand also upon the countries: and the land of Egypt shall not escape. But he shall have power over the treasures of gold and of silver, and over all the precious things of Egypt: and the Libyans and the Ethiopians shall be at his steps. But tidings out of the east and out of the north shall trouble him: therefore he shall go forth with great fury to destroy and utterly to make away many. And he shall plant the tabernacles of his palace between the seas in the glorious holy mountain; yet he shall come to his end, and none shall help him."*[11]

There are several notable things in this passage concerning the Antichrist and the events leading up to Armageddon.

We have already seen how he will magnify himself against God and will speak great things. Daniel says that he will not honor the God of his fathers. This has led to much speculation as to whether the Antichrist will have Jewish roots. He will not regard the desire of women. Though the meaning of this phrase is unclear, it could be that he will remain celibate during his tenure on earth or that he could be a homosexual. Others believe that it was the *desire* of Jewish women to give birth to the Messiah. Thus, the Antichrist will not acknowledge the Desire or Messiah of Israel. The only god that he will honor is the "god of force" and the "god of riches". I believe the phrase, *"Thus shall he do in the most strong holds with a strange god, whom he shall acknowledge and increase with glory: and he shall cause them to rule over many, and shall divide the land for gain"*, refers to his possession by the Devil who gives to him all his authority.[12] Dividing the Middle East for gain could be a reference to the oil supplies that are located there. All of this results in the other leaders of the world seeking to stop him from expanding his greed to their lands.

Daniel says that the king of the south will push toward him. This king will probably be leading a confederation of African and Arab armies that are marching to Israel. A king from the north will come down toward him like a whirlwind. These could be Russian troops and include soldiers from the Islamic states that surround it.

At first, the Antichrist's armies will gain the upper hand as *"many countries shall be overthrown"* by him. It is interesting though that Edom, Moab, and Ammon will be protected from his attacks. These areas make up the present-day country of Jordan, which is the area to where the Jews will flee. This would explain why he would be unable to attack these lands because God's supernatural protection will be over them for the Jews' sake.

He will be successful in fighting back the southern armies into Egypt, Libya, and Ethiopia where he will gain control of those countries' wealth.

Just when the Antichrist thinks he is about to be victorious he receives bad news. He has to divert his attention to the coming onslaught of the massive armies from the east and the north. He will go forth to fight these invading armies with a *"great fury"* and will wipe out many of them. This battle will take place on the plains of Israel in the valley of Megiddo and end in Jerusalem. Nevertheless, as Daniel says *"he shall come to his end, and none shall help him"*.

Armageddon

Even though by this time, the world will have been decimated and billions of people killed, there will still be billions of humans living on the earth. After all they will have gone through by this time, the only hope they may have left is to fight with the armies of the world in order to stay alive. The result of this will be hundreds of millions of soldiers converging on Israel from the north, the south, the east, and the west to fight to gain control of the wealth of the world.

The prophet Joel speaks of this gathering of the nations to the battle of Armageddon:

> *"Proclaim ye this among the Gentiles; Prepare war, wake up the mighty men, let all the men of war draw near; let them come up: Beat your plowshares into swords and your pruning hooks into spears: let the weak say, I am strong. Assemble yourselves, and come, all ye heathen, and gather yourselves together round about: there cause Your mighty ones to come down, O LORD. Let the heathen be wakened, and come up to the valley of Jehoshaphat: for there will I sit to judge all the heathen round about. Put ye in the sickle, for the harvest is ripe: come, get you down; for the press is full, the fats overflow; for their wickedness is great. Multitudes, multitudes in the valley of decision: for the day of the LORD is near in the valley of decision. The sun and the moon shall be darkened, and the stars shall withdraw their shining. The LORD also shall roar out of Zion, and utter His voice from Jerusalem; and the heavens and the earth shall shake: but the LORD will be the hope of His people, and the strength of the children of Israel. So shall ye know that I am the LORD your God dwelling in Zion, My holy mountain: then shall Jerusalem be holy, and there shall no strangers pass through her any more."*[13]

God tells the nations of the world to turn the instruments they use for peaceful means into weapons of war. Later on He will reverse this process but not until the earth is purged of this final rebellion.

God says for the multitudes of the world to gather in the valley of Jehoshaphat, the valley of decision. Though we do not know whether this is an actual geographical valley or a metaphor for the judgment of God, the nations will come together around Jerusalem. When they do swift judgment will come upon them by the hand of God: *"Put you in the sickle, for the harvest is ripe: come, get you down; for the press is full, the fats overflow; for their wickedness is great"*. The Book of Revelation makes mention of this event:

> *"And I looked, and behold a white cloud, and upon the cloud one sat like unto the Son of man, having on His head a golden crown, and in His hand a sharp sickle. And another angel came out of the Temple, crying with a loud voice to Him that sat on the cloud, Thrust in your sickle, and reap: for the time is come for you to reap; for the harvest of the earth is ripe. And He that sat on the cloud thrust in His sickle on the earth; and the earth was reaped. And another angel came out of the Temple which is in Heaven, he also having a sharp sickle. And another angel came out from the altar, which had power over fire; and cried with a loud cry to him that had the sharp sickle, saying, Thrust in your sharp sickle, and gather the clusters of the vine of the earth; for her grapes are fully ripe. And the angel thrust in his sickle into the earth, and gathered the vine of the earth, and cast it into the great winepress of the wrath of God. And the winepress was trodden without the city, and blood came out of the winepress, even unto the horse bridles, by the space of a thousand and six hundred furlongs."*[14]

The term here, "Son of man", is a title for Jesus Christ. It is used only twice in the Book of Revelation. The other time is in the first chapter where it is clearly speaking of Jesus Christ. It does seem strange that here an angel appears to command Jesus to thrust in the sickle to judge the armies of the earth. Yet I believe it is more along the lines of the angels declaring that they have prepared everything for the Lord to begin His judgment. It could also be that since this angel came out of the Temple in Heaven, he was speaking a command from the Father.

Both the Books of Joel and Revelation liken this final destruction of the armies of the world to a winepress. Just as the press squeezes out the juice from the grapes, so too will the blood pour out of the millions of soldiers who are lying dead and wounded for a distance of about *two hundred miles*.

The prophet Zechariah spoke an enigmatic prophecy concerning this battle when he said:

> *"And this shall be the plague wherewith the LORD will smite all the people that have fought against Jerusalem; Their flesh shall consume away while they stand upon their feet, and their eyes shall consume away in their holes, and their tongue shall consume away in their mouth."*[15]

This prophecy states that during the battle of Armageddon the soldiers' flesh, eyes, and tongues will melt away while they are still standing on their feet. Though this could be the result of a supernatural act of God it also is a description of what happens to humans killed by a nuclear explosion. Either way the rebellious armies will be destroyed.

The prophet Isaiah also foretells of the results of this final battle:

> *"Come near, ye nations, to hear; and hearken, you people: let the earth hear, and all that is therein; the world, and all things that come forth of it. For the indignation of the LORD is upon all nations, and His fury upon all their armies: He has utterly destroyed them, He has delivered them to the slaughter. Their slain also shall be cast out, and their stink shall come up out of their carcasses, and the mountains shall be melted with their blood. And all the host of heaven shall be dissolved, and the heavens shall be rolled together as a scroll: and all their host shall fall down, as the leaf falls off from the vine, and as a falling fig from the fig tree."*[16]

The smell of the wounded and dead soldiers and animals will cover the land of Israel. The Lord has poured out His final fury upon the armies of the world. This destruction includes that of the Antichrist and his False Prophet as we will see.

God states that the heavens will be dissolved. After the devastation and desolation of the Tribulation Period the world will need renovating. In Chapter 12, I will discuss this transformation of the earth into a beautiful and fruitful world.

Lastly, we read that the battle of Armageddon ends with the second coming of the Lord Jesus Christ:

> *"Behold, the day of the LORD comes, and your spoil shall be divided in the midst of you. For I will gather all nations against Jerusalem to battle; and the city shall be taken, and the houses rifled, and the women ravished; and half of the city shall go forth into captivity, and the residue of the people shall not be cut off from the city. Then shall the LORD go forth, and fight against those nations, as when he fought in the day of battle. And His feet shall stand in that day upon the mount of Olives, which is before Jerusalem on the east, and the mount of Olives shall cleave in the midst thereof toward the east and toward the west, and there shall be a very great valley; and half of the mountain shall remove toward the north, and half of it toward the south. And you shall flee to the valley of the mountains; for the valley of the mountains shall reach unto Azal: yea, you shall flee, like as you fled from before the earthquake in the days of Uzziah king of Judah: and the LORD my God shall come, and all the saints with thee. And it shall come to pass in that day, that the light shall not be clear, nor dark: But it shall be one day which shall be known to the LORD, not day, nor night: but it shall come to pass, that at evening time it shall be light. And it shall be in that day, that living waters shall go out from Jerusalem; half of them toward the former sea, and half of them toward the hinder sea: in summer and in winter shall it be. And the LORD shall be King over all the earth: in that day shall there be one LORD, and His name one."*[17]

The final battle of Armageddon will take place in and around the city of Jerusalem. The inhabitants will flee the city until the battle is consummated. The Lord will destroy all the armies and will stand on the Mount of Olives, which will cause it to cleave in two and create a new landscape around Jerusalem. We will see this fulfilled when Jesus descends to earth at His second coming with the saints of God.

Zechariah states that this day of the Lord's coming *"shall be known to the LORD"*. This corresponds to what Jesus said: *"But of that day and hour knows no man, no, not the angels of heaven, but*

My Father only".[18] When Jesus does come, He will put an end to the battle of Armageddon and to the Tribulation Period.

As horrible as the events of this and the previous chapter were, there are still two horrific judgments of God that will take place. The first is the judgment by Jesus Christ of those who survive the Tribulation Period. The second will take place 1000 years after Jesus sets up His Millennial Kingdom. I will discuss the former in the next chapter and the latter in Chapter 13.

---

1 *II Thessalonians 2:3*
2 *Daniel 7:25*
3 *Daniel 2:1-45*
4 *Daniel 2:40*
5 *Daniel 7:1-27*
6 *Daniel 7:7-8*
7 *Daniel 7:23-26*
8 *Revelation 13:1-2*
9 *Daniel 9:26*
10 *Revelation 12:13-17*
11 *Daniel 11:36-45*
12 *Revelation 13:2*
13 *Joel 3:9-17*
14 *Revelation 14:14-20*
15 *Zechariah 14:12*
16 *Isaiah 34-1-4*
17 *Zechariah 14:1-9*
18 *Matthew 24:36*

11 - The Second Coming of Jesus the Messiah

The first coming of Jesus Christ changed the world. His second coming will change the universe. The timing of His appearance is explicit in many Bible passages. He will come again to earth at the end of the battle of Armageddon. He will destroy the armies of the world, judge the inhabitants of the earth, and then set up His Messianic Kingdom.

Jesus promised to His disciples when He walked on the earth two thousand years ago that He would come again:

> *"Let not your heart be troubled: you believe in God, believe also in Me. In My Father's house are many mansions: if it were not so, I would have told you. I go to prepare a place for you. And if I go and prepare a place for you, I will come again, and receive you unto Myself; that where I am, there you may be also."*
>
> \- *John 14:1-3*

The writer of the Book of Hebrews also spoke of His second coming:

> *"So Christ was once offered to bear the sins of many; and unto them that look for Him shall He appear the second time without sin unto salvation."*
>
> *- Hebrews 9:28*

There is no doubt in the minds of the New Testament writers that Jesus Christ is literally coming to earth again.

Nevertheless, since it has been two thousand years since Jesus made His promise to return, many people have rejected this concept. The Book of Second Peter talks about this attitude of unbelief concerning His second coming:

> *"This second epistle, beloved, I now write unto you; in both which I stir up your pure minds by way of remembrance: That you may be mindful of the words which were spoken before by the holy prophets, and of the commandment of us the apostles of the Lord and Savior: Knowing this first, that there shall come in the last days scoffers, walking after their own lusts, And saying, Where is the promise of His coming? For since the fathers fell asleep, all things continue as they were from the beginning of the creation. For this they willingly are ignorant of, that by the word of God the heavens were of old, and the earth standing out of the water and in the water: Whereby the world that then was, being overflowed with water, perished: But the heavens and the earth, which are now, by the same word are kept in store, reserved unto fire against the day of judgment and perdition of ungodly men. But, beloved, be not ignorant of this one thing, that one day is with the Lord as a thousand years, and a thousand years as one day. The Lord is not slack concerning His promise, as some men count slackness; but is longsuffering to us-ward, not willing that any should perish, but that all should come to repentance. But the day of the Lord will come as a thief in the night; in the which the heavens shall pass away with a great noise, and the elements shall melt with fervent heat, the earth also and the works that are therein shall be burned up."*[1]

The apostle Peter states that scoffers and mockers of those who believe that Jesus Christ is coming to earth a second time will increase in the last days. He also says that what seems like a long time to humans is but one day to God. Peter gives the reason for this delay when he says that God is not willing for anyone to perish. Therefore, God is giving humanity time to come to a saving faith in

Jesus Christ. This correlates with what Jesus said about the preaching of the gospel occurring throughout the entire world before the end comes.

Peter mentions that the earth will burn up and the heavens pass away. He might be referring to the cosmic changes that take place in the latter part of the Tribulation Period. He also could be speaking of the renovation of the earth that occurs at the start of Jesus' Millennial Kingdom.

Every Eye Will See

There have been misguided individuals in history who have proclaimed that they were Jesus Christ come again.[2] Also, there is a religious sect that believes Jesus came secretly in the early part of the Twentieth Century.[3] Both of these concepts are not only biblically erroneous but they are also heretical.

The Bible makes it clear that when Jesus Christ comes again to set up His earthly kingdom, the whole world will witness it:

> *"Behold, He comes with clouds; and every eye shall see Him, and they also which pierced Him: and all kindreds of the earth shall wail because of Him. Even so, Amen. I am Alpha and Omega, the beginning and the ending, saith the Lord, which is, and which was, and which is to come, the Almighty."*[4]

This means that anyone claiming to be Jesus Christ, including the Antichrist, must come in the clouds with the whole world witnessing it. Otherwise, they are deceivers and manipulators and are worthy of denunciation and opposition.

In this passage there is also an allusion to the prophecy in Zechariah concerning the coming of the Messiah:

> *"And it shall come to pass in that day, that I will seek to destroy all the nations that come against Jerusalem. And I will pour upon the house of David, and upon the inhabitants of Jerusalem, the spirit of grace and of supplications: and they shall look upon Me whom they*

have pierced."[5]

The world will see Jesus, Whom they pierced at His crucifixion, when He comes during the final battle of the nations at Armageddon.

Jesus also spoke concerning His second coming and the universality of it:

> *"For as the lightning cometh out of the east, and shines even unto the west; so shall also the coming of the Son of man be."*[6]

The Bible is unyielding in teaching that all humanity will indeed witness the return of Jesus Christ to the earth. When that event occurs it will not happen in secret or in some mysterious fashion. The world will know that Jesus has returned as He said He would.

How will it be possible for everyone on earth to see this event since some will be living on the other side of the world? I do not believe this will occur through the medium of television or some other modern means of electronic transmissions, although that is possible. Rather, they will see His second coming with their naked eyes.

You may remember that the fifth bowl judgment results in darkness coming on the earth as Armageddon is occurring. When Jesus comes again the Bible declares that there will be a heavenly illumination accompanying this event:

> *"And then shall that Wicked* [i.e., the Antichrist] *be revealed, whom the Lord shall consume with the spirit of His mouth, and shall destroy with the brightness of His coming."*[7]

> *"Immediately after the tribulation of those days shall the sun be darkened, and the moon shall not give her light, and the stars shall fall from heaven, and the powers of the heavens shall be shaken: And then shall appear the sign of the Son of man in heaven: and then shall all the tribes of the earth mourn, and they shall see the Son of man coming in the clouds of heaven with power and great glory. And He shall send His angels with a great sound of a trumpet,*

and they shall gather together His elect from the four winds, from one end of heaven to the other."[8]

The brightness of Jesus' coming will overwhelm the darkened earth and illuminate the entire heavens so that the whole world will see it. The sound of a trumpet will accompany His appearance and a shaking of the heavenly realm occurs. In this second passage we once more see a reference to the mourning that will take place when Jesus comes again. The cause of this grief is the recognition by humanity that it had been responsible for the death of the Son of God because of their sinfulness.

The Second Coming

As mentioned in some of the passages above, the time of Jesus' second coming will occur during the battle of Armageddon. We read that the events leading up to this final battle encompass the Tribulation Period during which God punishes the world for its rebellion against Him and His Son.

The Book of Revelation offers the clearest description of His second coming:

"And I saw heaven opened, and behold a white horse; and He that sat upon him was called Faithful and True, and in righteousness He does judge and make war. His eyes were as a flame of fire, and on His head were many crowns; and He had a name written, that no man knew, but He Himself. And He was clothed with a vesture dipped in blood: and His name is called The Word of God. And the armies which were in heaven followed Him upon white horses, clothed in fine linen, white and clean. And out of His mouth goes a sharp sword, that with it He should smite the nations: and He shall rule them with a rod of iron: and He treads the winepress of the fierceness and wrath of Almighty God. And He has on His vesture and on His thigh a name written, KING OF KINGS, AND LORD OF LORDS. And I saw an angel standing in the sun; and he cried with a loud voice, saying to all the fowls that fly in the midst of heaven,

Come and gather yourselves together unto the supper of the great God; That you may eat the flesh of kings, and the flesh of captains, and the flesh of mighty men, and the flesh of horses, and of them that sit on them, and the flesh of all men, both free and bond, both small and great. And I saw the beast, and the kings of the earth, and their armies, gathered together to make war against Him that sat on the horse, and against His army. And the beast was taken, and with him the false prophet that wrought miracles before him, with which he deceived them that had received the mark of the beast, and them that worshipped his image. These both were cast alive into a lake of fire burning with brimstone. And the remnant were slain with the sword of Him that sat upon the horse, which sword proceeded out of His mouth: and all the fowls were filled with their flesh."[9]

John gives quite a graphic account of the return of Jesus Christ to the earth. Though we cannot know how many, if any, of the descriptive terms he uses are symbolic, it is clear that he saw Jesus' second coming as a visible, literal event.

John mentions that an army accompanies Jesus at His return. This army's uniforms are made of clean, white linen. Earlier, in this chapter from Revelation, John sees this "army" receive these linen robes. This occurred at the "marriage feast" that took place between Jesus and His bride, the Church:

"Let us be glad and rejoice, and give honor to Him: for the marriage of the Lamb is come and His wife has made herself ready. And to her was granted that she should be arrayed in fine linen, clean and white: for the fine linen is the righteousness of saints. And he says unto me, Write, Blessed are they which are called unto the marriage supper of the Lamb."[10]

The term "wife" in this passage refers to Christians who had either died or been raptured. Just as God unites a married couple through matrimony, so too Christians will be united with Jesus Christ forever. The word "saints" in this passage also refers to the same

Christians who have believed and accepted Jesus Christ as their Savior. Their righteousness is actually the righteousness of Jesus Christ that God imputes to those who believe in Him. Therefore, the believers who died and those whom Jesus raptured will fill out the ranks of His army. Post-Tribulationists believe that the Rapture occurs around this point in time. The intriguing little Book of Jude also mentions this army of believers:

> *"And Enoch also, the seventh from Adam, prophesied of these, saying, Behold, the Lord comes with ten thousands of His saints, To execute judgment upon all, and to convince all that are ungodly among them of all their ungodly deeds which they have ungodly committed, and of all their hard speeches which ungodly sinners have spoken against Him."*[11]

According to Jude, Enoch declared the culmination of the world's history at the beginning of its history. The Lord would come with those who accepted Him to exact punishment upon those who rejected Him. I get the sense that Jesus will actually do the fighting at Armageddon. His army of saints will only be a witness to it. This "fighting" against the nations of the world seems to consist of Jesus *speaking* destruction to their armies. His awesome appearance may also play a part in their obliteration. John sees a *"sharp sword"* proceeding from Jesus' mouth with which He smites the nations. The apostle Paul stated something similar:

> *"And then shall that Wicked be revealed, whom the Lord shall consume with the spirit of His mouth, and shall destroy with the brightness of His coming: Even him, whose coming is after the working of Satan with all power and signs and lying wonders, And with all deceivableness of unrighteousness in them that perish; because they received not the love of the truth, that they might be saved."*[12]

Paul says that the *"spirit"* of Jesus' mouth and His *"brightness"* will destroy the Antichrist and his followers. Whatever the means are that Jesus uses to accomplish this victory, the results from it are overwhelmingly gruesome.

The fowls of the air will devour the bodies of those who made war with Jesus at His coming. John mentions that Jesus treads the winepress of God's wrath. As we read in the last chapter, this press refers to the squeezing out of the blood from the dead so that it rises to the height of a horse's bridle. This will be a horrific scene indeed.

However, it seems the first action Jesus takes will be the casting of the Antichrist and his False Prophet into the lake of fire. I will be discussing Hell and its inhabitants, including the Devil, in a later chapter. For now though, this is a just punishment for those two deceivers of the human race who helped bring such devastation to the earth and its inhabitants.

The Final Destination

The Bible reveals the precise location where Jesus' second coming to earth will occur. Though we know that the final battle of Armageddon takes place around Jerusalem, the scriptures are even more detailed as to where Jesus will culminate His return.

In the Book of Acts when the disciples saw Jesus ascend to heaven from the Mount of Olives an angel said to them:

> *"Which also said, You men of Galilee, why stand you gazing up into heaven? This same Jesus, which is taken up from you into heaven, shall so come in like manner as you have seen Him go into heaven. Then returned they unto Jerusalem from the mount called Olivet, which is from Jerusalem a sabbath day's journey"*[13]

Two things are significant in this passage. The first is that the angel declares that as Jesus ascended into heaven, so too He will again descend to earth. This is another confirmation that the early Christians believed in a visible, literal second coming of Jesus. The second thing to note is that Jesus ascended from the Mount of Olives on the east side of Jerusalem. The angel states that just as the disciples saw Him depart from there, so too would His followers see Him return to there in the future.

The Old Testament confirms that the Mount of Olives will be Jesus' destination when He returns:

> *"For I will gather all nations against Jerusalem to battle; and the city shall be taken, and the houses rifled, and the women ravished; and half of the city shall go forth into captivity, and the residue of the people shall not be cut off from the city. Then shall the LORD go forth, and fight against those nations, as when He fought in the day of battle. And His feet shall stand in that day upon the mount of Olives, which is before Jerusalem on the east, and the mount of Olives shall cleave in the midst thereof toward the east and toward the west, and there shall be a very great valley; and half of the mountain shall remove toward the north, and half of it toward the south."*[14]

Again, the Bible references the battle of Armageddon in accordance with Jesus' second coming. Notice that when He does set His foot upon the Mount of Olives the renovation of the earth begins to take place.

At the conclusion of Armageddon Jesus sets up a kind of tribunal at which He will judge the surviving inhabitants of the earth.

Second Coming and the Jewish Feasts

At this time, I want to mention the timing at which Jesus' second coming may occur. If Pre-Tribulationists are correct in their belief, then the Rapture might take place before the Tribulation Period on the first or second day of Tishri. This would allow Jesus to fulfill the aforementioned Feast of Trumpets. This means that Jesus could then fulfill the sixth Jewish feast, the Day of Atonement, with His second coming. If so, then Jesus will return to earth on the 10th day of Tishri. Again, however, we still do not know the year of His second coming and therefore would not know the exact day of its occurrence.

Jesus' return on the Day of Atonement would coincide with God's purpose for ordaining the Jews to observe this holy day. On that day and that day only, the high priest went into the Temple and entered the innermost sanctum, the Holy of Holies, where the Ark of the

Covenant resided. The priest then sprinkled the blood of a sacrificed animal on the mercy seat that covered the Ark. This blood was to atone for the nation's sins from the previous year.[15] This act reconciled the Jews as a nation to God for the coming year.

The Book of Hebrews calls Jesus the true high priest, *"Wherefore, holy brethren, partakers of the heavenly calling, consider the Apostle and High Priest of our profession, Christ Jesus...Now of the things which we have spoken this is the sum: We have such an High Priest, Who is set on the right hand of the throne of the Majesty in the heavens; A Minister of the sanctuary, and of the true tabernacle, which the Lord pitched, and not man."*[16]

At Jesus' second coming God will do a mighty work among the Jewish people by reconciling them to Himself. This work will consummate one of the original purposes Jesus gave for coming the first time: Saving the *"lost sheep of the house of Israel"*.[17]

As mentioned earlier, the prophet Zechariah prophesied concerning the salvation of the Jews at the second coming of the Lord, *"And I will pour upon the house of David, and upon the inhabitants of Jerusalem, the spirit of grace and of supplications: and they shall look upon Me whom they have pierced, and they shall mourn for Him, as one mourns for his only son, and shall be in bitterness for Him, as one that is in bitterness for his firstborn."*[18] God will pour out His saving grace on the Jews when they finally recognize Jesus as the Messiah and true High Priest. They will then have obtained the *"everlasting righteousness"* that Daniel spoke of as a consummation of the "seventy weeks" that God determined to come upon the Jews.

God spoke of this salvation of the Jews to His prophet Ezekiel:

> *"And say unto them, Thus saith the Lord GOD; Behold, I will take the children of Israel from among the nations, where they be gone, and will gather them on every side, and bring them into their own land: And I will make them one nation in the land upon the mountains of Israel; and one King shall be King to them all: and they shall be no more two nations, neither shall they be divided into two kingdoms any more at all. Neither shall they defile themselves any more with their idols, nor with their*

> *detestable things, nor with any of their transgressions: but I will save them out of all their dwelling places, wherein they have sinned, and will cleanse them: so shall they be My people, and I will be their God. And David My Servant shall be King over them; and they all shall have one Shepherd: they shall also walk in My judgments, and observe My statutes, and do them. And they shall dwell in the land that I have given unto Jacob My servant, wherein your fathers have dwelt; and they shall dwell therein, even they, and their children, and their children's children for ever: and My servant David shall be their Prince for ever. Moreover I will make a covenant of peace with them; it shall be an everlasting covenant with them: and I will place them, and multiply them, and will set My Sanctuary in the midst of them for evermore. My Tabernacle also shall be with them: yea, I will be their God, and they shall be My people."*[19]

Jesus said that when He came again He would gather His elect, the Jews, from the four corners of the earth. Here, God says the same thing when He speaks of taking the Jews from all the nations of the world and bringing them back to Israel. There they will serve the Messiah, Jesus Christ (God uses the name of Israel's greatest king, David, as a metaphor for the Messiah). God's Temple will once again reside in Jerusalem and Jesus will reign from there. The Jews will be God's people and He will be their God.

Thus, it would be fitting indeed for Jesus to return on the Day of Atonement and thereby fulfill the true meaning of that feast. The Jews will be reconciled to God through their Messiah, Jesus. This leaves one ordained Jewish feast left to fulfill which I will discuss in the next chapter.

The belief of Post-Tribulationists that the Rapture and the second coming of Jesus Christ occur simultaneously also allows Jesus to fulfill the final three feasts of the Jews. As we read above, at His return a trumpet will sound. This could refer to the same trumpet that Paul spoke about in I Thessalonians concerning the Rapture. There Paul stated that Jesus would *"descend from heaven with a shout, with the voice of the archangel, and with the trump of God: and the dead in Christ shall rise first: Then we which are alive and remain shall be caught up together with them in the clouds, to meet the Lord in the air."* [20] If so then Jesus' second coming would occur on the first or second day of Tishri, which is the Feast of Trumpets. That would leave the final two ordained Jewish feasts for Him to fulfill.

The Sheep and the Goats

Jesus said that when He comes again He will judge the inhabitants of the earth:

> *"When the Son of man shall come in His glory, and all the holy angels with Him, then shall He sit upon the throne of His glory: And before Him shall be gathered all nations: and He shall separate them one from another, as a shepherd divides his sheep from the goats: And He shall set the sheep on His right hand, but the goats on the left. Then shall the King say unto them on His right hand, Come, you blessed of My Father, inherit the kingdom prepared for you from the foundation of the world: For I was hungry, you gave me meat: I was thirsty, and you gave Me drink: I was a stranger, and you took Me in: Naked, and you clothed Me: I was sick, and you visited Me: I was in prison, and you came unto Me. Then shall the righteous answer Him, saying, Lord, when saw we You hungry, and fed You? Or thirsty, and gave You drink? When saw we You a stranger, and took You in? or naked, and clothed You? Or when saw we You sick, or in prison, and came unto You? And the King shall answer and say unto them, Verily I say unto you, Inasmuch as you have done it unto one of the least of these My brethren, you have done it unto Me. Then shall He say also unto them on the left hand, Depart from Me, you cursed, into everlasting fire, prepared for the devil and his angels: For I was hungry, and you gave Me no meat: I was thirsty, and you gave Me no drink: I was a stranger, and you took Me not in: naked, and you clothed Me not: sick, and in prison, and you visited Me not. Then shall they also answer Him, saying, Lord, when saw we You hungry,*

> *or athirst, or a stranger, or naked, or sick, or in prison, and did not minister unto You? Then shall He answer them, saying, Verily I say unto you, Inasmuch as you did it not to one of the least of these, you did it not to Me. And these shall go away into everlasting punishment: but the righteous into life eternal."*[21]

There has been much debate concerning several of the issues surrounding this passage. The position one holds in this dispute centers around whether you believe the Rapture takes place before the Tribulation Period or after it.

The subject of the next chapter is the Millennial Kingdom of Jesus Christ. However, I need to mention it now because it has some bearing on the answers to these issues.

Soon after Jesus destroys the armies of the world at Armageddon He is going to set up His kingdom on earth. His reign will last for a thousand years after which God brings down the curtain on human history and eternity begins. Therefore, the judgment listed above takes place after Armageddon yet before eternity begins.

When precisely does this judgment by Jesus Christ take place? Pre-Tribulationists believe that it occurs after the Battle of Armageddon but before Jesus sets up His Millennial Kingdom in Jerusalem. Post-Tribulationists have a variety of beliefs as to when this judgment takes place. One is that it occurs after Jesus has been crowned King over the earth at the beginning of His millennial reign. Another belief is that this judgment is the same as the Great White Throne Judgment that takes place after the end of the Millennium. However, I believe the Book of Daniel can shed some light as to the precise timing of the "sheep and goats" judgment.

Daniel's 1260, 1290, 1335 Days

In Chapter 5, I illustrated how the "seventy weeks" prophecy of Daniel referred to seventy sevens of years. Each of these years consisted of 360 days according to the lunar calendar that the Jews used. In Chapter 9, I discussed how the final seven years of this prophecy encompassed the seven-year Tribulation Period. This means that the Tribulation Period lasts a total of 2520 days. At the midpoint of this period or 1260 days from its beginning, we saw that the Antichrist is going to enter the third Jewish Temple and declare himself God. The final 1260 days will consist of the "Great Tribulation" when God's pours out His full wrath upon the earth. Daniel, in speaking of the second half of the Tribulation Period, introduces some new numbers that indicate when the events in question might take place:

> *"And I heard the man clothed in linen, which was upon the waters of the river, when he held up his right hand and his left hand unto heaven, and swore by Him that lives for ever that it shall be for a time, times, and an half; and when He shall have accomplished to scatter the power of the holy people, all these things shall be finished. And I heard, but I understood not: then said I, O my Lord, what shall be the end of these things? And he said, Go thy way, Daniel: for the words are closed up and sealed till the time of the end. Many shall be purified, and made white, and tried; but the wicked shall do wickedly: and none of the wicked shall understand; but the wise shall understand. And from the time that the daily sacrifice shall be taken away, and the abomination that makes desolate set up, there shall be a thousand two hundred and ninety days. Blessed is he that waits, and comes to the thousand three hundred and five and thirty days. But go you your way till the end be: for you shall rest, and stand in your lot at the end of the days."*[22]

Daniel states that from the time the "abomination of desolation" abolishes the Temple sacrifice, 1290 days will pass before *"all these things shall be finished"*. In Chapter 9, we saw that the abomination of desolation refers to the Antichrist entering the Temple and declaring Himself God. When he performs this blasphemous act there will be 1260 days left during which the Great Tribulation takes place. At the end of the Tribulation Period Jesus Christ comes down to earth. Therefore, Daniel is saying that something occurs during the 30 days after the second coming of Jesus. Though he does not specify what this occurrence is I believe that it is possible that the "sheep and goats" judgment takes place during that time. My reasoning for this is that Daniel associates the extra 30 days with the Tribulation Period. Since this is a judgment of the inhabitants of the earth who survived the Tribulation Period this would be a reasonable speculation. I will discuss below and in the next chapter the "1335 days" prophecy mentioned in this passage.

Where and How will this judgment take place?

Pre-Tribulationists believe that Jesus is going to judge the "sheep and the goats" outside the walls of Jerusalem. They base this belief upon a prophecy that the prophet Joel spoke:

> *"For, behold, in those days, and in that time, when I shall bring again the captivity of Judah and Jerusalem, I will also gather all nations, and will bring them down into the valley of Jehoshaphat, and will plead with them there for My people and for My heritage Israel, whom they have scattered among the nations, and parted My land."*[23]

Scholars do not know whether the valley of Jehoshaphat is a geographical location or a metaphor for the judgment of God. The word Jehoshaphat in Hebrew means "Yahweh judges". Since Jesus returns to the Mount of Olives on the east side of Jerusalem it is possible that He will set His throne there to judge the people.

Post-Tribulationists believe that Jesus will already be sitting in the Temple to perform His judgment of the nations. Jesus said, *"When the Son of man shall come in His glory, and all the holy angels with Him, then shall He sit upon the throne of His glory: And before Him shall be gathered all nations: and He shall separate them one from another, as a shepherd divides his sheep from the goats."*[24] Since we know that Jesus will rule the earth from the Temple in Jerusalem it is possible that this judgment does takes place when He is sitting upon His Temple throne. Yet, I will submit another possibility.

I believe that Jesus is going to judge the nations from His throne, which will be set up on the Mount of Olives. However, according the prophet Zechariah, the topography in that area will change when Jesus sets His foot upon the Mount of Olives. The mount splits in two and this creates a new valley that runs east and west. It is possible that this valley will be the "valley of Jehoshaphat or judgment" that Joel mentions. Of course, after the judging takes place Jesus' throne would need to be moved to the Temple from where He will rule the earth. This could be a part of some type of coronation procession. As we will see in the next chapter, Jesus will participate in a "new" triumphal entry into Jerusalem after His second coming. He will enter Jerusalem through the Eastern or Golden Gate and go into the newly rebuilt fourth Jewish Temple.

It is interesting that when you face Jerusalem from the Mount of Olives, the valley of Kidron runs below you and to the right around the city. The valley of Hinnom runs to left around the city. The valley of Hinnom was the place where the ancient Jerusalemites constantly burned their refuse. Jesus used the name of the Hinnom valley, which in Greek is the word "gehenna", as a metaphor for the eternal flames of Hell. During the judgment of the "sheep and the goats", Jesus sends the blessed "sheep" or humans to the right and the condemned "goats" or humans to the left. To enter the Eastern or Golden Gate that leads to the Temple, you would have to go down and to the right across the Kidron Valley. To go away from the holy city you would go to the left toward the Hinnom Valley. Thus, it is possible that the separation of the sheep and goats judgment does take place on the Mount of Olives.

There is one other reason I have for believing that Jesus will not enter the Temple until some time after this judgment takes place. In the above passage from Daniel, he mentioned that those people who survive until the 1335th day after the Antichrist enters the Temple would be blessed. If Jesus' return to earth takes place on the 10th of Tishri, the Day of Atonement, then that would be the 1260th day of the second half of the Tribulation Period. That means 75 days later or the 1335th day since the Antichrist entered the Temple would occur on the 25th of the Jewish month Kislev. That is a very significant day in Jewish history.

In 167 B.C., Antiochus Epiphanes IV, one of the Greek successors to the empire of Alexander the Great, conquered Jerusalem. He proceeded to desecrate the Jewish Temple by sacrificing a pig to Zeus on the Temple altar. Many scholars consider Antiochus Epiphanes to be a type of the Antichrist who also will desecrate the Temple at the middle of the Tribulation Period. Three years later the Jewish leader Judah Maccabee and his forces defeated Antiochus and regained control of Jerusalem and its Temple. The Jews had to cleanse and rededicate the Temple so that they could use it again for their religious observances. This cleansing started on the 25th of Kislev. Every year since then, Jews celebrate the festival of Chanukah on the 25th of Kislev in commemoration of the rededicated Temple. Even though Chanukah is not one of the seven Jewish feasts ordained by God, Jesus did celebrate it when He was on the earth the first time. His disciple John wrote in his Gospel:

> *"And it was at Jerusalem the feast of the dedication, and it was winter. And Jesus walked in the temple in Solomon's porch. Then came the Jews round about Him, and said unto Him, How long do You make us to doubt? If You be the Messiah, tell us plainly."*[25]

Therefore, I believe that Jesus Christ will enter the newly rebuilt Temple on the 25th of Kislev, 1335 days after the Antichrist entered the previous Temple and show the world *"plainly"* that He is the Messiah. Whether Jesus builds the Temple (as the prophets say the Messiah is to do) in the preceding days or whether He just supernaturally builds it in one moment is not clear. But just as He fulfilled the Jewish spring feasts to the exact day with His first coming and may fulfill the autumn feasts with His second coming, so too it is possible that He will fulfill the winter feast of Chanukah with His triumphal entry into Jerusalem on the 25th of Kislev.

Who are the sheep and the goats?

The people whom Jesus judges at His second coming will be those persons who survive the Tribulation Period. Pre-Tribulationists believe that these "sheep" will consist of both Jews and Gentiles who accept Jesus as their Savior during the Tribulation Period. Jesus said that those who treat His brethren, the Jews, with kindness during that time would enter the Millennial Kingdom to repopulate the earth. The Jews who receive Jesus as their Messiah at His second coming will also enter into His earthly kingdom. Those who receive the mark of the beast during the Tribulation will be the "goats" that He casts into everlasting fire.

Post-Tribulationists have a more difficult time explaining who these people will be. If the Rapture occurs at the second coming then that means Jesus takes all the saved people off the earth at that time. This leaves only the Jews who receive salvation at His appearing and possibly the "sealed" 144,000 Jewish evangelists to repopulate the earth during the Millennium. However, Post-Tribulationists counter this by saying it is the "nations" and not individuals whom Jesus judges as the sheep and goats. Therefore, God allows some unsaved persons to enter the Millennial Kingdom on earth. The problem with this belief is that in the passage under discussion, Jesus uses personal relationships as the measure of His judgment. Nations do not visit individuals in prison as one of the charges read. The giving of water, food, and clothing to people in this context also connotes personal interaction between individuals. Post-Tribulationists also say there will be millions of children of those who received the beast's mark who are alive at that time. Consequently, God will not punish those who are under the age of accountability and will allow them to enter His kingdom on earth also.

There is one other point that Post-Tribulationists make to support the idea that unsaved persons enter into the Millennial Kingdom. Several Old Testament passages state that "heathen" or unsaved people will inhabit the earth at that time. They say that this proves that unsaved persons will survive the Tribulation and live in Jesus' earthly kingdom. However, saved persons can have offspring who reject Jesus as their Savior. The same will be true for the Gentile "sheep" who enter the Millennial Kingdom and produce many children. Some of their children could rebel and therefore make up the "heathen" alluded to in the Old Testament. As we will see in the next chapter though, Jesus will rule with a "rod of iron" and will quash any overt rebellion against God.

The Quick and the Dead

There is one final aspect to the second coming of Jesus that I need to address. Up to this point, I have only dealt with those persons who have accepted Jesus as their Lord and Savior. The Rapture of the saints by Jesus Christ speaks to the fact that God will resurrect and glorify those who had previously accepted His Son as their Messiah. The second coming of Jesus addresses the issue of allowing the rest of humanity to enter His earthly kingdom. What about the Old Testament saints such as Abraham, Isaac, and Jacob? What happens to the prophets such as Isaiah, Daniel, Zechariah or others who believed in God who did not have a chance to accept Jesus as their Savior? The Bible does speak to their fates also.

The apostle Paul uses an interesting phrase in a letter he wrote to Timothy, one of the Christians that he was mentoring in the Lord:

> *"I charge you therefore before God, and the Lord Jesus Christ, Who shall judge the quick and the dead at His appearing and His kingdom. Preach the word; be instant in season, out of season; reprove, rebuke, exhort with all long suffering and doctrine."*[26]

We have seen how Jesus will judge the "living" at His second coming with His judgment of the "sheep and the goats". Who are the "dead" that Paul refers to here? I believe He is speaking of two distinct groups of people in this verse.

The first will consist of those believers who died during the Tribulation Period. John describes this event in the Book of Revelation as he witnessed it:

> *"And I saw an angel come down from heaven, having the key of the bottomless pit and a great chain in his hand. And he laid hold on the dragon, that old serpent, which is the Devil, and Satan, and bound him a thousand years, And cast him into the bottomless pit, and shut him up, and set a seal upon him, that he should deceive the nations no more, till the thousand years should be fulfilled: and after that he must be loosed a little season. And I saw thrones, and they sat upon them, and judgment was given unto them: and I saw the souls of them that were beheaded for the witness of Jesus, and for the word of God, and which had not worshipped the beast, neither his image, neither had received his mark upon their foreheads, or in their hands;*

and they lived and reigned with Christ a thousand years. But the rest of the dead lived not again until the thousand years were finished. This is the first resurrection. Blessed and holy is he that has part in the first resurrection: on such the second death has no power, but they shall be priests of God and of Christ, and shall reign with Him a thousand years."[27]

I will discuss the binding of Satan and the reigning of the saints in the next chapter. I only include them here for the sake of context. John sees those persons martyred during the Tribulation Period. These individuals refused to receive the mark of the Antichrist or to worship him. They also suffered death for preaching the gospel to the unsaved during that time. However, John sees that God has resurrected them. Sequentially, this resurrection takes place immediately after the second coming, which is described in chapter 19 of Revelation. John states that this is the *"first resurrection"*. The term "first" here cannot refer to a numerical sequence since Jesus experienced the first and truly permanent resurrection that took place in the First Century A.D. There were a few persons resurrected in the Old Testament and some in the New Testament. However, each of them died again and is now waiting for a final resurrection. Therefore, God will resurrect the Tribulation saints around the time following the second coming of Jesus.

Some believe that God will resurrect the Old Testament saints at the Rapture.[28] However, the Old Testament seems to indicate that God will raise these pre-Christian era saints at the end of the Tribulation Period. Returning to the Book of Daniel we read:

"And at that time shall Michael [the archangel] stand up, the great prince which stands for the children of your people: and there shall be a time of trouble, such as never was since there was a nation even to that same time: and at that time your people shall be delivered, every one that shall be found written in the book. And many of them that sleep in the dust of the earth shall awake, some to everlasting life, and some to shame and everlasting contempt."[29]

The phrase "*time of trouble, such as never was since there was a nation even to that same time*" is an obvious reference to the Tribulation Period. As we have already seen the Jews must experience the "time of Jacob's trouble" or the Tribulation Period. Therefore, the resurrection of Daniel's people, the Old Testament Jews, takes place after this time. This resurrection will also include those non-Jews such as Noah and others. Thus, it seems that God will resurrect all the Old Testament saints at the same time He resurrects the Tribulation saints. They, along with all the other glorified saints, will rule with Jesus during the Millennial Kingdom.

As for the unsaved dead, God will resurrect them at a final judgment after the thousand-year reign of Jesus. The prophet Isaiah speaks of the delay in the final judgment of the non-believers when he prophesied concerning the end of the Tribulation Period:

> *"Behold, the LORD makes the earth empty, and makes it waste, and turns it upside down, and scatters abroad the inhabitants thereof...The land shall be utterly emptied, and utterly spoiled: for the LORD has spoken this word. The earth mourns and fades away, the world languishes and fades away, the haughty people of the earth do languish. The earth also is defiled under the inhabitants thereof; because they have transgressed the laws, changed the ordinance, broken the everlasting covenant. Therefore has the curse devoured the earth, and they that dwell therein are desolate: therefore the inhabitants of the earth are burned, and few men left...Fear, and the pit, and the snare, are upon you, O inhabitant of the earth. And it shall come to pass, that he who flees from the noise of the fear shall fall into the pit; and he that comes up out of the midst of the pit shall be taken in the snare: for the windows from on high are open, and the foundations of the earth do shake. The earth is utterly broken down, the earth is clean dissolved, the earth is moved exceedingly. The earth shall reel to and fro like a drunkard, and shall be removed like a cottage; and the transgression thereof shall be heavy upon it; and it shall fall, and not rise again. And it shall come to pass in that day, that the LORD shall punish the host of the*

high ones that are on high, and the kings of the earth upon the earth. And they shall be gathered together, as prisoners are gathered in the pit, and shall be shut up in the prison, and after many days shall they be visited."[30]

First, Isaiah gives the reason for the punishment of the inhabitants of the earth. The people have arrogantly rebelled against the truths of God and His laws. The Lord will judge them through the Tribulation Period and only a *"few men are left"*. Of course, this few is in relation to the billions who entered into the Tribulation.

Next, Isaiah talks about the terror that grips the inhabitants of the earth. God will cast them into the pit and then ensnare the Devil *"that comes up out of the midst of the pit"*. He then shakes the foundations of the earth, which causes so much damage to the world that God will have to renovate it.

Lastly, Isaiah declares that God will keep the rebellious unsaved persons in the prison of the pit. After many days, one thousand years to be exact, they *"will be visited"* at which time God will judge them. I will talk about this horrific judgment in Chapter 13.

With the return of Jesus Christ to the earth, God will usher in a new era in human history. Christians call this era the Millennium. It is to that subject that we now turn our attention to.

---

1 *II Peter 3:1-10*

2 Persons such as David Koresh, Jim Jones, Sun Myung Moon and others have either implied that they were Jesus Christ or some being greater than Him.

3 The Jehovah Witnesses state that Jesus returned in 1914 to set up an *invisible* kingdom. As you read through this chapter you will see that this is the exact opposite of what the Bible definitively states concerning the second coming of Jesus Christ.

4 *Revelation 1:7-8*

5 *Zechariah 12:9-10*

6 *Matthew 24:27*

7 *II Thessalonians 2:8*

8 *Matthew 24:29-31*

9 *Revelation 19:11-21*

10 *Revelation 19-7-9*

11 *Jude 14-15*

[12] *II Thessalonians 2:8-10*
[13] *Acts 1:11-12*
[14] *Zechariah 14:2-4*
[15] *Leviticus 16:1-34*
[16] *Hebrews 3:1; 8:1-2*
[17] *Matthew 15:24*
[18] *Zechariah 12:10*
[19] *Ezekiel 37:21-27*
[20] *I Thessalonians 4:16-17*
[21] *Matthew 25:31-46*
[22] *Daniel 12:7-13*
[23] *Joel 3:1-2*
[24] *Matthew 25:31-32*
[25] *John 10:22-24*
[26] *II Timothy 4:1-2*
[27] *Revelation 20:1-6*
[28] The pre-Tribulation Bible scholar, Cyrus Ingerson Scofield, writes in his Bible that Jesus will include the Old Testament saints when He raptures His followers. ["The Scofield Study Bible", C.I. Scofield, p. 1269, footnote 1 (Oxford University Press 1909, 1917)]
[29] *Daniel 12:1-2*
[30] *Isaiah 24:1,3-6,17-22*

12 - Utopia: Paradise on Earth

For thousands of years humans have looked for a utopia on earth. Sadly, one does not exist at this time anywhere on the planet. It did exist in the Garden of Eden but humans gave up the right to that utopia and their right to dwell there.

In Eden, Adam and Eve chose to obey Satan and rebel against God. Satan, in the form of a serpent, told them that if they disobey God and eat the fruit from the tree of knowledge of good and evil they would become like Him. They used the free will that God had given them and chose to listen to Satan instead of God.[1] This first sinful act committed by humans gave the Title Deed of the earth to Satan. The apostle Paul confirmed this when he wrote:

> *"In whom the god of this world has blinded the minds of them which believe not, lest the light of the glorious gospel of Christ, Who is the image of God, should shine unto them."*
>
> *- II Corinthians 4:4*

The bad news is that Satan does indeed have reign over the earth at the current time. The good news is that Jesus Christ reclaimed the Title Deed of the earth with His sacrificial death and resurrection. With His crucifixion He defeated the power of Satan and the power of death over humankind. As the writer of Hebrews states:

> *"Forasmuch then as the children are partakers of flesh and blood, He also himself likewise took part of the same; that through death He might destroy him that had the power of*

death, that is, the devil; And deliver them who through fear of death were all their lifetime subject to bondage."
- Hebrews 2:14-15

Jesus now has the authority to redeem the earth from the power of Satan at the time of His choosing. As we read in the Book of Revelation, Jesus will start the reclamation process with the Tribulation Period. Before John saw this Period beginning, he wept because he didn't think anyone was worthy to perform the act of starting this process. However, he soon saw the only One who was worthy:

"And I saw in the right hand of Him that sat on the throne a book written within and on the backside, sealed with seven seals. And I saw a strong angel proclaiming with a loud voice, Who is worthy to open the book, and to loose the seals thereof? And no man in heaven, nor in earth, neither under the earth, was able to open the book, neither to look thereon. And I wept much, because no man was found worthy to open and to read the book, neither to look thereon. And one of the elders said unto me, Weep not: behold, the Lion of the tribe of Judah, the Root of David, has prevailed to open the book, and to loose the seven seals thereof. And I beheld, and, lo, in the midst of the throne and of the four beasts, and in the midst of the elders, stood a Lamb as it had been slain, having seven horns and seven eyes, which are the seven Spirits of God sent forth into all the earth. And He came and took the book out of the right hand of Him that sat upon the throne. And when He had taken the book, the four beasts and four and twenty elders fell down before the Lamb, having every one of them harps, and golden vials full of odors, which are the prayers of saints. And they sung a new song, saying, You are worthy to take the book, and to open the seals thereof: for You were slain, and have redeemed us to God by Your blood out of every kindred, and tongue, and people, and nation."
- *Revelation 5:1-9*

Jesus opens the sealed book in chapter 6 of Revelation and thereby begins to redeem the earth from the power of Satan. The process is complete after Jesus comes to earth again and judges the nations of the world. He then establishes His reign in place of Satan's by ruling from the Temple in Jerusalem. According to the Book of Revelation, He will rule for a thousand years:

> *"And I saw an angel come down from heaven, having the key of the bottomless pit and a great chain in his hand. And he laid hold on the dragon, that old serpent, which is the Devil, and Satan, and bound him a thousand years, And cast him into the bottomless pit, and shut him up, and set a seal upon him, that he should deceive the nations no more, till the thousand years should be fulfilled: and after that he must be loosed a little season. And I saw thrones, and they sat upon them, and judgment was given unto them: and I saw the souls of them that were beheaded for the witness of Jesus, and for the word of God, and which had not worshipped the beast, neither his image, neither had received his mark upon their foreheads, or in their hands; and they lived and reigned with Christ a thousand years."*
>
> *- Revelation 20:1-4*

Christians call this period of Jesus' rule "The Millennium". There are many aspects to this time on earth. However, I will only discuss a few of them in this chapter.

The Purpose of the Millennium

The purpose of the Tribulation Period was to punish the inhabitants of earth for their rebellion against God. It also allowed the Jewish people to accept Jesus as the Messiah. The Millennium has a purpose too.

I believe the primary reason that God is going to rule the earth for a thousand years through His Son Jesus is to show humanity what He wanted for them all along.

In the Garden of Eden God conversed daily with Adam and Eve. He made the earth beautiful and bountiful for His human children to enjoy. God also gave Adam and Eve dominion over the animal kingdom. These animals would not harm them but live in harmony with them. All Adam and Eve had to do was dwell there and fellowship with God. He told them to enjoy the pleasurable experience of procreation and to fill the earth with their children and their children's children. However, God did not want humans to be robots so He gave them a mind and a freedom to exercise their will with it. He hoped that of their own volition they would love Him as their Creator Father. Sadly, they wanted more than what God was offering them.

Adam and Eve wanted to become "Gods" themselves. The result of this was their expulsion from paradise and a life of toil and hardship. God still loved them and made clothes for them from animal skins to protect them. However, their relationship with Him was no longer on the same intimate level that it had been in the Garden. Humans now had to offer sacrifices to fellowship with God. Since that day (with the exception that occurred during Jesus' first coming), mankind can only interact with God on a spiritual level.

The good news is that in the Millennium God will again dwell in the midst of His Creation. As we will see, the animal kingdom will once more live peacefully with humans. Life spans will increase to the lengths of those at the beginning of human history. However, humans will still have free will to act. This time though, God restrains Satan for the duration of the Millennium so he will not be able to exacerbate any sinful human behavior. One other thing that will be different during this time is what will happen to those who think about sinning against others. Jesus will be ruling with a "rod of iron" and will not tolerate any overt rebellion by humans. He will punish them immediately for their sins. Lastly, the fact that there will still be aberrant behavior by some persons means that the Millennial Kingdom of Jesus Christ on earth will not be a perfect utopia. In Chapter 14, I will discuss a time when, finally, only perfection will exist.

Satan Bound

We saw that at Jesus' second coming, one of the first acts He commits is the casting of the Antichrist and the False Prophet into the lake of hellfire. Yet He allows Satan to exist one thousand more years before He brings down His final judgment upon him. This will not be much of an "existence" since God is going to restrain Satan until at the very end of those thousand years.

After John sees Jesus return to the earth and after Jesus judges the nations of the world, he wrote what he witnessed next:

> *"And I saw an angel come down from heaven, having the key of the bottomless pit and a great chain in his hand. And he laid hold on the dragon, that old serpent, which is the Devil, and Satan, and bound him a thousand years, And cast him into the bottomless pit, and shut him up, and set a seal upon him, that he should deceive the nations no more, till the thousand years should be fulfilled: and after that he must be loosed a little season."*[2]

With this action the angel of the Lord removes satanic influence from the earth. The humans who repopulate the earth during the Millennium will be freed from the Devil's authority to harass and oppress them. They will still have free will though to make good and bad decisions. If their bad choices adversely affect others Jesus will judge them swiftly with a "rod of iron". At the end of the Millennium God allows Satan to be loosed for one final battle. God will deal summarily with him and bring him to his final fate.

Renovation of the Earth

The devastation to the earth that occurs during the Tribulation will make the world uninhabitable for any extended length of time. The judgments of God and very possibly the use of nuclear weapons will burn up large parts of the earth. The catastrophic events that take place will render the majority of the water on the planet undrinkable. God will have to renovate the earth so that humans can dwell on it. He will accomplish this between the judgment of the nations and Jesus' triumphal entry into the Temple in Jerusalem.

God spoke of the restoration of the earth through His prophet, Isaiah:

> *"For, behold, I create new heavens and a new earth: and the former shall not be remembered, nor come into mind. But be you glad and rejoice for ever in that which I create: for, behold, I create Jerusalem a rejoicing, and her people a joy...For as the new heavens and the new earth, which I will make, shall remain before Me, says the LORD, so shall your seed and your name remain. And it shall come to pass, that from one new moon to another, and from one Sabbath to another, shall all flesh come to worship before Me, says the LORD. And they shall go forth, and look upon the carcasses of the men that have transgressed against Me: for their worm shall not die, neither shall their fire be quenched; and they shall be an abhorring unto all flesh."*[3]

This passage use to trouble me from a doctrinal aspect. God states here that He will create a *"new heavens and a new earth"*. The context of this prophecy clearly relates to the Tribulation Period and the Millennium. He says that humans will look upon the dead bodies of those who transgressed against Him during the Tribulation. He also mentions the moon and the Sabbaths. Since there will be no time references nor a sun or moon in eternity this has to refer to the Millennium.[4] The problem I had was the fact that the in the Book of Revelation John saw a new heavens and earth at the beginning of eternity.[5] Thus, I couldn't reconcile the use of the same phrase *"new heavens and earth"* with the idea that God was speaking prophetically of two different new creations. However, the descriptions used in both of these prophecies led me to conclude that God will indeed recreate the cosmos and earth twice in the future. For the omnipotent Creator of the universe this will be but a simple matter as the prophet Isaiah declares:

> *"Who has directed the Spirit of the LORD, or being His counselor has taught Him? With whom took He counsel, and who instructed Him, and taught Him in the path of judgment, and taught Him knowledge, and showed to Him the way of understanding? Behold, the nations are as a drop of a bucket, and are counted as the small dust of the balance: behold, He takes up the isles as a very little thing."*[6]

I believe this renovation of the earth starts with Jesus' second coming when He sets His foot upon the Mount of Olives. As we read previously the mount will split in two which creates a new valley. After that and before Jesus enters the new Temple in Jerusalem, the Lord will restore the rest of the earth. He will somehow protect those humans that survive the judgment of the "sheep and goats" while this renovation takes place. Once He is finished the earth will once again be like the Garden of Eden:

> *"For the LORD shall comfort Zion: He will comfort all her waste places; and He will make her wilderness like Eden, and her desert like the garden of the LORD; joy and gladness shall be found therein, thanksgiving, and the voice of melody."*[7]

> *"And they shall build the old wastes, they shall raise up the former desolations, and they shall repair the waste cities, the desolations of many generations. And strangers shall stand and feed your flocks, and the sons of the stranger shall be your plowmen and your vinedressers...For as the earth brings forth her bud, and as the garden causes the things that are sown in it to spring forth; so the Lord GOD will cause righteousness and praise to spring forth before all the nations."*[8]

The prophet Joel also speaks of the bountiful fruitfulness of this renewed earth:

> *"And it shall come to pass in that day, that the mountains shall drop down new wine, and the hills shall flow with milk, and all the rivers of Judah shall flow with waters, and a fountain shall come forth out of the Temple of the LORD, and shall water the valley of Shittim."*[9]

The earth will truly be the paradise that God had originally created it to be. It will be ready for humans to dwell in and multiply. However, before that can occur two events must take place.

The Millennial Temple

The first one is the rebuilding of the Temple in Jerusalem. This will be the fourth and final Temple built on the earth. The Bible states that the Messiah will build the Temple for the Millennial Kingdom:

> *"And speak unto him, saying, Thus speaks the LORD of hosts, saying, Behold the Man whose name is the BRANCH; and He shall grow up out of His place, and He shall build the Temple of the LORD. Even He shall build the Temple of the LORD; and He shall bear the glory, and shall sit and rule upon His throne; and He shall be a Priest upon His throne: and the counsel of peace shall be between them both."*[10]

In Chapter 3, I mentioned that the Old Testament uses the appellation "Branch" as another name for the Messiah. Therefore, Jesus will rebuild the Temple at the beginning of the Millennium. The third or Tribulation Temple that the Antichrist enters and defiles will be destroyed at some stage during the Tribulation by one of the earthquakes that occurs or by the armies of the Antichrist. The Temple that Jesus builds will be a magnificent edifice.

The first description that Ezekiel provides is that the Temple will sit on a high mountain in Jerusalem:

> *"In the five and twentieth year of our captivity, in the beginning of the year, in the tenth day of the month, in the fourteenth year after that the city was smitten, in the selfsame day the hand of the LORD was upon me, and brought me there. In the visions of God brought He me into the land of Israel, and set me upon a very high mountain, by which was as the frame of a city on the south."*[11]

Though Jerusalem currently rises above its surrounding area, it is not located on a *"very high mountain"*. However, we read that when Jesus sets His foot upon the Mount of Olives an earthquake occurs and splits the mount in two. This event must also change the surrounding topography sufficiently enough to create this new mountain in Jerusalem. Ezekiel continues and gives the specific dimensions of the Temple in the rest of this prophecy.

Isaiah confirmed the fact that the Millennial Temple will sit on a high mountain when he wrote:

> *"And it shall come to pass in the last days, that the mountain of the LORD's house shall be established in the top of the mountains, and shall be exalted above the hills; and all nations shall flow unto it"*[12]

It is possible that this mountain could be the highest one in the world after the renovation takes place. In any case all the inhabitants of the earth will visit it.

This Temple appears not to have any of the furnishings of the previous Temples except for the altar. Ezekiel does not mention seeing the Ark of the Covenant, Table of Shewbread, or the Menorah. I believe the reason Jesus omits these things is because He Himself will visibly reside in the Temple.

The Ark was the means by which the Jewish high priest entered into God's presence once a year. Now, God will be present in His Son Jesus who will be sitting on His throne. The prophet Jeremiah confirms the fact that the Ark of the Covenant will not be in the Millennial Temple:

> *"And it shall come to pass, when you be multiplied and increased in the land, in those days, says the LORD, they shall say no more, The Ark of the Covenant of the LORD: neither shall it come to mind: neither shall they remember it; neither shall they visit it; neither shall that be done any more. At that time they shall call Jerusalem the throne of the LORD; and all the nations shall be gathered unto it, to the name of the LORD, to Jerusalem"*[13]

The Table of Shewbread was where the priests placed twelve loaves of bread, which were symbols of God's presence among the twelve tribes of Israel. Again, Jesus' presence renders this furnishing as unnecessary. He told His disciples at His first coming, *"And Jesus said unto them, I am the bread of life: he that comes to Me shall never hunger; and he that believes on Me shall never thirst."*[14]

Lastly, the menorah or seven-branched candlestick gave light to the inside of the Temple. Jesus declared, *"I am the light of the world: he that follows Me shall not walk in darkness, but shall have the light of life."*[15] As the prophet Haggai declares, the glory of Jesus' presence will illuminate the Millennial Temple:

> *"For thus says the LORD of hosts; Yet once, it is a little while, and I will shake the heavens, and the earth, and the sea, and the dry land; And I will shake all nations, and the Desire of all nations shall come: and I will fill this house with glory, says the LORD of hosts."*[16]

The *"Desire"* of the nations is another appellation for the Messiah who will bring the true peace and righteousness that the world has desired. His glory will fill the Temple.

Ezekiel does see an altar in the Temple courtyard:

> *"And He said unto me, Son of man, thus says the Lord GOD; These are the ordinances of the altar in the day when they shall make it, to offer burnt offerings thereon, and to sprinkle blood thereon. And you shall give to the priests the Levites that be of the seed of Zadok, which approach unto Me, to minister unto Me, says the Lord GOD, a young bullock for a sin offering. And you shall take of the blood thereof, and put it on the four horns of it, and on the four corners of the settle, and upon the border round about: thus shall you cleanse and purge it. You shall take the bullock also of the sin offering, and he shall burn it in the appointed place of the house, without the sanctuary."*[17]

The fact that Ezekiel sees an altar and the people offering sacrifices on it during the Millennium has troubled some Christians for centuries. They don't see why sacrifices would be offered in the future since Jesus was the perfect sacrifice that God accepted on behalf of humanity.

First, I want to point out that John, in writing about the Millennial Kingdom in the Book of Revelation, declares that the resurrected and gloried saints of God will act as priests:

> *"Blessed and holy is he that has part in the first resurrection: on such the second death hath no power, but they shall be priests of God and of Christ, and shall reign with him a thousand years."*[18]

From this passage I must conclude that the glorified saints will be the priests offering the sacrifices in the Millennial Temple. These offerings are for the benefit of the people living during the Millennium. However, I do not believe they will be redemptive in nature. They will be more along the lines of commemorative sacrifices. The people will remember daily the sacrificial death of Jesus and the shedding of His blood. Today, Christians commemorate the death of Jesus by receiving communion. This sacrament involves the eating of Jesus' "body" and drinking of His "blood" as a sign that they have received Him as their Savior. So too will the people of the Millennium commemorate Jesus' sacrificial death through these sacrifices.

It appears that Jesus Himself will also offer sacrifices on behalf of the people just as He offered Himself as a sacrifice at His first coming:

> *"And it shall be the Prince's part to give burnt offerings, and meat offerings, and drink offerings, in the feasts, and in the new moons, and in the Sabbaths, in all solemnities of the house of Israel: He shall prepare the sin offering, and the meat offering, and the burnt offering, and the peace offerings, to make reconciliation for the house of Israel."*[19]

Again though I do not believe these sacrifices will be redemptive in essence. They will be a sign that the people have accepted Jesus as their Messiah and received His sacrificial death for their own salvation. These sacrifices will be evidence of their relationship with

God through His Son Jesus. By performing these sacrifices Jesus will show them that God's original purpose for ordaining the animal sacrifices for the Jews was to point to the death of His Son as the perfect redemptive sacrifice.

There is one other feature to the Millennial Temple that I want to mention. Ezekiel saw in his vision of the future a stream of water flowing from the Temple:

> *"Afterward He brought me again unto the door of the Temple; and, behold, waters issued out from under the threshold of the Temple eastward: for the forefront of the Temple stood toward the east, and the waters came down from under from the right side of the house, at the south side of the altar...Then said He unto me, These waters issue out toward the east country, and go down into the desert, and go into the sea: which being brought forth into the sea, the waters shall be healed. And it shall come to pass, that every thing that lives, which moves, wherever the rivers shall come, shall live: and there shall be a very great multitude of fish, because these waters shall come there: for they shall be healed; and every thing shall live whether the river comes...And by the river upon the bank thereof, on this side and on that side, shall grow all trees for food, whose leaf shall not fade, neither shall the fruit thereof be consumed: it shall bring forth new fruit according to His months, because their waters they issued out of the Sanctuary: and the fruit thereof shall be for food, and the leaf thereof for medicine."*[20]

This life-giving stream will flow east from under the Temple into the Dead Sea. The water will *"heal"* the Dead Sea of its saltiness and fish will be abundant in it. The prophet Zechariah states that this stream will also flow to the Mediterranean Sea:

> *"And it shall be in that day, that living waters shall go out from Jerusalem; half of them toward the former sea, and half of them toward the hinder sea: in summer and in*

> *winter shall it be. And the LORD shall be King over all the earth: in that day shall there be one LORD, and His name one."*[21]

Just as there were fruit trees in the Garden of Eden that had supernatural qualities, so too will the fruit trees in the Millennium. As Zechariah declared, this will all be part of the Messiah's Kingdom when the LORD shall rule over all the earth.

It is interesting that in the Book of Revelation John sees a similar life-giving river flowing out of Heavenly Temple in eternity. He also sees similar life-giving fruit trees along the banks of this river.[22] According to the writer of the Book of Hebrews, the previous earthly Temples were patterned after the Heavenly Temple.[23] Therefore, I believe that the Millennial Temple is also a type of the eternal Heavenly Temple that John saw.

Lastly, I want to discuss the timing of the rebuilding of this Temple. Before God ordained King Solomon to build the first "permanent" stone Temple, He commanded the Jews under the leadership of Moses to construct a temporary Temple.[24] This structure was actually a large tent surrounded by canvas-type walls. The Old Testament calls this Temple the "Tabernacle". God's glory burned like a pillar of fire above the Tabernacle by night and a cloud pillar by day. The Tabernacle was to be set in the middle of the Israelite camp during their wanderings in the wilderness.

After God had delivered the Jews from their bondage in Egypt, He led them safely into the wilderness between Egypt and Israel. During this exodus from Egyptian slavery the Jews had to build temporary shelters or booths to live in. God's glory resided in the midst of the Israelite camp in the Tabernacle. When He moved the temporary camp went with Him. He commanded the Jews to commemorate this deliverance by making booths or tabernacles each year:

> *"In the fifteenth day of the seventh month, when you have gathered in the fruit of the land, you shall keep a feast unto the LORD seven days: on the first day shall be a Sabbath, and on the eighth day shall be a Sabbath. And you shall*

> *take you on the first day the boughs of goodly trees, branches of palm trees, and the boughs of thick trees, and willows of the brook; and you shall rejoice before the LORD your God seven days. And you shall keep it a feast unto the LORD seven days in the year. It shall be a statute forever in your generations: you shall celebrate it in the seventh month. You shall dwell in booths seven days; all that are Israelites born shall dwell in booths: That your generations may know that I made the children of Israel to dwell in booths, when I brought them out of the land of Egypt: I am the LORD your God."*[25]

This is the seventh and final God-ordained Jewish feast called the Feast of Tabernacles. The Jews were to observe this feast starting on the 15th of Tishri.

I believe Jesus will "construct" the Temple on the 15th of Tishri in order to fulfill this feast. Previously I had said that He might return to earth on the 10th of Tishri to fulfill the sixth Jewish festival, the Day of Atonement. Just as God commanded the Jews to build their booths or tabernacles on the 15th of Tishri, so too will Jesus build His tabernacle, the Temple, on that day. This would complete the fulfillment of the seven feasts that God ordained the Jews to keep.

I mentioned at the end of the last chapter that there is one more feast day spoken of in the Bible. Although this feast called Chanukah was not ordained by God, I believe Jesus will fulfill it nonetheless.

Jesus' Second Triumphal Entry

The second event that must take place, before humans spread out across the new earth, is the coronation of Jesus as the King-Messiah.

When Jesus came to earth the first time the Jewish people proclaimed Him as the Messiah. This proclamation took place when Jesus rode on a lowly donkey from the Mount of Olives down and across the Kidron Valley and back up through the Golden Gate into the Temple:

> *"And when they drew near unto Jerusalem, and were come to Bethphage, unto the mount of Olives, then sent Jesus two*

disciples, Saying unto them, Go into the village over against you, and straightway you shall find a donkey tied, and a colt with her: loose them, and bring them unto Me. And if any man says anything to you, you shall say, The Lord has need of them; and straightway he will send them. All this was done, that it might be fulfilled which was spoken by the prophet, saying, 'Tell ye the daughter of Zion, Behold, your King comes unto you, meek, and sitting upon a donkey, and a colt the foal of a donkey'. And the disciples went, and did as Jesus commanded them, And brought the donkey, and the colt, and put on them their clothes, and they set Him thereon. And a very great multitude spread their garments in the way; others cut down branches from the trees, and strewed them in the way. And the multitudes that went before, and that followed, cried, saying, 'Hosanna to the son of David: Blessed is He that cometh in the name of the Lord; Hosanna in the highest'."[26]

Christians refer to this entrance into Jerusalem as the "Triumphal Entry". Sadly though, at Jesus' crucifixion many of the Jews rejected Him as the Messiah.

When Jesus sets up His Millennial Kingdom on earth He will once again ride from down the Mount of Olives and up through the renovated Golden or Eastern Gate. Every human on earth will still be dwelling temporarily around Jerusalem after the judgment of the "sheep and the goats". They all will participate in the coronation process. This time however, the Jews and Gentiles will proclaim Jesus the Messiah and this proclamation will stand.

Jesus will not be riding upon a lowly donkey but will be riding upon the mighty, white horse that John saw Him descending from heaven on. This will truly be a "Triumphal Entry" into Jerusalem and into the Temple. He will enter through the Eastern Gate. The prophet Ezekiel saw the glory of God entering through this gate in the Millennial Jerusalem:

"Afterward He brought me to the gate, the gate facing east. And behold, the glory of the God of Israel came from the

> *east; and the sound of His coming was like the sound of many waters; and the earth shone with His glory. And the vision I saw was like the vision which I had seen when He came to destroy the city, and like the vision which I had seen by the river Chebar; and I fell upon my face. As the glory of the LORD entered the Temple by the gate facing east, the Spirit lifted me up, and brought me into the inner court; and behold, the glory of the LORD filled the Temple."*[27]

It is interesting that the Muslims took this prophecy so seriously that they sealed up the current Eastern or Golden Gate and placed a cemetery in front of it. Their purpose in doing this was to keep the Jewish Messiah from entering Jerusalem since any Jew walking on graves would become unclean. This was an exercise in futility as Jesus will clear the way and open the gate when He comes at His triumphal entry:

> *"Then He brought me back to the outer gate of the Sanctuary, which faces east; and it was shut. And He said to me, "This gate shall remain shut; it shall not be opened, and no one shall enter by it; for the LORD, the God of Israel, has entered by it; therefore it shall remain shut. Only the Prince may sit in it to eat bread before the LORD; He shall enter by way of the vestibule of the gate, and shall go out by the same way."*[28]

Jesus will enter the gate and proceed into the Temple. From there He will reign over the earth. Ezekiel witnessed His entry into the Temple:

> *"While the man was standing beside me, I heard one speaking to me out of the Temple; and He said to me, "Son of man, this is the place of My throne and the place of the soles of My feet, where I will dwell in the midst of the people of Israel for ever."*[29]

I believe the "one" speaking to Ezekiel was Jesus Christ Himself. He uses the first person to declare that He will walk in the Temple and will sit on His throne there. Just as God was surrounded by the Israelites in His Tabernacle in the wilderness, so too the Messiah will be surrounded by the Jews in the Millennial Temple.

As I stated earlier, I believe that Jesus will enter the Temple on the 25th of Kislev. This will be the 1335th day after the Antichrist defiled the Tribulation Temple as prophesied by the prophet Daniel.[30] On that day the Jews celebrate the rededication of their Temple after Antiochus Epiphanies had defiled it. That rededication involved the lighting of the menorah for eight days. The Jews call this day the Feast of Dedication or Chanukah in the Hebrew language. In the Millennial Temple there will not be a menorah to light. However, when Jesus enters the Temple He will illuminate it with the light of His glory.

After Jesus' coronation as King of the Earth I believe He will give the resurrected, glorified saints their "assignments" for the Millennium. John spoke of this in the Book of Revelation:

> *"Blessed and holy is he who shares in the first resurrection! Over such the second death has no power, but they shall be priests of God and of Christ, and they shall reign with him a thousand years."*[31]

Jesus will send the saints around the earth to govern in the different lands. Since these saints will be in their final, perfected, eternal states, their judgments will also be righteous and just. Other saints will have the honor of ministering as priests in the Temple. The interaction between glorified beings and humans will be a normal occurrence during the Millennium. After all the supernatural events that the survivors of the Tribulation Period witnessed, their contact with these eternal beings will be accepted as an ordinary part of their lives.

This will complete the renovation of the world. Now the people who survived the Tribulation Period and the judgment of Jesus can inhabit the earth.

Humanity Renovated

In the Millennium, there will be a new relationship between humans and God, each other, and the animal kingdom:

> *"For, behold, I create new heavens and a new earth: and the former shall not be remembered, nor come into mind. But be you glad and rejoice for ever in that which I create: for, behold, I create Jerusalem a rejoicing, and her people a joy. And I will rejoice in Jerusalem, and joy in My people: and the voice of weeping shall be no more heard in her, nor the voice of crying. There shall be no more then an infant of days, nor an old man that has not filled his days: for the child shall die an hundred years old; but the sinner being an hundred years old shall be accursed. And they shall build houses, and inhabit them; and they shall plant vineyards, and eat the fruit of them. They shall not build, and another inhabit; they shall not plant, and another eat: for as the days of a tree are the days of My people, and My elect shall long enjoy the work of their hands. They shall not labor in vain, nor bring forth for trouble; for they are the seed of the blessed of the LORD, and their offspring with them. And it shall come to pass, that before they call, I will answer; and while they are yet speaking, I will hear. The wolf and the lamb shall feed together, and the lion shall eat straw like the bullock: and dust shall be the serpent's food. They shall not hurt nor destroy in all My holy mountain, says the LORD."*[32]

God states that He will be in Jerusalem rejoicing in His people. No longer will humans have to wait for an answer from God to their prayers. He declares, *"before they call, I will answer; and while they are yet speaking, I will hear"*. Jesus will be sitting in the Temple in Jerusalem speaking personally with the inhabitants of the earth.

Humans will reap the benefits of their own labors. Criminals will not be able to infringe upon another person's life. Jesus will rule with a rod of iron as the Psalmist says:

"You are my Son; this day have I begotten You. Ask of me, and I shall give You the heathen for your inheritance, and the uttermost parts of the earth for your possession. You shall break them with a rod of iron; You shall dash them in pieces like a potter's vessel. Be wise now therefore, O you kings: be instructed, you judges of the earth. Serve the LORD with fear, and rejoice with trembling. Kiss the Son, lest He be angry, and you perish from the way, when His wrath is kindled but a little. Blessed are all they that put their trust in Him."[33]

Not only will Jesus not tolerate any criminal behavior, He will stop it before it occurs. Just as He will hear the thoughts of His people before they speak, so too will He know the thoughts of those who wish to do evil. His judgment will fall on them immediately. There will be no lawyers to get their clients off on a technicality for Jesus' judgment will be righteous and true.

In this passage God alludes to the idea that those humans who re-populate the earth during the Millennium will once again live to great ages. A human will be as an infant at one hundred years of age. Some will probably live the full length of the Millennium while others will die because of their sinful attitudes.

Isaiah also said that the dangerous animals would live peacefully together. In another passage, he declares that the animal kingdom will also live peacefully with humans during the Millennium:

"The wolf also shall dwell with the lamb, and the leopard shall lie down with the kid; and the calf and the young lion and the fatling together; and a little child shall lead them. And the cow and the bear shall feed; their young ones shall lie down together: and the lion shall eat straw like the ox. And the sucking child shall play on the hole of the cobra, and the weaned child shall put his hand on the viper's den."[34]

Children will be able to play with the animals that previously would have harmed them. The animals will no longer have territorial disputes and will eat grass instead of attacking each other. The world will return to the utopian state that God had originally created for Adam and Eve. There they had lived in harmony with nature and the animals in the Garden of Eden.

There will be no more wars between humans during this time. God declared in an earlier prophecy that He gave to Isaiah:

> *"And it shall come to pass in the last days, that the mountain of the LORD's house shall be established in the top of the mountains, and shall be exalted above the hills; and all nations shall flow unto it...And He shall judge among the nations, and shall rebuke many people: and they shall beat their swords into plowshares, and their spears into pruning hooks: nation shall not lift up sword against nation, neither shall they learn war any more."*[35]

After the false peace treaty that the Antichrist made with the world at the beginning of the Tribulation Period the earth will finally know true peace under the rule of the true Messiah. There will be no more wars until the end of the Millennium when God defeats Satan.

There will also be a lasting peace between the Arabs and the Jews. The prophet Isaiah foresaw the time at the end when the Arab nations would accept the God of Israel for their own:

> *"In that day shall there be an altar to the LORD in the midst of the land of Egypt, and a pillar at the border thereof to the LORD. And it shall be for a sign and for a witness unto the LORD of hosts in the land of Egypt: for they shall cry unto the LORD because of the oppressors, and He shall send them a Savior, and a great one, and He shall deliver them. And the LORD shall be known to Egypt, and the Egyptians shall know the LORD in that day, and shall do sacrifice and oblation; yea, they shall vow a vow unto the LORD, and perform it. And the LORD shall smite Egypt: He shall smite and heal it: and they shall return even to the LORD, and He shall be entreated of them, and shall heal them. In that day shall there be a highway out of Egypt to Assyria, and the Assyrian shall come into Egypt, and the Egyptian into Assyria, and the Egyptians shall serve with*

the Assyrians. In that day shall Israel be the third with Egypt and with Assyria, even a blessing in the midst of the land: Whom the LORD of hosts shall bless, saying, Blessed be Egypt My people, and Assyria the work of My hands, and Israel Mine inheritance."[36]

Isaiah states that someone oppresses Egypt in the future. I believe this oppressor is the Antichrist. In Chapter 10 I mentioned that the king of the south would come against the Antichrist in a battle leading up to Armageddon. The prophet Daniel stated that this king would command a confederation of Arab countries to fight the Antichrist:

"[The Antichrist] shall stretch forth his hand also upon the countries: and the land of Egypt shall not escape. But he shall have power over the treasures of gold and of silver, and over all the precious things of Egypt; and the Libyans and the Ethiopians shall follow in his train."[37]

Daniel said that Egypt would not immediately escape from the wicked, oppressive hand of the Antichrist. However, Isaiah said that God would send a Savior to deliver the Egyptians at the end. They will accept this Savior and turn to the LORD God of Israel. Assyria, which then consisted of what is now the modern countries of Turkey, Syria, Lebanon, Iran, Kuwait, and Egypt, will also accept the God of Israel for their own. The Middle East will finally experience true peace, as all of the Arab countries will worship alongside of the Jews.

The Millennial Kingdom of Jesus Christ will truly be an unprecedented time in human history. The world will live together in harmony with creation just as God meant for it to do from the beginning.

However, there is a saying that all good things must end. This is true with the Millennium. John wrote in the Book of Revelation:

"And when the thousand years are ended, Satan will be loosed from his prison and will come out to deceive the

nations which are at the four corners of the earth, that is, Gog and Magog, to gather them for battle; their number is like the sand of the sea. And they marched up over the broad earth and surrounded the camp of the saints and the beloved city; but fire came down from heaven and consumed them, and the devil who had deceived them was thrown into the lake of fire and sulphur where the beast and the false prophet were, and they will be tormented day and night for ever and ever."[38]

God is going to culminate the long history of humankind by defeating the one being who did more to destroy it then any other force in the universe. At the end of the Millennium God is going to give Satan one last opportunity to defeat His plans.

After one thousand years the earth's population will have grown exponentially. Those who were the last to be born during this time will probably be the ones who will want to rebel against God and His Messiah. Up to this point Jesus will have immediately judged those who sought to hurt others. Now though He lets Satan gather them together as an army where God will judge them all at once. This too is a parallel to the beginning of human history. In the Garden of Eden God allowed humans to choose to obey Him or to follow Satan. This will be the last time that humans will be able to make this choice. Sadly, there will be humans that make the same fatal choice as Adam and Eve. They will side with the Devil and suffer the consequences. God brings fire down from heaven and devours the entire army of rebels. Then He casts Satan into Hell for eternity.

Isaiah, in a prophetic allusion to this demise of Satan, declared:

"When the LORD has given you rest from your pain and turmoil and the hard service with which you were made to serve, you will take up this taunt against the king of Babylon: "How the oppressor has ceased, the insolent fury ceased! The LORD has broken the staff of the wicked, the scepter of rulers, that smote the peoples in wrath with unceasing blows, that ruled the nations in anger with unrelenting persecution. The whole earth is at rest and quiet; they break forth into singing. The cypresses rejoice

at you, the cedars of Lebanon, saying, 'Since you were laid low, no hewer comes up against us.' Sheol beneath is stirred up to meet you when you come, it rouses the shades to greet you, all who were leaders of the earth; it raises from their thrones all who were kings of the nations. All of them will speak and say to you: 'You too have become as weak as we! You have become like us!' Your pomp is brought down to Sheol, the sound of your harps; maggots are the bed beneath you, and worms are your covering. "How you are fallen from heaven, O Day Star, son of Dawn! How you are cut down to the ground, you who laid the nations low! You said in your heart, 'I will ascend to heaven; above the stars of God I will set my throne on high; I will sit on the mount of assembly in the far north; I will ascend above the heights of the clouds, I will make myself like the Most High.'" But you are brought down to Sheol, to the depths of the Pit. Those who see you will stare at you, and ponder over you: 'Is this the man who made the earth tremble, who shook kingdoms, who made the world like a desert and overthrew its cities, who did not let his prisoners go home?'"[39]

At the beginning of human history Satan had stirred the people of the earth's hearts to rebel against God. He influenced them to build a tower at Babylon in order to make a name for themselves apart from God. Isaiah speaks of the *"king of Babylon"* here as an allusion to Satan. He wanted to ascend on high and become God but instead was cast down into the deepest part of Hell. The nations of the world will look on him and see him as he really is. They ask rhetorically, "Is this the one who created such terror for the human race?" Sadly he is, but he himself will now suffer the terror of Hell for eternity.

With this God brings an end to human history. The time has now come for the most horrific event since the beginning of the universe to take place.

---

1 *Genesis 2:8-9; 3:1-24*
2 *Revelation 20:1-3*
3 *Isaiah 65:17-18; 66:22-24*
4 *Revelation 21:23*

[5] *Revelation 21:1*
[6] *Isaiah 40:13-15*
[7] *Isaiah 51:3*
[8] *Isaiah 61:4-5, 11*
[9] *Joel 3:18*
[10] *Zechariah 6:12-13*
[11] *Ezekiel 40:1-2*
[12] *Isaiah 2:2*
[13] *Jeremiah 3:16-17*
[14] *John 6:35*
[15] *John 8:12*
[16] *Haggai 2:6-7*
[17] *Ezekiel 43:18-21*
[18] *Revelation 20:6*
[19] *Ezekiel 45:17*
[20] *Ezekiel 47:1, 8-9,*
[21] *Zechariah 14:8-9*
[22] *Revelation 22:1-2*
[23] *Hebrews 8:1-5*
[24] *Exodus 25:9-26:37*
[25] *Leviticus 23:39-43*
[26] *Matthew 21:1-9*
[27] *Ezekiel 43:1-5*
[28] *Ezekiel 44:1-3*
[29] *Ezekiel 43:6-7*
[30] *Daniel 12:11-12*
[31] *Revelation 20:6*
[32] *Isaiah 65:17-25*
[33] *Psalms 2:7-12*
[34] *Isaiah 11:6-8*
[35] *Isaiah 2:2, 4*
[36] *Isaiah 19:19-25*
[37] *Daniel 11:42-43*
[38] *Revelation 20:7-10*
[39] *Isaiah 14:3-17*

13 - The Great White Throne and Hell

There are three biblical concepts that I consider the most terrifying in their essence and horrifying in their results. The thought that any or all three of them could apply to my life has troubled me greatly at various times.

The first is that I was afraid I might commit blasphemy of the Holy Spirit. Jesus said that God would forgive every sin except this one. Thankfully, I heard a pastor teach that if a person was concerned that they might have committed this sin then they can rest assured that they have not. If they had committed it their conscience would have become so seared that they would not care if they had committed it.

The second concept that disturbed me was that the Book of Hebrews *seems* to say that if a Christian sins willfully after they received the salvation of Jesus Christ then there was no more forgiveness for them. However, every born-again Christian sins until the day they die. Many of these sins will be committed willfully because we are still in our corruptible flesh. The danger lies in the fact that if we keep abusing God's grace then eventually we will harden our hearts and turn from Him.

The final concept is one that terrified me as a child. I used to lie on my bed at night and think about the possibility that I might go to Hell. This thought brought a terror to me unlike anything else ever could. At that time, I like many people, believed that the only way a person could avoid going to Hell was by going to church every Sunday and being a good person. As we will see shortly I was greatly mistaken in this belief.

Let me say that all three of these concepts share a common theme: A willful rejection of the saving truths of God and the finality of that rejection. The results of rejecting God by any one of these methods are dreadful and eternal. Most people are interested in how to get to heaven. The three concepts listed above answer the question, "How do I go to Hell?"

In this chapter, I will discuss the concept of Hell and the judgment of God that will send people there.

The Great White Throne

After John saw the Devil cast into Hell, he wrote what he witnessed next:

> *"And I saw a great white throne, and Him that sat on it, from whose face the earth and the heaven fled away; and there was found no place for them. And I saw the dead, small and great, stand before God; and the books were opened: and another book was opened, which is the book of life: and the dead were judged out of those things which were written in the books, according to their works. And the sea gave up the dead which were in it; and death and hell* [lit. hades] *delivered up the dead which were in them: and they were judged every man according to their works. And death and hell* [lit. hades] *were cast into the lake of fire. This is the second death. And whosoever was not found written in the book of life was cast into the lake of fire."*
>
> *- Revelation 20:11-15*

Now that human history and time are completed John sees the awful event that ushers in eternity. The Millennial earth and heavens dissolve before the eternal glory of God. All that he sees now is God sitting on His white throne and the unsaved dead whom He resurrected.

These resurrected dead include some of the greatest men and women who ever lived and others whom history does not remember. Sadly, these persons are those who for one reason or another rejected the saving truths of God and His Son Jesus Christ. God will judge each of these persons according to the works they did while they were alive.

Many people believe and many religions teach that a person can enter heaven based on the good deeds that they perform during their lifetimes. If you ask most people how will they get to heaven they usually respond by saying that they try to be good persons and do good things. However, the Bible dispels this notion of earning one's salvation:

> *"But we are all as an unclean thing, and all our righteousnesses are as filthy rags; and we all do fade as a leaf; and our iniquities, like the wind, have taken us away."*[1]

The prophet Isaiah states that all of our "righteousnesses" or good deeds are as filthy rags. The Hebrew word translated here as "filthy" actually means "menstrual". Therefore, according to the Bible our good works have the equivalent value of used menstrual rags if we do them apart from the will of God.

The apostle Paul addressed this issue in a letter He wrote to the Christians living in Corinth, Greece:

> *"Though I speak with the tongues of men and of angels, and have not love, I am become as sounding brass, or a tinkling cymbal. And though I have the gift of prophecy, and understand all mysteries, and all knowledge; and though I have all faith, so that I could remove mountains, and have not love, I am nothing. And though I bestow all my goods to feed the poor, and though I give my body to be burned, and have not love, it profits me nothing."*[2]

The love Paul speaks about here is the Greek word "agape" which denotes unconditional love, the highest form of the expression of love. The apostle John wrote, *"And we have known and believed the love that God has to us. God is* [agape] *love; and he that dwells in love dwells in God, and God in him."*[3] Therefore, if we do not have the love of God in us then as Paul says all our good works are in vain. We can give all of our money to the poor yet if we do not have the love of God inside us it is to no avail.

Paul wrote about the sinful condition of humans in a letter to the Christians living in Rome:

> *"No, in no wise: for we have before proved both Jews and Gentiles, that they are all under sin; As it is written, There is none righteous, no, not one: There is none that understands, there is none that seeks after God. They are all gone out of the way, they are together become unprofitable; there is none that does good, no, not one...For all have sinned, and come short of the glory of God."*[4]

Every human being that has ever lived is a sinner. Paul states that it is not in us to do righteous deeds from a pure heart. Many other biblical passages make the same point concerning the "good" works of humankind. However, there is one work that we can do to "earn" our way into heaven:

> *"Then said they unto Him, What shall we do, that we might work the works of God? Jesus answered and said unto them, This is the work of God, that you believe on Him Whom He has sent."*[5]

Jesus states that the only "work" that a person can do to enter heaven is to believe in Him, God's only Son. None of our other works will earn us one second in heaven. The apostle Paul confirms this truth in a letter he wrote to the Church at Ephesus:

> *"For by grace are you saved through faith; and that not of yourselves: it is the gift of God: Not of works, lest any man should boast."*[6]

It is only by God's merciful grace that He saves any human beings from the punishment of Hell. There is not one good deed that we can do to enter heaven. Going to church every Sunday will not save anyone nor will giving away all our money.

Paul, in writing to a Christian named Titus affirmed this truth:

> *"For we ourselves also were sometimes foolish, disobedient, deceived, serving diverse lusts and pleasures, living in malice and envy, hateful, and hating one another. But after that the kindness and love of God our Savior toward man appeared, Not by works of righteousness which we have done, but according to His mercy He saved us, by the washing of regeneration, and renewing of the Holy Ghost; Which He shed on us abundantly through Jesus Christ our Savior; That being justified by His grace, we should be made heirs according to the hope of eternal life."*[7]

The Bible makes it abundantly clear that it is only by God's loving mercy and grace that any human beings will be saved. Since the unsaved have rejected the grace that is available only through Jesus Christ, God will judge them based on their works. As we just read these works will have no saving value by themselves.

Therefore, the unsaved will be standing (or more likely prostrate) alone before God at the Great White Throne judgment. Sadly, they could have had the perfect attorney as the apostle John wrote:

> *"My little children, these things write I unto you, that you sin not. And if any man sin, we have an Advocate with the Father, Jesus Christ the righteous."*[8]

However, since they rejected Jesus Christ as their Lord and Savior they will appear all alone before God's judgment seat.

I do not believe that any of the accused will try to give a defense of the lives that they chose to live. They will be standing before the *Omnipotent, Omniscient, and Omnipresent God of Eternity.* God, the One who is an all-consuming fire according to the Book of Hebrews[9], will be their Righteous Judge. We read earlier how people were awestricken in the presence of angels. What will happen to them in the presence of the Almighty God?

The Book of Isaiah describes what happened to a righteous servant of God when he entered into the presence of God:

> *"In the year that king Uzziah died I saw also the LORD sitting upon a throne, high and lifted up, and His train filled the Temple. Above it stood the seraphims: each one had six wings; with two he covered his face, and with two he covered his feet, and with two he did fly. And one cried unto another, and said, Holy, holy, holy, is the LORD of hosts: the whole earth is full of His glory. And the posts of the door moved at the voice of him that cried, and the house was filled with smoke. Then said I, Woe is me! for I am undone; because I am a man of unclean lips, and I dwell in the midst of a people of unclean lips: for mine eyes have seen the King, the LORD of hosts. Then flew one of the seraphims unto me, having a live coal in his hand, which he had taken with the tongs from off the altar: And he laid it upon my mouth, and said, Lo, this has touched your lips; and your iniquity is taken away, and your sin purged."*[10]

The prophet Isaiah, who had been a faithful servant of the Lord, was devastated when he entered into the presence of God. He felt the excruciating weight of all the sins he had ever committed when he stood before the holiness of God. How much more overwhelmed will those persons be who have rejected God when they stand before Him at the Great White Throne? They too will feel the incomprehensible uncleanness of every sin they ever committed.

Jesus made an intriguing statement concerning human sin to the religious leaders during His earthly ministry because they had rejected Him as the Messiah:

> *"And He said unto them, You are from beneath; I am from above: you are of this world; I am not of this world. I said therefore unto you, that you shall die in your sins: for if you believe not that I am He, you shall die in your sins."*[11]

Since they rejected the only sacrifice that God accepts for human sin, when they die they will have all their sins as part of their eternal souls. And since God cannot have sin in His holy presence because He is a *"consuming fire"* He will have to remove these sinful beings from His presence. The writer of the Book of Hebrews declares this truth concerning the only sacrifice for sins available for humankind:

> *"For if we sin willfully after that we have received the knowledge of the truth, there remains no more sacrifice for sins, But a certain fearful looking for of judgment and fiery indignation, which shall devour the adversaries. He that despised Moses' law died without mercy under two or three witnesses: Of how much sorer punishment, suppose you, shall he be thought worthy, who has trodden under foot the Son of God, and has counted the blood of the covenant, wherewith He was sanctified, an unholy thing, and has insulted the Spirit of grace? For we know Him that has said, Vengeance belongs unto Me, I will recompense, says the Lord. And again, The Lord shall judge His people. It is a fearful thing to fall into the hands of the living God."*[12]

Indeed, it will truly be a fearful thing for the unsaved at the Great White Throne judgment when they *"fall into the hands of the living God"*.

The Millennial Saints

Before I address the punishment that God metes out to these persons there is one more aspect to the Great White Throne judgment that I want to discuss. What happened to the people who were saved during the Millennial Kingdom? The short answer is that the Bible is unclear on this issue but it may hint as to what might happen to them.

As I stated in the last chapter, I believe the Millennium was God's way of showing humanity what His plans were for it from the beginning. I also pointed out some of the parallels between that time and the end-times. One more correlation I would like to make concerning the beginning of human history and the end of it might answer the question above.

In the book of Genesis, there is a genealogical list of humans from Adam on. The seventh descendant of Adam was a man named Enoch. The Bible makes an interesting statement concerning him:

> *"And Enoch lived sixty and five years, and begat Methuselah: And Enoch walked with God after he begat Methuselah three hundred years, and begat sons and daughters: And all the days of Enoch were three hundred sixty and five years: And Enoch walked with God: and he was not; for God took him."*[13]

This passage states that Enoch walked with God. The implication is that he was a faithful and obedient servant of the Lord. All the humans named in this genealogy died except for Enoch. This verse simply says that Enoch was no more because God took him. This must have been a type of Rapture because it does not say that Enoch died yet he went to be with God. With the possible exception of the prophet Elijah, all the other godly persons mentioned in the Old Testament died. Why did God choose to rapture the little-known Enoch for this honor? No one knows but it is possible that God is teaching us something through this incident.

In the Bible the number "7" is sometimes representative of perfection or completion. Enoch was the seventh generation of humans on the earth. It is possible that just as God raptured Enoch right before the flood, which completed the first stage of human history, so too He will rapture the Millennial saints just before He completes the last stage of human history. Of course this is mere speculation on my part but again it ties the beginning of human history with the end of it.

Another possibility is that the Millennial saints will be judged with the unsaved dead at the Great White Throne judgment. Why else would God open the Book of Life at this judgment if He were only going to judge the unsaved persons? None of their names would be written in it so it would seem to be a superfluous act if that were the case. Therefore, it is possible that God will transform the bodies of these saints at that time. Even though the Bible is unclear on this point God will have to change the Millennial saints' mortal bodies into immortal bodies at some point so that they can exist in eternity.

Hades

Now we come to the punishment of the unsaved after God judges them. John wrote what he saw:

> *"And death and hell were cast into the lake of fire. This is the second death. And whosoever was not found written in the book of life was cast into the lake of fire."*[14]

The word *hell* here is actually *hades* in the Greek and refers to the abode of the dead. This is the place where the souls of all the dead went until the resurrection of Jesus Christ. Jesus spoke of this place in a parable:

> *"There was a certain rich man, who was clothed in purple and fine linen, and fared sumptuously every day: And there was a certain beggar named Lazarus, who was laid at his gate, full of sores, And desiring to be fed with the crumbs which fell from the rich man's table: moreover the dogs came and licked his sores. And it came to pass, that the beggar died, and was carried by the angels into Abraham's bosom: the rich man also died, and was buried; And in hell* [lit. hades] *he lift up his eyes, being in torments, and sees Abraham afar off, and Lazarus in his bosom. And he cried and said, Father Abraham, have mercy on me, and send Lazarus, that he may dip the tip of his finger in water, and cool my tongue; for I am tormented in this flame."*[15]

Though this is a parable I believe Jesus is actually describing the place where the souls of the dead went before His resurrection. He uses the word "hades" when speaking of the place where Lazarus and the rich man went after their deaths. It appears that Hades was divided into two sections. The righteous persons of God were in "Abraham's bosom" while the unrighteous were in a place of torment. When Jesus ascended into heaven He took the souls of the righteous with Him and left the unsaved in Hades to await their final judgment at God's Great White Throne:

> *"Wherefore he said, When He ascended up on high, He led captivity captive, and gave gifts unto men. (Now that He ascended, what is it but that He also descended first into the lower parts of the earth? He that descended is the same also that ascended up far above all heavens, that He might fill all things.)"*[16]

Thus, John sees God cast "death" and "hades" into the lake of fire. However, God resurrects the unsaved from Hades before he does this. These two afflictions of humanity will no longer have the power to hold humans captive. Since John is seeing this in the eternal dimension it is possible that God literally throws these two concepts into the fire.

Finally, the punishment of the unsaved occurs. John states that those found guilty before God will be cast into the lake of fire. This truly will be a horrific event for those who reject God's Son as their Savior. This punishment is what Jesus came to save all these people from but now it will be too late.

Hell

Some people reject the idea that a God of love could send people to suffer in Hell for eternity. However, think about that conjecture. God so loved the world that God the Son died so that people wouldn't have to spend eternity separated from Him. He made a way for everyone to escape the flames of Hell. Yet some people do not want anything to do with God and His sacrifice for them. If they do not want to spend their earthly lives in fellowship with Him why would they want to spend their eternal lives with Him?

Which one of us would not rejoice to see the death of a dictator who was responsible for deaths of millions of people? Yet God, who *is* loving, declares:

> *"But if the wicked will turn from all his sins that he has committed, and keep all My statutes, and do that which is lawful and right, he shall surely live, he shall not die. All his transgressions that he has committed, they shall not be mentioned unto him: in his righteousness that he has done*

> *he shall live. As I live, says the Lord GOD, I have no pleasure in the death of the wicked; but that the wicked turn from his way and live: turn you, turn you from your evil ways."*[17]

And:

> *"The Lord is not slack concerning His promise, as some men count slackness; but is longsuffering to us-ward, not willing that any should perish, but that all should come to repentance."*[18]

God knows the horrors of Hell and does not wish any one of His creations to go there. Yet He gives humans the free will to choose where they want to spend eternity.

Some may say that the punishment doesn't fit the crime. Why should God punish the average human who tries to live a good life (although they will sin throughout their life) with the same punishment as Adolph Hitler?

At first glance it appears that people who believe that it would be unfair of God to send a person to Hell have a point. However, let me submit a question to you. Let's say that a person steals an item from a store. The police catch him and take him before a judge for a trial. The judge finds him guilty and sentences him to death. Would you say that the judge was unfair in his sentence? Indeed this judge ruled unfairly in this case. Therefore, if a person commits the sin of stealing isn't God also being unfair in sentencing them to Hell for eternity? The answer to this question is no. God is not sending them to Hell because they stole something. This crime is just a symptom of a deeper problem. That problem is the sin nature of human beings. As we read above all people have sinned and there is none righteous. In turn, our sinful nature is reflective of our rebellious nature toward God. Therefore, it is not because of any particular sin, great or small, that causes God to sentence us to Hell. Sin is an extension of our rebellion and separation from God. Our sinful natures will cause us to spend eternity in Hell. As the prophet Isaiah declares, sin separates us from God:

> *"Behold, the LORD's hand is not shortened, that it cannot save; neither His ear heavy, that it cannot hear: But your iniquities have separated between you and your God, and your sins have hid His face from you, that He will not hear."*[19]

God is a consuming fire who consumes sin by His holy presence. Thus, those who die in their sins will be removed from His presence.

There are two deeper aspects to this issue that I believe will give you a better understanding of the justice of God in this matter.

The first is that Jesus indicated that there would be different degrees of punishment for unsaved people:

> *"But I say unto you, It shall be more tolerable for Tyre and Sidon at the day of judgment, than for you. And You, Capernaum, which are exalted unto heaven, shall be brought down to hell: for if the mighty works, which have been done in you, had been done in Sodom, it would have remained until this day. But I say unto you, That it shall be more tolerable for the land of Sodom in the day of judgment, than for you."*[20]

Jesus was upbraiding the cities that He visited during His earthly ministry for not believing in Him. He had done mighty miracles before these people yet they had rejected Him as the Messiah. He states here that although the people of Tyre, Sidon, and Sodom were wicked, God will punish them less severely than He will the people of the towns that Jesus had visited. The Bible is unclear as to exactly how this occurs yet Jesus states that there will be different levels of punishment. God will punish those persons whose works were more evil than others more severely. God will not punish everyone with the exact same punishment.

The second aspect has to do with our lack of understanding the significance of the consequences of sin. Humans are finite beings who exist in the dimensions of space and time. With our limited minds we cannot understand how sin operates in the spiritual and eternal realms. We may consider an act that we commit as a little sin yet in the spiritual world it may have a more dreadful significance.

I mentioned above how the prophet Isaiah reacted when he saw his sins against the holiness of God. God had brought Isaiah into the eternal dimension and immediately Isaiah saw himself against the standard of God's perfection. He said, "*Woe is me! for I am undone; because I am a man of unclean lips, and I dwell in the midst of a people of unclean lips: for mine eyes have seen the King, the LORD of hosts.*"[21] Isaiah was devastated by this experience, an experience that no other human being had ever had. He saw the true nature of sin in the eternal dimension. I believe that if God had asked Isaiah at that exact moment if He should send him to Hell because of his sins, Isaiah would have answered *"Yes"*. He was distraught and could not cope with his sinfulness. If Isaiah, a great man of God, felt this way when confronted with his sin, how much more undone will the unsaved feel when they appear before God?

Therefore, what we finite humans may feel to be unfair by our standards in the temporal realm may seem extremely fair to us in the spiritual realm.

Our sins have such an impact in the spiritual realm that it appears Jesus will bear the marks of His crucifixion for eternity. After His resurrection He showed the disciples the marks in His hands and feet and side, which were made by the Roman nails and spear. Since this was Jesus' resurrected body it may very well be that He will carry them in His glorified body forever.

The Bible gives other examples of human actions on earth affecting the eternal, spiritual realm. Jesus described one such event after His disciples had returned from a missionary trip that He had sent them on:

> *"And the seventy [disciples] returned again with joy, saying, Lord, even the devils are subject unto us through Your name. And He said unto them, I beheld Satan as lightning fall from heaven."*[22]

Jesus had instructed His disciples to go throughout Israel preaching the gospel and healing the sick. They successfully carried out this mission and returned rejoicing. Jesus stated that because of their efforts He saw Satan fall from Heaven in the spiritual realm.

The simple preaching of the gospel and the miraculous healing of the sick by humans had a tremendous effect in the eternal realm.

One other example of this takes place when a human receives the salvation offered through Jesus Christ:

> *"I say unto you, that likewise joy shall be in heaven over one sinner that repents, more than over ninety and nine just persons, which need no repentance...Likewise, I say unto you, there is joy in the presence of the angels of God over one sinner that repents."*[23]

The act of a human being accepting Jesus as their Savior, though done in the earthly realm, has an impact in the spiritual realm with eternal results.

Jesus raised the seriousness of sin in His Sermon on the Mount. He declared that God sees sin differently than humans do:

> *"You have heard that it was said of them of old time, Thou shalt not kill; and whosoever shall kill shall be in danger of the judgment: But I say unto you, That whosoever is angry with his brother without a cause shall be in danger of the judgment: and whosoever shall say to his brother, Raca, shall be in danger of the council: but whosoever shall say, You fool, shall be in danger of hell fire."*[24]

And:

> *"You have heard that it was said by them of old time, Thou shalt not commit adultery: But I say unto you, That whosoever looks on a woman to lust after her has committed adultery with her already in his heart."*[25]

In the first instance Jesus equates hatred of a fellow human being with the sin of murder. In the second passage He equates the act of lusting after another person with the actual act of adultery. We humans see hatred and lust as minor offenses yet God sees them as murder and adultery. This points out how sin in the temporal realm has a different, more significant aspect to it in the spiritual realm.

I do not believe that we are able to grasp the seriousness of our sins as they pertain to the eternal dimension. We may think that it is unfair of God to sentence a person to Hell because of their sins. However, we will not understand the significance or damage that is done in the eternal dimension by the sins we commit until we enter that dimension ourselves. Otherwise, we sit in judgment of God if we say that He is unfair for punishing people for eternity. God declares:

> *"Seek you the LORD while He may be found, call you upon Him while He is near: Let the wicked forsake his way, and the unrighteous man his thoughts: and let him return unto the LORD, and He will have mercy upon him; and to our God, for He will abundantly pardon. 'For My thoughts are not your thoughts, neither are your ways My ways, saith the LORD. For as the heavens are higher than the earth, so are My ways higher than your ways, and My thoughts than your thoughts.'"*[26]

God, who dwells in all dimensions, is omniscient and infinite. Humans, who dwell in four dimensions, are finite and limited in their thoughts. We will not understand God's ways until we are with Him in eternity.

Gehenna

Many religions teach that Hell is a place of punishment. However, the Christian Bible describes this concept in its most graphic, terrifying terms. The primary source in the New Testament for the doctrine of Hell is Jesus Christ.

I mentioned in the Chapter 11 that Jesus used the Greek word "gehenna" as a metaphor for the eternal flames of Hell. This word refers to the Valley of Hinnom outside the walls of Jerusalem. It was there that the Jerusalemites constantly burned their refuse. The Old Testament Hebrew equivalent for the word "gehenna" is "Gai Ben Hinnom" which is sometimes contracted to "Gai Hinnom".[27] It means the Valley of the Son of Hinnom. However, the Jewish concept of Hell and the Christian concept of Hell differ in that the Jews believe that Hell is only a temporary place of punishment. The

New Testament unequivocally states that punishment in Hell is for eternity.

Jesus used the term "gehenna" seven times in His teachings, some of which are repeated in the different Gospels:

> *"You have heard that it was said of them of old time, You shall not kill; and whosoever shall kill shall be in danger of the judgment: But I say unto you, That whosoever is angry with his brother without a cause shall be in danger of the judgment: and whosoever shall say to his brother, Raca, shall be in danger of the council: but whosoever shall say, You fool, shall be in danger of [gehenna] fire."*
>
> *- Matthew 5:21-22*

Jesus says that we should love our fellow human beings. Those who would belittle God's children by calling them fools are in danger of spending eternity in Hell. Of course, saying this would reflect the attitude that they have toward God Himself. Jesus associates the Greek word "puros", which means fire, with the word Hell.

> *"You have heard that it was said by them of old time, You shall not commit adultery: But I say unto you, That whosoever looks on a woman to lust after her has committed adultery with her already in his heart. And if your right eye offends you, pluck it out, and cast it from you: for it is profitable for you that one of your members should perish, and not that your whole body should be cast into [gehenna]. And if your right hand offends you, cut it off, and cast it from you: for it is profitable for you that one of your members should perish, and not that your whole body should be cast into [gehenna]."*
>
> *- Matthew 5:27-30*

It would be a tragedy if someone took the words of Jesus here literally and actually maimed themselves to keep from sinning. What He is actually saying here is that it is so important, eternally important, that we turn from our sinful attitudes that if it were necessary, we should maim ourselves to accomplish this. Thankfully, it is not necessary. Accepting the forgiveness of Jesus and receiving the Holy Spirit to guide us allows us to walk in His ways without taking such drastic measures. The alternative to heeding His warning is spending eternity in Hell.

> *"And fear not them which kill the body, but are not able to kill the soul: but rather fear Him which is able to destroy both soul and body in [gehenna]."*
>
> *- Matthew 10:28*

It is interesting that several times during Jesus' ministry He told the people to "fear not" and "be not afraid". Yet here He told them that Hell was something *they should fear.* The implication is that if a person does not fear God, and therefore lives a life of rebellion, then that person will spend eternity in Hell. One other noteworthy aspect to this saying of Jesus is the fact that there will not be disembodied souls or spirits suffering in Hell. Just as believers in Jesus receive an eternal, glorified body for their souls and spirits, so too will the unsaved have eternal bodies.

> *"And whoso shall receive one such little child in My name receives Me. But whoso shall offend one of these little ones which believe in Me, it were better for him that a millstone were hanged about his neck, and that he were drowned in the depth of the sea. Woe unto the world because of offences! for it must needs be that offences come; but woe to that man by whom the offence comes! Wherefore if your hand or your foot offends you, cut them off, and cast them from you: it is better for you to enter into life halt or maimed, rather than having two hands or two feet to be cast into everlasting fire. And if your eye offends you, pluck it out, and cast it from you: it is better for you to enter into life with one eye, rather than having two eyes to be cast into [gehenna] fire."*

- Matthew 18:5-9

Jesus declares here that anyone who causes a child to turn from God will regret it for eternity. Again, He states the importance of turning from a life of sin rather than spending eternity in Hell. Notice too that Jesus refers to Hell as *everlasting* fire.

> *"Woe unto you, scribes and Pharisees, hypocrites! for you travel around sea and land to make one proselyte, and when he is made, you make him twofold more the child of [gehenna] than yourselves."*
>
> *- Matthew 23:15*

> *"You serpents, you generation of vipers, how can you escape the damnation of [gehenna]?"*
>
> *- Matthew 23:33*

The harshest words that Jesus spoke while on the earth were to the religious leaders of His day. Instead of turning the people to the true worship of God they were placing all types of rules and regulations upon them. Instead of teaching the people to obey the commandments of God, the religious leaders were teaching them to obey their traditions. God will hold teachers accountable for the way they represent Him to the people.

There is no doubt that Jesus spoke of there being an eternal punishment for humans in a place called Hell. Though some have tried, there is absolutely no other way interpret His words. If Hell were not real, why would He tell people to fear it? Why would He tell people to seemingly maim themselves rather than enter into to Hell? Hell is a real place of suffering and torment and people who reject God will dwell there forever.

Where is Hell?

There is much speculation as to where the location of Hell is. I believe it is in a dimension different from the four we live in (height, width, length, which together equals "space" and the fourth one, which is time). Some physicists believe there might be ten dimensions and others believe there may be hundreds of dimensions. The Bible declares that God dwells in timeless eternity and therefore He exists in another dimension. Since Hell exists for eternity it must also be in the eternal dimension.

When God let John see the future described in the Book of Revelation, He showed Him Hell:

> *"And the devil that deceived them was cast into the lake of fire and brimstone, where the beast and the false prophet are, and shall be tormented day and night for ever and ever."*[28]

John does not say where he was when he saw the lake of fire. He did say that the Devil and his cohorts would be tormented there forever. Hell is not a place of temporary punishment.

Personally, I don't want to know where Hell is nor do I desire to see anyone suffering there. But the Bible makes it clear that there will be people suffering there forever and ever.

A Living Hell

Thankfully, anyone who accepts the shed blood of Jesus' sacrificial death for their sins can spend eternity with God instead of with the Devil. However, there are going to be many people who lived on the earth during its long history who will no longer have a choice of where they spend eternity. The Book of Hebrews declares:

> *"And as it is appointed unto men once to die, but after this the judgment: So Christ was once offered to bear the sins of many; and unto them that look for Him shall He appear the second time without sin unto salvation."*
>
> \- *Hebrews 9:27-28*

There will be no second chance after a person dies. The Bible does not teach the doctrines of reincarnation or purgatory. If a person rejects God in this life, God will reject them in the next.

The tragic part is that God did not create Hell as a place of punishment for His human creations. Jesus stated:

> *"Then shall He say also unto them on the left hand, Depart from Me, you cursed, into everlasting fire, prepared for the devil and his angels."*[29]

God's plan was to punish the Devil and his angelic followers who rebelled against Him by sending them to Hell for eternity. However, when humans rebelled against God, He declared that they too would be punished in Hell forever.

John wrote in Revelation who will go to Hell:

> *"And whosoever was not found written in the book of life was cast into the lake of fire."*[30]

In chapter 21 of Revelation, John describes the Book of Life as referring to the saving work of the Lamb of God, Jesus Christ:

> *"And there shall in no wise enter into it* [i.e., New Heaven] *any thing that defiles, neither whatsoever works abomination, or makes a lie: but they which are written in the Lamb's book of life."*[31]

Anyone who has not been saved by accepting the shed blood of Jesus Christ's sacrificial death, which is the only sacrifice that can take away their sins, will be cast into Hell. When a person accepts Jesus as their Savior then their name is in the Book of Life. If a person refuses Jesus as their Savior then their name is not in the Book of Life and they will suffer in Hell for eternity.

There is a religious sect[32] that rejects the concept of Hell and denies that any unsaved persons will suffer punishment forever. They believe that those whom God does not choose for salvation will become non-existent rather than suffer for eternity. As we have read this is contradictory to the plain teachings of the Bible.

Those who end up in Hell will be alive and in torment forever. Jesus declared that nothing dies in Hell and the fire is everlasting:

> *"And if your hand offends you cut it off: it is better for you to enter into life maimed, than having two hands to go into hell, into the fire that never shall be quenched: Where their worm dieth not, and the fire is not quenched."*[33]

> *"Then shall He say also unto them on the left hand, Depart from Me, you cursed, into everlasting fire, prepared for the devil and his angels...And these shall go away into everlasting punishment: but the righteous into life eternal."*[34]

Not even the worms will die in the fires of Hell. Jesus says that those who reject God will suffer *everlasting* punishment. If the fire consumed them as soon as they entered Hell then their punishment would not be everlasting. If they became non-existent they would not know that God was punishing them. Also, if all the unsaved immediately cease to exist in Hell, why then is it necessary for the fire to be *"everlasting"*?

John also described the punishment of Hell as lasting for eternity:

> *"And the third angel followed them, saying with a loud voice, If any man worship the beast and his image, and receive his mark in his forehead, or in his hand, The same shall drink of the wine of the wrath of God, which is poured out without mixture into the cup of His indignation; and he shall be tormented with fire and brimstone in the presence of the holy angels, and in the presence of the Lamb: And the smoke of their torment ascends up for ever and ever: and they have no rest day nor night, who worship the beast and his image, and whosoever receives the mark of his name."*[35]

John heard the angel declare that the punishment of those who worship the Devil and his Antichrist will be suffering forever. The unsaved will have no rest day or night for eternity. He later describes the types of persons who will end up suffering in Hell:

> *"And He that sat upon the throne said, Behold, I make all things new. And He said unto me, Write: for these words are true and faithful. And He said unto me, It is done. I am Alpha and Omega, the beginning and the end. I will give unto him that is athirst of the fountain of the water of life freely. He that overcomes shall inherit all things; and I will be his God, and he shall be My son. But the fearful, and unbelieving, and the abominable, and murderers, and whoremongers, and sorcerers, and idolaters, and all liars, shall have their part in the lake which burns with fire and brimstone: which is the second death."*[36]

The horror of Hell is unimaginable to our finite minds. However, I believe there will be a worse pain than that caused by the flames. Jesus made an intriguing statement when He spoke in a parable about the punishment that awaits the unsaved:

> *"And cast you the unprofitable servant into outer darkness: there shall be weeping and gnashing of teeth."*[37]

Although this verse is part of a parable I believe that Jesus is stating a truth about eternal punishment. The next verse after this one starts the description of the judgment of the sheep and the goats and the punishment meted out to the people by Jesus Christ. Here He describes the place of punishment as *"outer darkness"*. Whether this is part of the different degrees or levels of punishment that I mentioned above is unclear. It could also be that once a person is thrown into the lake of fire, they descend into darkness beneath the surface. If so, I believe that these tormented souls will no longer be able to feel the presence of God.

Even in the fallen world we live in now we can still feel God's presence. We may not know that it is His presence we are feeling but nonetheless it is here. Those in Hell may suffer most by not being able to sense God anywhere around them. This will lead to an unimaginable loneliness that will cause them to weep and grind their teeth (an allusion to the physical bodies that will exist in eternity).

I have heard people say that they are going to "party" in Hell with their friends. As you have just read, Hell will be anything but a party. On the contrary, Hell is a real, living horror that we humans cannot comprehend. Mercifully, God has made a way for His human creations to escape the fires of Hell. He did this by coming down in the person of His Son, Jesus Christ, and suffering Himself by dying for the sins of humanity:

> *"For God so loved the world, that He gave His only begotten Son, that whosoever believeth in Him should not perish, but have everlasting life. For God sent not His Son into the world to condemn the world; but that the world through Him might be saved. He that believeth on Him is not condemned: but he that believeth not is condemned already, because he hath not believed in the name of the only begotten Son of God."*[38]

Fire and Brimstone

I wrote at the beginning of this chapter that the concept of Hell has always scared me. As I wrote this last section on Hell, I realized this concept still puts the fear of God in me. Some people believe that modern-day preachers should not preach on the subject of Hell. I strongly disagree with this assertion for the simple fact that people should know what awaits them if they continue rejecting the truth of God and His Son Jesus Christ.

The New Testament writer Jude, possibly a brother of Jesus, also states that preaching Hell needs to be done in some cases:

> *"Keep yourselves in the love of God, looking for the mercy of our Lord Jesus Christ unto eternal life. And of some have compassion, making a difference: And others save with fear, pulling them out of the fire; hating even the garment spotted by the flesh. Now unto Him that is able to keep you from falling, and to present you faultless before the presence of His glory with exceeding joy, To the only*

> *wise God our Savior, be glory and majesty, dominion and power, both now and ever. Amen."*[39]

Jude says that we can save some persons by showing them the compassion and mercy of God. However, he states that others need to be saved by putting the fear of God in them and thereby "*pulling them out of the fire*".

If after reading this chapter you are unsure of where you will spend eternity, please go to the Chapter 19 in this book. There I will tell how you can be saved from an eternity of Hell and instead experience an unimaginable joy for eternity in Heaven. After you have read that chapter return to the next chapter. There I will discuss what the Bible has to say about what awaits us when we will be with the Almighty God who created us forever and ever.

---

1 *Isaiah 64:6*
2 *I Corinthians 13:1-3*
3 *I John 4:16*
4 *Romans 3:9-12, 23*
5 *John 6:28-29*
6 *Ephesians 2:8-9*
7 *Titus 3:3-7*
8 *I John 2:1*
9 *Hebrews 12:29*
10 *Isaiah 6:1-7*
11 *John 8:23-24*
12 *Hebrews 10:26-31*
13 *Genesis 5:21-24*
14 *Revelation 20:14-15*
15 *Luke 16:19-24*
16 *Ephesians 4:8-10*
17 *Ezekiel 18:21-23*
18 *II Peter 3:9*
19 *Isaiah 59:1-2*
20 *Matthew 11:22-24*
21 *Isaiah 6:5*
22 *Luke 10:17-18*
23 *Luke 15:7, 10*
24 *Matthew 5:21-22*
25 *Matthew 5:27-28*

[26] *Isaiah 55:6-9*

[27] *Joshua 18:16; II Chronicles 28:3, 33:6; Jeremiah 7:31-32, 19:2-6*

[28] *Revelation 20:10*

[29] *Matthew 25:41*

[30] *Revelation 20:15*

[31] *Revelation 21:27*

[32] Charles Taze Russell founded a religious movement that would become the Jehovah Witnesses. Because he couldn't reconcile the idea of the mercy of God with the punishment of God, Russell rejected the concept of Hell. This rejection is continued by the modern day Jehovah Witnesses.

[33] *Mark 9:43-44*

[34] *Matthew 25:41, 46*

[35] *Revelation 14:9-11*

[36] *Revelation 21:5-8*

[37] *Matthew 25:30*

[38] *John 3:16-18*

[39] *Jude 21-25*

14 – Eternity

Now we come to my favorite chapter in the whole Bible, Revelation 21. Every time I read it my spirit becomes tender at the awesome beauty that John tries his best to describe. It makes me regret every sin that I have committed because they might have kept me from going to such a place.

If you have never read this chapter in Revelation in its entirety you may want to take a moment and do so. I believe it will inspire you to want to draw closer to God in this life.

A New Heaven, A New Earth, and a New Jerusalem

After John saw the final judgment of the unsaved God showed him what eternity would be like for the saved:

> *"And I saw a new heaven and a new earth: for the first heaven and the first earth were passed away; and there was no more sea. And I John saw the holy city, new Jerusalem, coming down from God out of heaven, prepared as a bride adorned for her husband."*
>
> *- Revelation 21:1-2*

John sees the newly made eternal Heaven and Earth and Jerusalem. There is no more existence in any dimension except the eternal one. This new earth will not contain any seas or oceans. There will be at least one river as we shall see but it seems there will not be any other bodies of water on this new earth. Later we will also read that there may not be any other celestial bodies in eternity either.

Everyone will have a glorified body with which they will move about. This will be the beginning of eternity, which is a concept that our finite minds are not able to grasp. Then however, we will understand eternity as the apostle Paul states:

> *"For now we see through a glass, darkly; but then* [i.e. eternity] *face to face: now I know in part; but then shall I know even as also I am known."*[1]

> *"And I heard a great voice out of heaven saying, Behold, the tabernacle of God is with men, and He will dwell with them, and they shall be His people, and God Himself shall be with them, and be their God."*
>
> *- Revelation 21:3*

I find it interesting when Christians say that when they get to Heaven they want to talk to the apostle Paul or the other disciples or Moses and the other great men and women of God spoken of in the Bible. I too would like to speak to every one of them and I am sure that we will throughout eternity. However, I believe that we are going to be so overwhelmed by being in the presence of God and His heavenly creations that what we currently desire to do will become secondary to what we will want to do when we get there.

The next thing John says should make humans, who have suffered and toiled in this life, very joyful:

> *"And God shall wipe away all tears from their eyes; and there shall be no more death, neither sorrow, nor crying, neither shall there be any more pain: for the former things are passed away. And He that sat upon the throne said, Behold, I make all things new."*
>
> \- *Revelation 21:4-5a*

There will be no more death or sorrow or weeping or pain. Some people wonder if they will remember their loved ones who did not accept Jesus Christ as their Savior and therefore will be separated from them for eternity. I believe the answer is that since the former things have passed away we will not have a memory of them. However, I hope that our loved ones will be in Heaven with us to experience the unimaginable joy that we will have in the presence of God.

The beauty of eternity is unfathomable in our current state yet John is still able to give us a sense of its awesomeness:

> *"And there came unto me one of the seven angels which had the seven bowls full of the seven last plagues, and talked with me, saying, Come here, I will show thee the bride, the Lamb's wife. And he carried me away in the spirit to a great and high mountain, and showed me that great city, the holy Jerusalem, descending out of heaven from God, Having the glory of God: and her light was like unto a stone most precious, even like a jasper stone, clear as crystal; And had a wall great and high, and had twelve gates, and at the gates twelve angels, and names written thereon, which are the names of the twelve tribes of the children of Israel: On the east three gates; on the north three gates; on the south three gates; and on the west three gates. And the wall of the city had twelve foundations, and in them the names of the twelve apostles of the Lamb. And he that talked with me had a golden reed to measure the city, and the gates thereof, and the wall thereof. And the city lies foursquare, and the length is as large as the breadth: and he measured the city with the reed, twelve thousand furlongs. The length and the breadth and the height of it are equal. And he measured the wall thereof, an hundred and forty and four cubits, according to the measure of a man, that is, of the angel. And the building of the wall of it was of jasper: and the city was pure gold, like unto clear glass. And the foundations of the wall of the city were garnished with all manner of precious stones. The first foundation was jasper; the second, sapphire; the third,*

a chalcedony; the fourth, an emerald; The fifth, sardonyx; the sixth, sardius; the seventh, chrysolyte; the eighth, beryl; the ninth, a topaz; the tenth, a chrysoprasus; the eleventh, a jacinth; the twelfth, an amethyst. And the twelve gates were twelve pearls: every several gate was of one pearl: and the street of the city was pure gold, as it were transparent glass."

- Revelation 21:9-21

The angel takes John to where he can witness the New Jerusalem descending to the New Earth from Heaven. What he sees astonishes him as he describes the city as having the glory of God and likens it to a precious stone.

The city is fifteen hundred miles wide, long, and high. He sees a wall surrounding it that is two-hundred and sixteen feet high. The city consists of pure gold and the wall is jasper, which would suggest a swirl of colors. The wall had twelve gates made of pearl that lead into the city. The streets are made of pure gold and are transparent. I think the most beautiful description John gives is that of the foundation stones of the city. There are twelve rows of the most precious stones and gems known to us that are built one upon another. Although he does not say how big each stone is there are foundation stones in the modern city of Jerusalem that weigh more than forty tons. Here John is describing the foundation stones for a city that is *fifteen hundred miles high.* These stones must be incredibly large. It is hard to imagine a sapphire, emerald, or topaz weighing hundreds of tons yet this is what John sees. I believe that God created the New Jerusalem with transparent walls, foundation stones, and streets so that we will be able to see the light of His glory shining everywhere. I cannot imagine what the experience of dwelling in such a place will be like. Well said by the apostle Paul when he wrote, *"But as it is written, Eye has not seen, nor ear heard, neither have entered into the heart of man, the things which God has prepared for them that love Him."*[2]

> *"And I saw no temple therein: for the Lord God Almighty and the Lamb are the Temple of it. And the city had no need of the sun, neither of the moon, to shine in it: for the glory of God did lighten it, and the Lamb is the light thereof. And the nations of them which are saved shall walk in the light of it: and the kings of the earth do bring their glory and honor into it. And the gates of it shall not be shut at all by day: for there shall be no night there. And they shall bring the glory and honor of the nations into it. And there shall in no wise enter into it any thing that defiles, neither whatsoever works abomination, or makes a lie: but they which are written in the Lamb's book of life."*
>
> *- Revelation 21:22-27*

The only light we will need in eternity will be the light of God's glory and that of His Son Jesus Christ. Just as we cannot currently understand the significance of sin's impact in the eternal realm, so too we cannot grasp the glorious effulgence of the holy presence of God that exists there. There will be no darkness either in the corporeal nature of the New Jerusalem or in the hearts of those who will dwell there.

> *"And he showed me a pure river of water of life, clear as crystal, proceeding out of the throne of God and of the Lamb. In the midst of the street of it, and on either side of the river, was there the tree of life, which bare twelve manner of fruits, and yielded her fruit every month: and the leaves of the tree were for the healing of the nations. And there shall be no more curse: but the throne of God and of the Lamb shall be in it; and His servants shall serve Him: And they shall see His face; and His name shall be in their foreheads. And there shall be no night there; and they need no candle, neither light of the sun; for the Lord God gives them light: and they shall reign for ever and ever."*
>
> *- Revelation 22:1-5*

The river of life could very well be a manifestation of the Holy Spirit. Jesus spoke of the Spirit in these terms, *"He that believes on Me, as the scripture has said, out of his belly shall flow rivers of living water. (But this spoke He of the Spirit, which they that believe on Him should receive: for the Holy Ghost was not yet given; because that Jesus was not yet glorified.)"*[3] We will be able to see God face to face and we will serve Him. However, this service will not consist of toil and labor. God cursed the earth when Adam and Eve sinned in the Garden of Eden, *"And unto Adam He said, Because you have hearkened unto the voice of your wife, and have eaten of the tree, of which I commanded thee, saying, Thou shall not eat of it: cursed is the ground for your sake; in toil shall you eat of it all the days of thy life; Thorns also and thistles shall it bring forth to you; and you shall eat the herb of the field; In the sweat of your face shall you eat bread, till you return unto the ground; for out of it were you taken: for dust you are, and unto dust shall you return."*[4] John declared that the curse will be removed in eternity. It will be a pleasurable experience to serve God forever.

"And he said unto me, These sayings are faithful and true: and the Lord God of the holy prophets sent His angel to show unto His servants the things which must shortly be done. Behold, I come quickly: blessed is he that keeps the sayings of the prophecy of this book. And I John saw these things, and heard them. And when I had heard and seen, I fell down to worship before the feet of the angel which showed me these things. Then said he unto me, See you do it not: for I am thy fellow servant, and of your brethren the prophets, and of them which keep the sayings of this book: worship God. And he said unto me, Seal not the sayings of the prophecy of this book: for the time is at hand. He that is unjust, let him be unjust still: and he which is filthy, let him be filthy still: and he that is righteous, let him be righteous still: and he that is holy, let him be holy still."

- Revelation 22:6-11

The Book of Revelation was ordained by God to be written to show *"His servants the things which must shortly be done."* God sees time from a different perspective than humans do. Though it has been nearly two thousand years since John wrote these words, God declared that these events would occur *"shortly"*. A prayer of Moses recorded in a Psalm declared, *"For a thousand years in your sight are but as yesterday when it is past, and as a watch in the night."*[5] The apostle Peter also affirmed that God sees time differently than we do, *"But, beloved, be not ignorant of this one thing, that one day is with the Lord as a thousand years, and a thousand years as one day."*[6] Therefore, it has only been "two days" since God revealed His plans for the future. I believe that the end-times are going to happen shortly by our standards too as we will see in Part Three of this book.

John was so overwhelmed by the vision of eternity that he fell down at the angel's feet to worship him. The angel immediately told him not to do that because he was a servant of God just like the human servants of God. In Chapter 6 of this book, I quoted this verse as one of the examples that illustrate that Jesus is God. The Bible records several instances where humans tried to worship angels or other humans because they sensed God's presence around them. In each case they were told by the objects of their veneration not to worship them. They were to worship God alone. The only exception to this was when people fell before Jesus' feet to worship Him. Not once did He tell them not to worship Him. There can only be one reason Jesus did not stop them in their adoration of Him: He is God in the personage of His Son.

Jesus states in this passage that He will bless the one who observes the prophecies of the Book of Revelation. This is a reaffirmation of the words that John wrote at the beginning of Revelation, *"Blessed is he that reads, and they that hear the words of this prophecy, and keep those things which are written therein: for the time is at hand."*[7] This is the only book in the Bible that declares a person will be blessed for reading, hearing, and observing it. I find it ironic that throughout Church history many teachers have avoided teaching on the Book of Revelation because it seems to be hard to understand. Yet God declares a blessing on those who do read it.

The angel commanded John not to keep these prophecies to himself. He wanted the followers of Jesus Christ to know what waited for them after a lifetime of serving God and His Son Jesus Christ.

Some people have wondered that if after they die, could they still sin and be removed from Heaven. John makes it clear here that the answer to that question is *"no"*. Whatever condition a person dies in will be their state forever. Those made holy and righteous through the blood of Jesus Christ will remain holy and righteous for eternity. Those who die apart from Jesus Christ will be unjust and filthy forever. As I stated earlier, there is no second chance for a person after they die.

> *"And, behold, I come quickly; and My reward is with Me, to give every man according as his work shall be. I am Alpha and Omega, the beginning and the end, the first and the last. Blessed are they that do His commandments, that they may have right to the tree of life, and may enter in through the gates into the city. For without are dogs, and sorcerers, and whoremongers, and murderers, and idolaters, and whosoever loves and makes a lie."*
>
> *- Revelation 22:12-15*

Jesus Christ is the consummate being and the reason that eternity exists. Alpha and Omega are the first and last letters of the Greek language. The entire New Testament was originally written in Greek. The purpose of the New Testament is to testify of Jesus Christ and His redeeming grace. From the first Greek letter written in Matthew 1:1 to the last Greek letter written in Revelation 22:21, God's entire plan of salvation through His Son Jesus Christ is laid out for all to see. Those who receive God's plan of salvation will enter in the gates of the New Jerusalem and abide with God forever. Those who reject it will be separated from the glorious splendor of eternity with God and be cast into Hell where they will not sense God's presence ever again.

> *"I Jesus have sent mine angel to testify unto you these things in the churches. I am the root and the offspring of David,*

and the bright and morning star. And the Spirit and the bride say, Come. And let him that hears say, Come. And let him that is thirsty come. And whosoever will, let him take the water of life freely. For I testify unto every man that hears the words of the prophecy of this book, If any man shall add unto these things, God shall add unto him the plagues that are written in this book: And if any man shall take away from the words of the book of this prophecy, God shall take away his part out of the book of life, and out of the holy city, and from the things which are written in this book. He which testifies these things says, Surely I come quickly. Amen. Even so, come, Lord Jesus. The grace of our Lord Jesus Christ be with you all. Amen."

- *Revelation 22:16-21*

Jesus Himself ordained that the future be shown to His followers in the Book of Revelation. The Holy Spirit declares that the offer to live in eternity with God is open to anyone who thirsts after the righteousness of God. It is so important that the truths of God are represented accurately to people that a curse is pronounced upon those who would change the truths that are in the Book of Revelation.

The last verses in the Bible offer hope to those who have been burdened by life. Jesus is coming again and sooner rather than later. If you accept His free gift of salvation, then His grace will be with you in this life and for eternity.

This concludes Part Two of my book and the prophecies that Jesus will fulfill with His second coming. As we just read, Jesus said that He was coming quickly. It has been nearly two thousand years since He spoke these words. That means that we are two thousand years closer to His second coming and the fulfillment of all these prophecies. As I stated at the beginning of this book, I believe that God has given us the timing of these events in His word, the Holy Bible. I will now address that subject in Part Three.

---

[1] *I Corinthians 13:12*
[2] *I Corinthians 2:9*
[3] *John 7:38-39*
[4] *Genesis 3:17-19*
[5] *Psalm 90:4*
[6] *II Peter 3:8*
[7] *Revelation 1:3*

<u>Part Three</u>

God's Timepiece: The Land Of Israel

Introduction to Part Three

In Part One of this book I illustrated how Jesus of Nazareth fulfilled all the biblical prophecies concerning the suffering Messiah with His first coming. In Part Two, I listed the biblical prophecies concerning the triumphant Messiah that Jesus will fulfill with His second coming. Here in Part Three, I will show how the Land of Israel and the Jewish people are at the center of God's timing for the end-times events.

Jesus, Paul, and some of the other prophets of the Bible gave signs for Jesus' followers to watch for so that they would know when the end-times were beginning. I will be discussing some of these signs in Chapter 18. However, I believe the Bible makes it clear that all the end-times prophecies revolve around the Jewish presence in the modern state of Israel.

In this section, I will lay down a biblical foundation to support the premise that I am proposing. Chapter 18 will consummate the purpose of this book by showing that we are indeed living on the brink of the last days.

15 - Eretz Yisrael: The Land of Israel

I believe the second greatest country in the history of the world is the United States of America. God has blessed our country with resources and creative people many times over. Our country was founded upon the principle of religious freedom and the Judeo-Christian ethic. American missionaries have taken the lead in the propagation of the gospel to the four corners of the earth. No country in history has had the military power that the United States has wielded to fight for freedom in this country and around the world. Americans have shared their wealth with the poor and hurting people of the world. With all its historical and current shortcomings, I am proud to be an American citizen. Of course, I am more thankful that God has granted me citizenship in His kingdom for eternity.

However, I believe the greatest country in history is the historical nation of Israel. That is because God chose it as His dwelling place and has granted it His divine favor:

> *"For the LORD has chosen Zion; He has desired it for His habitation. This is My rest for ever: here will I dwell; for I have desired it. I will abundantly bless her provision: I will satisfy her poor with bread. I will also clothe her priests with salvation: and her saints shall shout aloud for joy. There will I make the Horn of David to bud: I have ordained a lamp for Mine Anointed. His enemies will I clothe with shame: but upon Himself shall His crown flourish."*[1]

God, the omnipotent Creator of the universe, chose Zion or Israel as the place of His habitation. Out of all the beautiful countries in the world He chose this small strip of land along the eastern Mediterranean Sea to be His dwelling place.

God has a special affection for the land of Israel:

> *"And that you may prolong your days in the land [of Israel], which the LORD swore unto your fathers to give unto them and to their seed, a land that flows with milk and honey. For the land, where you go in to possess it, is not as the land of Egypt, from where you came out, where you sowed your seed, and watered it with your foot, as a garden of herbs: But the land, where you go to possess it, is a land of hills and valleys, and drinks water of the rain of heaven: A land which the LORD your God cares for: the eyes of the LORD your God are always upon it, from the beginning of the year even unto the end of the year."*[2]

God gave the land of Israel to the Jews and promised it would be a land flowing with *"milk and honey"*. Here the Bible declares that God *cares* about the land of Israel and that His eyes are *always* watching it.

Just as God has a special affection for the land, so too He has a special affection for the people that He gave it to, the Jews:

> *"When the Most High divided to the nations their inheritance, when He separated the sons of Adam, He set the bounds of the people according to the number of the children of Israel. For the LORD's portion is His people; Jacob* [i.e., Israel] *is the lot of His inheritance. He found him in a desert land, and in the waste howling wilderness; He led him about, He instructed him, He kept him as the apple of His eye."*[3]

When God set up the boundaries for the nations of the world He gave the land of Israel to the Jews and gave them the special appellation: *"The apple of His eye"*. Just as our children are the apples of our eyes, so too is the Jewish nation of Israel the pleasure of His eye.

Though God has disciplined His children many times in history because of their rebellion, He always protects them from complete destruction and punishes those who seek to destroy them:

> *"Deliver yourself, O Zion, that dwell with the daughter of Babylon. For thus saith the LORD of hosts; After the glory has He sent Me unto the nations which spoiled you: for he that touches you touches the apple of His eye. For, behold, I will shake Mine hand upon them, and they shall be a spoil to their servants: and you shall know that the LORD of hosts has sent Me. Sing and rejoice, O daughter of Zion: for, lo, I come, and I will dwell in the midst of you, saith the LORD. And many nations shall be joined to the LORD in that day, and shall be My people: and I will dwell in the midst of you, and you shall know that the LORD of hosts has sent Me unto you. And the LORD shall inherit Judah His portion in the Holy Land, and shall choose Jerusalem again. Be silent, O all flesh, before the LORD: for He is raised up out of His holy habitation."*[4]

God had allowed the Babylonian empire to punish Israel for their rebellion against Him by conquering it. However, God declared that He would never leave them in a state of captivity. He would send the Messiah to set them free and He will dwell in the midst of Israel. God refers to Israel as the *"Holy Land"*, a reference that Jews and Christians still use to this day.

The Babylonian captivity was just one of many times that God punished the Jews for their disobedience to Him. In this case He brought the Jews back to the Land of Israel after seventy years of captivity.

At other times God allowed foreign powers to rule over the Jews while they were living in Israel. It was at such a time when the Romans were occupying the land that God sent His Son to deliver the Jews, not from foreign oppression but the oppression of sin, which is more deadly than any earthly power.

Forty years after the Jews as a nation rejected Jesus as their Messiah, God dispersed them throughout the known world. As we will see though, God was not through with the Jewish people. His word declares many times that He will return the Jews to the land of Israel once and for all.

The reason for this is that God promised the land of Israel to Abraham and His Jewish descendants until the ordinances of the celestial bodies cease to exist.[5] Though modern Islam and even some Christian organizations and churches reject this premise, the Bible does not.

The Abrahamic Covenant

Throughout the Bible God makes various covenants or contracts with His human creations. Some of these covenants have conditions attached to them while others are unconditional. One example is the New Testament or Covenant, which has the condition that if we accept God's Son, Jesus Christ, as our Savior and receive forgiveness through His sacrificial death, then we will be saved for eternity. However, the covenant that I will discuss in this section is unconditional.

Almost four thousand years ago God chose a man named Abraham to fulfill His purpose for the human race. Abraham faithfully served God for the rest of his life. This faithfulness resulted in three of the world's major religious faiths: Judaism, Christianity, and Islam. It also led to Abraham's Jewish descendants having the honor of giving God's Son and Messiah to the world.

God had spoken to Abraham while he was living in the city of Haran, which was located near the modern Syrian-Turkey border. It was there that God made His first promise to Abraham (originally his name was Abram until God changed it):

> *"Now the LORD had said unto Abram, Get you out of your country, and from your kindred, and from your father's house, unto a land that I will show you: And I will make of you a great nation, and I will bless you, and make your name great; and you shall be a blessing: And I will bless them that bless you, and curse him that curses you: and in you shall all families of the earth be blessed. So Abram departed, as the LORD had spoken unto him; and Lot went*

> *with him: and Abram was seventy and five years old when he departed out of Haran. And Abram took Sarai* [changed later to Sarah] *his wife, and Lot his brother's son, and all their substance that they had gathered, and the souls that they had gotten in Haran; and they went forth to go into the land of Canaan; and into the land of Canaan they came."*[6]

God tells Abraham to leave the land of his fathers and go to the land of Canaan, which would later become Israel. The first promise that God made to Abraham was that He would make a great nation out of his descendants. God then tells him that He will bless those that bless him and his descendants and curse those who curse him and his descendants. Lastly, God tells Abraham that all the earth will be blessed because of him. This blessing came when the Messiah was born to one of Abraham's descendants. Thus, Abraham departed from Haran as the Lord had instructed him to.

After Abraham arrived in Canaan God made another promise to him:

> *"And Abram passed through the land unto the place of Shechem, unto the plain of Moreh. And the Canaanite was then in the land. And the LORD appeared unto Abram, and said, Unto your seed will I give this land: and there built he an altar unto the LORD, who appeared unto him."*[7]

God declares here that He is giving the land of Israel to Abraham's descendants. As we will see in a moment, God specifies that it is the *Jewish* descendants of Abraham who are entitled to the land of Israel.

Next, God gives to Abraham the boundaries of the land of Israel that his descendants will inherit:

> *"And [Abraham] went on his journeys from the south even to Bethel, unto the place where his tent had been at the beginning, between Bethel and Ai; Unto the place of the altar, which he had made there at the first: and there Abram called on the name of the LORD...And the LORD*

said unto Abram, after that Lot was separated from him, Lift up now your eyes, and look from the place where you are northward, and southward, and eastward, and westward: For all the land which you see, to you will I give it, and to your seed for ever."[8]

The city of Bethel is located about ten miles north of Jerusalem. From there Abraham could see the land of Israel spreading out before him. God promises Abraham that all this land will belong to his descendants *forever.*

Abraham moved south and dwelt in the city of Hebron, which is located about twenty miles south of Jerusalem. While Abraham was living there God appeared to him and made him another promise:

"After these things the word of the LORD came unto Abram in a vision, saying, Fear not, Abram: I am your shield, and your exceeding great reward. And Abram said, LORD God, what will You give me, seeing I go childless, and the steward of my house is this Eliezer of Damascus? And Abram said, Behold, to me You have given no seed: and, lo, one born in my house is my heir. And, behold, the word of the LORD came unto him, saying, This shall not be your heir; but he that shall come forth out of your own bowels shall be your heir. And He brought him forth abroad, and said, Look now toward heaven, and tell the stars, if you be able to number them: and He said unto him, So shall your seed be. And he believed in the LORD; and He counted it to him for righteousness."[9]

Abraham was concerned because he had no physical heirs to inherit his legacy. He told God the only person that was close to being his heir was his steward Eliezer. God tells him that Eliezer will not be his heir but that He will give Abraham a son who will inherit the blessings that God gives to Abraham. His son will come out of Abraham's loins and his descendants will be as many as the stars in heaven. Because Abraham believed God's word, God counted him as a righteous man.

Immediately after this God makes a covenant with Abraham:

"And He said unto him, I am the LORD that brought you out of Ur of the Chaldees, to give you this land to inherit it. And he said, LORD God, whereby shall I know that I shall inherit it? And He said unto him, Take Me an heifer of three years old, and a she goat of three years old, and a ram of three years old, and a turtledove, and a young pigeon. And he took unto him all these, and divided them in the midst, and laid each piece one against another: but the birds divided he not. And when the fowls came down upon the carcasses, Abram drove them away. And when the sun was going down, a deep sleep fell upon Abram; and, lo, an horror of great darkness fell upon him. And He said unto Abram, Know for certain that your seed shall be a stranger in a land that is not theirs, and shall serve them; and they shall afflict them four hundred years; And also that nation, whom they shall serve, will I judge: and afterward shall they come out with great substance. And you shall go to your fathers in peace; you shall be buried in a good old age. But in the fourth generation they shall come here again: for the iniquity of the Amorites is not yet full. And it came to pass, that, when the sun went down, and it was dark, behold a smoking furnace, and a flaming torch that passed between those pieces. In the same day the LORD made a covenant with Abram, saying, Unto your seed have I given this land, from the river of Egypt unto the great river, the river Euphrates: The Kenites, and the Kenizzites, and the Kadmonites, And the Hittites, and the Perizzites, and the Rephaims, And the Amorites, and the Canaanites, and the Girgashites, and the Jebusites."[10]

This passage is the foundation of the current Israeli-Arab conflict that exists in the Middle East. It is crucial that you understand exactly what took place here.

Although Abraham had no trouble believing that God was going to give him a son, for some reason he wanted reassurance that God was also going to give him and his descendants the land of Israel forever. Thus, God instructs Abraham to get a heifer, a goat, a ram, a turtledove, and a young pigeon and bring them before the Lord. It is interesting that God will later tell the Jews that each of these animals will be an acceptable Temple sacrifice to Him under the laws given to Moses. Abraham did as God told him to do and cut each of these dead animals in half, except for the birds. He laid the halves of the animals opposite each other and left a small pathway between them. Then God caused a deep sleep to come over Abraham during which he suffered a nightmare. God tells him that his descendants will be strangers in a strange land [Egypt] and shall be that people's slaves for four hundred years. However, God declares that He will punish Egypt and return Abraham's descendants to the land of Israel. The reason for the delay is because God will allow time for the people currently living in the land of Israel, the Amorites, to repent of their sins. Since God knows that they will not repent, He promises that Abraham's people will take the land from the Kenites, the Kenizzites, the Kadmonites, the Hittites, the Perizzites, the Rephaims, the Amorites, the Canaanites, the Girgashites, and the Jebusites.

Then to confirm this promise God performs a strange ritual. While Abraham is sleeping, yet with some comprehension of what is taking place, a flaming torch that seemingly represents the Lord passes through the animal carcasses. This ritual was God's way of making Abraham understand that He was making a covenant or contract with him. By performing this deed God was telling Abraham that He would indeed give the land of Israel to him and his descendants.

There are a couple of things to note here that are of extreme importance. The first is that this covenant was unconditional. Abraham did not have to do anything for God to give him the land of Israel. He did not have to serve God faithfully or perform any other act in order for God to give him the land. God declared He would give possession of the land to Abraham without any strings attached. This is evidenced by the fact that Abraham was asleep during the making of this covenant. This becomes an important component in Chapter 17 of this book where I discuss a doctrine called "Replacement Theology".

The other noteworthy item in this passage is that God states that Abraham's descendants would displace the current residents of the land. In recent history Arabs have made unsubstantiated claims that their ancestors were the ancient Canaanites. They claim this to support their position that the land of Israel belongs to them since their ancestors predated the ancient Hebrews. There is absolutely no historical evidence that they are related to the Canaanites. Even if by some stretch of the imagination their claims were true, God states here that He took the land from them and gave it to the Jews.

Abraham, Ishmael, and the Arabs

God promised Abraham that he would have a son who would inherit the promises that God gave to him. As sometimes happens with humans, we take it upon ourselves to "help" God out in fulfilling His will. Such is the case with Abraham and his wife Sarai whose name God would later change to Sarah:

> *"Now Sarai Abram's wife bore him no children: and she had an handmaid, an Egyptian, whose name was Hagar. And Sarai said unto Abram, Behold now, the LORD has restrained me from bearing: I pray you, go in unto my maid; it may be that I may obtain children by her. And Abram hearkened to the voice of Sarai. And Sarai, Abram's wife, took Hagar her maid the Egyptian, after Abram had dwelt ten years in the land of Canaan, and gave her to her husband Abram to be his wife. And he went in unto Hagar, and she conceived: and when she saw that she had conceived, her mistress was despised in her eyes. And Sarai said unto Abram, My wrong be upon you: I have given my maid into your bosom; and when she saw that she had conceived, I was despised in her eyes: the LORD judge between me and you."*[11]

Just like Abraham, Sarah also wanted a child. It appears though that she was not willing to wait for God to fulfill His promise. In the culture that she lived in, it was permissible for a man to marry more than one woman at a time. Since Sarah was barren she told her husband to marry her servant Hagar in order that she might have a child by her. Abraham fulfilled his wife's wishes and Hagar became pregnant. This caused Hagar to believe that she was blessed of God and that her mistress, Sarah, was rejected by God. Understandably this led to a conflict between Sarah and Hagar:

> *"But Abram said unto Sarai, Behold, your maid is in your hand; do to her as it pleases you. And when Sarai dealt harshly with her, she fled from her face. And the angel of the LORD found her by a fountain of water in the wilderness, by the fountain in the way to Shur. And he said, Hagar, Sarai's maid, whence camest you? and where will you go? And she said, I flee from the face of my mistress Sarai. And the angel of the LORD said unto her, Return to your mistress, and submit yourself under her hands. And the angel of the LORD said unto her, I will multiply your seed exceedingly, that it shall not be numbered for multitude. And the angel of the LORD said unto her, Behold, you are with child and shall bear a son, and shall call his name Ishmael; because the LORD has heard your affliction."*[12]

Because Sarah had mistreated Hagar in response to her haughtiness, she fled from the presence of her mistress. The angel of the Lord told Hagar she needed to return and continue serving Sarah. He then promised her that she would bear a son whose name would be Ishmael. Through him the Lord would multiply Hagar's descendants exceedingly. This is almost the exact promise that God had made to Abraham. Hagar did return and gave birth to Ishmael when Abraham was eighty-six years old. However, it would not be until fourteen years later that God fulfilled His promise to Abraham by giving him a son by his wife Sarah.

God made a new covenant with Abraham that also reinforced the land covenant that He had made previously with him:

> *"And when Abram was ninety years old and nine, the LORD appeared to Abram, and said unto him, I am the Almighty God; walk before Me, and be you perfect. And I will make My covenant between Me and you, and will multiply you exceedingly. And Abram fell on his face: and God talked with him, saying, As for Me, behold, My covenant is*

> *with you, and you shall be a father of many nations. Neither shall your name any more be called Abram, but your name shall be Abraham; for a father of many nations have I made you. And I will make you exceeding fruitful, and I will make nations of you, and kings shall come out of you. And I will establish My covenant between Me and you and your seed after you in their generations for an everlasting covenant, to be a God unto you, and to your seed after you. And I will give unto you, and to your seed after you, the land wherein you are a stranger, all the land of Canaan, for an everlasting possession; and I will be their God. And God said unto Abraham, You shall keep My covenant therefore, you, and your seed after you in their generations. This is My covenant, which you shall keep, between Me and you and your seed after you; Every man child among you shall be circumcised. And you shall circumcise the flesh of your foreskin; and it shall be a token of the covenant between Me and you. And he that is eight days old shall be circumcised among you, every man child in your generations, he that is born in the house, or bought with money of any stranger, which is not of your seed."*[13]

God tells Abraham that he will be the father of many peoples. He also promises that He will be God to Abraham's descendants. Unlike the first covenant this promise or covenant does have a condition attached to it. It is to be an *everlasting* covenant and as a sign of Abraham's acceptance of this covenant with God he is to circumcise all the males in his family. Abraham's descendants are to do the same from generation to generation as a sign of their relationship with God.

God then declares that He will give the land of Israel to these descendants. At the time that God offered this covenant to Abraham, the only heir that he had was his son Ishmael, whom he later circumcises. Therefore, are Ishmael's descendants entitled to the land of Israel? God answers this question immediately after offering this covenant to Abraham:

> *"And God said unto Abraham, As for Sarai your wife, you shall not call her name Sarai, but Sarah shall her name be. And I will bless her, and give you a son also of her: yes, I will bless her, and she shall be a mother of nations; kings of people shall be of her. Then Abraham fell upon his face, and laughed, and said in his heart, Shall a child be born unto him that is an hundred years old? and shall Sarah, that is ninety years old, bear? And Abraham said unto God, O that Ishmael might live before you! And God said, Sarah your wife shall bear you a son indeed; and you shall call his name Isaac: and I will establish My covenant with him for an everlasting covenant, and with his seed after him. And as for Ishmael, I have heard you: Behold, I have blessed him, and will make him fruitful, and will multiply him exceedingly; twelve princes shall he beget, and I will make him a great nation. But My covenant will I establish with Isaac, which Sarah shall bear unto you at this set time in the next year."*[14]

Abraham still believes that God is going to fulfill this covenant through his son Ishmael. However, God straightens him out on this matter. He is not going to fulfill this covenant through Ishmael but through the son that God had originally promised to Abraham, Isaac. God does declare that he is going to bless Ishmael with many descendants.

The modern Arabs claim that Ishmael is the patriarch of their people. If this is true then God did indeed fulfill His promise to bless Ishmael with many descendants. The crucial point is that in this passage God explicitly states that it will be Abraham's descendants through his son Isaac who will inherit the land of Israel. *There is no other possible interpretation of this verse.*

How do the Muslims of today get around this passage in the Bible? By simply declaring that the Jews changed the wording of it so that instead of Ishmael being the true heir, they made Isaac the heir to God's covenant with Abraham. There are many problems with this theory. The biggest one is that the last book of the Old Testament was written one thousand years before the birth of Mohammed. There was no religion of Islam in existence until six hundred years after Jesus Christ came to earth. Therefore, the Jews had to be extraordinarily prescient, by one thousand years, to know that one day there would be a dispute over a small strip of land on the eastern Mediterranean seacoast. If the Jews had switched the names then that means the entire New Testament is based on a false premise.

The Bible makes it clear that the Messiah was to be a descendant of Abraham through Isaac and the seed of the Jewish King David. This would make Jesus a false prophet since He claimed numerous times to be the Son of David as a fulfillment of Messianic prophecy. However, this would conflict with Islamic claims that Jesus or "Isa" as they call Him is a prophet of Allah (though Muslims reject the idea that He is the Son of God). Since the Muslims know this is a fallacious argument they resort to other means to claim the land of Israel for their own. I mentioned one above concerning modern Arab-claims that they are the descendants of the Canaanites who predated the ancient Hebrews and thereby are the rightful heirs to the land of Israel. Nevertheless, God's word clearly disagrees with modern Arab-claims and declares that the Jews are the sole heirs to the land of Israel.

Abraham confirms this just before he dies when he gives all of his possessions to Isaac and not Ishmael:

> *"And Abraham gave all that he had unto Isaac...And these are the days of the years of Abraham's life which he lived, an hundred threescore and fifteen years. Then Abraham gave up the ghost, and died in a good old age, an old man, and full of years; and was gathered to his people. And his sons Isaac and Ishmael buried him in the cave of Machpelah, in the field of Ephron the son of Zohar the Hittite, which is before Mamre."*[15]

There was no question in Abraham's mind that Isaac was to be the heir through whom God would fulfill His covenants. God further delineates the family line of succession from Abraham through Isaac through Isaac's son, Jacob:

"And Isaac entreated the LORD for his wife, because she was barren: and the LORD was entreated of him, and Rebekah his wife conceived. And the children struggled together within her; and she said, If it be so, why am I thus? And she went to enquire of the LORD. And the LORD said unto her, Two nations are in your womb, and two manner of people shall be separated from your bowels; and the one people shall be stronger than the other people; and the elder shall serve the younger. And when her days to be delivered were fulfilled, behold, there were twins in her womb. And the first came out red, all over like an hairy garment; and they called his name Esau. And after that came his brother out, and his hand took hold on Esau's heel; and his name was called Jacob: and Isaac was threescore years old when she bore them."[16]

Isaac married Rebekah and she gave birth to twins, Jacob and Esau. Even though Esau was born first God declared that Jacob would have precedence over him. He later promises Jacob that he will be the recipient of the covenants that He made with his grandfather Abraham and his father Isaac:

"And [Jacob] came upon a certain place, and tarried there all night, because the sun was set; and he took of the stones of that place, and put them for his pillows, and lay down in that place to sleep. And he dreamed, and behold a ladder set up on the earth, and the top of it reached to heaven: and behold the angels of God ascending and descending on it. And, behold, the LORD stood above it, and said, I am the LORD God of Abraham your father, and the God of Isaac: the land whereon you lie, to you will I give it, and to your seed; And your seed shall be as the dust of the earth, and you shall spread abroad to the west, and to the east, and to the north, and to the south: and in you and in your seed shall all the families of the earth be blessed. And, behold, I am with you, and will keep you in all places where you go, and will bring you again into this land; for I will not leave you, until I have done that which I have

> *spoken to you of. And Jacob awaked out of his sleep, and he said, Surely the LORD is in this place; and I knew it not."*[17]

God tells Jacob that He will fulfill the covenants He made with his fathers through his descendants. Consequently, the promise of the land of Israel will go through Isaac's son Jacob instead of his other son Esau. God also reaffirms the Messianic promise that He will bless the nations of the earth through Jacob's descendants.

A little while after this experience God again visits Jacob and changes his name:

> *"And he said unto him, What is your name? And he said, Jacob. And he said, Your name shall be called no more Jacob, but Israel: for as a prince have you power with God and with men, and have prevailed."*[18]

This is the first time in the Bible that the word "Israel" is used. At this point God declares that this is Jacob's new name. Later, it becomes synonymous with the name of the land where Jacob's descendants dwell.

Jacob ends up having thirteen children, twelve sons and one daughter. He names one of his sons "Judah". It is from this word that the appellation "Jew" derives and eventually is applied to all the descendants of Jacob's children.

When Jacob is old a famine sweeps through Israel. He and his family move down to Egypt. At first, they are welcomed but later they become captives and slaves of the Egyptians. This fulfilled the prophecy that God had spoken to Abraham when He made the original covenant with him. God told Abraham that his descendants would become slaves for four hundred years. Then He would bring them back to the land of Israel. He accomplished this deliverance through His servant Moses. It was Moses' successor, Joshua, who led the children of Israel into the "promised land" of Israel.

The Jews dwelt there off and on for the next fifteen hundred years. What happened after that is the subject of the next chapter.

Before leaving this section I want to mention one other aspect to the Jews' right to live in the land of Israel.

Christian Zionism

Many Christians such as myself fully support the Jews' right to the land of Israel. The fact that some Christian Zionists are excited that the Jews are back in Israel after nineteen hundred years is upsetting to some Jews. This is because they believe that these Christians only care about the fulfillment of end-times prophecy. Though I too, believe the return of the Jews to Israel is a fulfillment of prophecy that is not why I support the Jews' right to the land of Israel. I support them for the simple fact that God gave this land to the Jews. God, the Creator of the universe, can give anything He wants to whomever He wants. He declares in Isaiah, *"I am the LORD, your Holy One, the Creator of Israel, your King."*[19] Therefore, since He created Israel He can give it to whomever He desires. As we have seen, He gave the land of Israel to the Jews forever. That is the sole reason that I believe the land of Israel belongs to the Jews and them alone.

---

1 *Psalm 132:13-18*
2 *Deuteronomy 11:9-12*
3 *Deuteronomy 32:8-10*
4 *Zechariah 2:7-13*
5 *Jeremiah 31:35-37*
6 *Genesis 12:1-5*
7 *Genesis 12:6-7*
8 *Genesis 13:3-4, 14-15*
9 *Genesis 15:1-5*
10 *Genesis 15:7-21*
11 *Genesis 16:1-5*
12 *Genesis 16:6-11*
13 *Genesis 17:1-12*
14 *Genesis 17:15-21*
15 *Genesis 25:5, 7-8*
16 *Genesis 25:21-26*
17 *Genesis 28:11-16*
18 *Genesis 32:27-28*
19 *Isaiah 43:15*

16 - Israel No More?

From around 1400 B.C. to 135 A.D. the Jews dwelt in the land of Israel. During that time God raised up many prophets to warn, reprove, and encourage the Jews to live their lives according to the truths of His word. Sometimes He allowed foreign countries to conquer them as a form of chastisement. Other times He blessed them with bountiful harvests. The greatest blessing He gave to them was His Son, Jesus Christ. Regrettably, as a nation they rejected Him as their Messiah. This led to their dispersion throughout the world, which lasted until 1948 A.D.

After the last book of the Old Testament was written around 400 B.C., God allowed the Greek armies, under the leadership of Alexander the Great, to conquer the land of Israel. The Jews suffered greatly under his successors until the Jewish commander, Judah Maccabee, started a revolt against them in 167 B.C. This uprising eventually led to the defeat of the Greek armies and restored Jewish rule in Israel for one hundred years. After that, a new threat appeared on the scene, one that would change Jewish history forever.

The Dreadful and Terrible Beast

In Chapter 10 I discussed a vision that God gave to Daniel concerning the future of his people and the nation of Israel. In this vision Daniel saw four beasts that represented four kingdoms that would conquer Israel in succession. The first three beasts were the Babylonian Empire, the Medo-Persian Empire, and the Greek Empire under Alexander the Great. However, the fourth beast was worse than the first three. Daniel described it in graphic terms:

> *"After this I saw in the night visions, and behold a fourth beast, dreadful and terrible, and strong exceedingly; and it had great iron teeth: it devoured and broke in pieces, and stamped the residue with the feet of it: and it was diverse from all the beasts that were before it; and it had ten horns."*[1]

This beast represented the Roman Empire, the most powerful force ever to rule the world until that time. The Roman conquest of the Mediterranean region began in the Fourth Century B.C. In 63 B.C. the Roman general, Pompey the Great, invaded and conquered Jerusalem and thereby fulfilled this prophecy of Daniel's. The Jews would suffer under Roman oppression for the next two hundred years.

It was during that time that God sent His Son, Jesus Christ, to deliver the Jews from the oppression of sin. However, the Jewish religious leaders rejected Jesus as the Messiah and had the Romans crucify Him. The week of Jesus' passion, He talked about the future of Israel and the center of Jewish worship, the Temple in Jerusalem:

> *"And Jesus went out, and departed from the Temple: and His disciples came to Him for to show Him the buildings of the Temple. And Jesus said unto them, See you not all these things? Truly I say unto you, There shall not be left here one stone upon another, that shall not be thrown down."*[2]

> *"Behold, your house is left unto you desolate: and verily I say unto you, You shall not see Me, until the time come when you shall say, Blessed is He that comes in the name of the Lord."*[3]

Within forty years of Jesus speaking this first prophecy the Temple was indeed destroyed. The fulfillment of the second prophecy occurred sixty-five years after the destruction of the Temple. The desolation of the House or Nation of Israel transpired when the Romans defeated the Jews in a final Jewish revolt.

What led up to these events was a century and a half of suffering under Roman rule. A segment of the Jewish population known as Zealots finally decided to take on the Roman Empire.

The Jewish Revolt

From the time that Pompey the Great conquered Jerusalem in 63 B.C., the Jews had endured Roman procurators, governors and puppet-kings. In 66 A.D. an incident occurred that would change Israel's history for nearly two thousand years.

The last of the Roman procurators, Gessius Florus, seized a large sum of money from the Jewish Temple treasury. Shortly thereafter, the Jewish masses rioted in protest against this action and defeated the Roman garrison stationed in Jerusalem. The Romans responded by sending a large army from Syria to quell the rebellion. This force swept down through northern Israel in the region of Galilee. There they captured or killed thousands of Jews. Eventually the Roman troops made their way south to the outskirts of Jerusalem. After several days of trying to breach the city's walls, the Roman forces pulled back. At this point, the Roman emperor, Nero, placed General Vespasian in charge of the Roman army.

Although the Jewish forces had some successes early on in the revolt there was severe infighting among the many factions of their people. This weakened their position before the Romans and eventually led to disaster for them. Vespasian sought to take advantage of this situation by immediately laying siege to Jerusalem. However, the political situation in Rome changed with the death of the emperor Nero and caused a delay in his efforts to conquer Jerusalem. Vespasian went to Rome to become the new emperor and left Jerusalem in the hands of his son Titus. Finally, in the spring of 70 A.D., Titus began the army's assault on Jerusalem. By summer they had penetrated the city walls and prepared to attack the Jewish rebels who were defending the Temple.

The Romans tried to break through the inner massive walls that surrounded the Temple complex but were unsuccessful. Eventually they achieved their objective by burning the gates that led into the Temple area. The Roman soldiers entered the complex, slaughtered the Jewish defenders, and set fire to the Temple. As Jesus had prophesied forty years earlier, the destruction of the Jewish Temple was complete.

Though the Roman Empire had dealt the Jews an ignominious defeat and reduced the Jewish presence in Jerusalem through death and exile, the nation of Israel continued to exist for another sixty-five years.

However, because of the Jewish Revolt the Jews no longer had an organized religious system by which they could worship God. There would be no more Temple sacrifices and the Jewish religious leadership was in disarray. Out of this uncertainty the Pharisees became the uncontested leaders of the Jewish nation. They redefined the Jewish system of worship and set about developing it for the next several generations. The synagogue replaced the Temple as a place for Jews to worship. The rabbis replaced the Temple priests as the religious leaders of Judaism. Lastly, the study of Jewish religious writings, prayer services, and the performing of good deeds replaced the system of Temple sacrifices.

Although the Jews continued to dwell in Jerusalem and Israel, they did so without any Jewish civil authority. That all changed in 132 A.D. when a second Jewish revolt against Rome occurred. This time it led to the downfall of ancient Israel and to the dispersion of the Jews throughout the world for the next eighteen hundred years.

The End of Ancient Israel: The Son of the Star

Forty-seven years after the Romans destroyed the second Jewish Temple, a new emperor reigned in Rome. At first He put down some final outbreaks of Jewish rebellion around the eastern part of the empire. However, some time later it appeared to the Jews that this emperor, Hadrian, was going to show favor to them. They even believed that he was going to allow them to rebuild the Temple. As it turned out, such was not the case.

In 130 A.D. Hadrian came to Jerusalem with the intention of establishing a Roman colony there and renaming it Aelia Capitolina. On top of this, he issued decrees against Judaism such as the one forbidding circumcision. These developments along with the fact that it did not appear that the Romans were going to allow the Jews to rebuild their Temple after all led to an uprising among the Jewish population. A man by the apparent name of Shimon ben-Kosiva emerged as the leader of this second rebellion. For the next three years he would gain the upper hand against the Roman forces that occupied Israel. Although history is a little vague as to ben-Kosiva's real name, it is very clear as to name given to him by his followers.

One of the leading Jewish rabbis at that time was Akiva (or Akiba) ben-Joseph. He came to believe that ben-Kosiva was the Messiah who would deliver the Jews from Roman oppression and rebuild their Temple. Thus, he applied a Messianic prophecy in the Book of Numbers to him:

> *"I shall see Him, but not now: I shall behold Him, but not near: there shall come a Star out of Jacob, and a Scepter shall rise out of Israel, and shall smite the corners of Moab and destroy all the children of Sheth."*[4]

Rabbi Akiva declared that ben-Kosiva was this Messianic "Star" and called him "Shimon bar-Kokhba", which is Hebrew for: "Simon, son of the star". As it turned out, although bar-Kokhba was a charismatic and strong leader, he was not able ultimately to defeat the Roman Empire. After three years of fierce fighting his forces were defeated, Rabbi Akiva was tortured to death by the Romans, and he was slain in the Judean hills.

After quashing this second Jewish rebellion the Romans were determined not to let a third Jewish revolt happen ever again. They accomplished this by exiling most of the Jewish population from the land of Israel.

For the next eighteen hundred years the Jews were dispersed throughout the world. Tragically, in most of the countries they migrated to, non-Jews, including the Christian Church persecuted them mercilessly. Though many of these nations tried to destroy their Jewish identity, their efforts were in vain. The Jews continued to observe the Sabbath, study their religious writings, and celebrate the Jewish feasts ordained by God. They always concluded the Passover feast by reciting their eternal hope of living in the land of Israel: *"Next year in Jerusalem!"* As we will see, it would not be until 1948 that they were able to realize this dream.

Post-Jewish Israel

Almost two hundred years after the bar-Kokhba revolt, the Roman/Byzantine emperor Constantine adopted Christianity for his religion. After nearly three centuries of persecution, Christianity had finally gained a legal status in the Roman Empire. By this time however, the number of Gentile Christians dwarfed the number of Jewish Christians. Many of these Christians migrated to Israel and built churches and monasteries around the holy sites mentioned in the Bible. A lot of them treated the Jewish population still dwelling in Israel in a very un-Christian manner. They would not allow Jews to enter Jerusalem except for one day a year to mourn the destruction of their Temple. This was just the beginning of a long succession of foreign dominance in the land of Israel.

After a brief and ultimately unsuccessful Persian invasion of Israel in the early part of the Seventh Century to defeat the Byzantine army, a new threat appeared on the horizon.

Mohammed was born in 570 A.D. in what is now Saudi Arabia. He founded the religion of Islam, which spread quickly throughout the Arab lands. A few years after Mohammed's death his followers invaded and conquered Israel and dwelt there for the next four centuries. They too placed some restrictions on the Jewish population. It was during this time that the Muslims built the Dome of the Rock shrine on the Temple mount, which is still located there in Jerusalem.

In 1099 A.D. the Europeans invaded Israel and defeated the Muslim armies in the name of the Christian Church. For the next eighty-eight years they maintained power in Israel and once again treated the non-Christian population harshly. However, their dominion over Israel was short-lived.

A Muslim army under the leadership of Saladin defeated the Christian Crusaders in 1187 A.D. By 1291 A.D., the Egyptian or Mamluk (or Mameluks) Muslim army completely eradicated the European influence in Israel. Under the rule of the Mamluks, the land of Israel declined into ruin.

The Ottoman Turks, in turn, conquered the Mamluks in 1517 A.D. It was under the reign of the Turkish Sultan, Suleiman the Magnificent, that the current walls of Jerusalem were built. During this period Jewish presence in Israel increased significantly. However, the Ottoman rulers placed many restrictions on the Jews that hindered but did not deter the Jews from reclaiming the land. One limitation was that the Turkish administration prohibited the Jews from purchasing any land in Israel without the permission of the government in Istanbul. But the rule of the Ottoman empire was about to end.

In 1897 an event took place that would have a profound effect on the land of Israel. In August of that year, the leading Jewish Zionist, a writer and journalist by the name of Theodore Herzl, convened the First Zionist Congress in Basel, Switzerland. Because of his efforts the Jews began to believe that they would once again live as a nation in the land of Israel. Jewish immigration to Israel increased and they created many settlements throughout the land.

When World War I erupted in 1914, the countries of the world chose sides. The primary combatants were the Allies consisting of Britain, France, and Russia and the Central Powers who were the Germans and the Austro-Hungarians. The Ottoman Turks decided to fight with Germany in this conflict. In December of 1917, the British army, under the command of General Edmund Allenby, defeated the Turks and conquered Jerusalem.

In November of 1917, the British foreign secretary, Lord Arthur James Balfour, issued a written pledge to the Jewish Zionist, Chaim Weizmann, to establish in Palestine a National Home for the Jewish people. To implement this policy, the newly formed world-governing council called the League of Nations mandated that Great Britain govern in Palestine. They were to help the Jews immigrate to Israel and organize a new Jewish nation. At the same time the British were to respect the rights of the Arab population that was also dwelling in the land. However, it did not take long for the Arabs to resist any effort that would allow the Jews to establish a country.

In 1929, rioting by the Arabs led to the deaths of numerous Jews in Jerusalem and around the country. More Arab uprisings occurred in the 1930s to resist the increasing immigration of Jews to Israel. It was during this time when the British government considered the idea of partitioning Israel into two sections, one for the Jews and the other for the Arabs. Both sides had problems with this solution and therefore the British did not attempt to implement it.

It was during the 1930s that Germany began wholesale persecution of the Jews. This eventually led to the Holocaust whereby the Nazis exterminated 6,000,000 Jews during World War II. A large part of this tragedy could have been avoided if the governments of the world had allowed the Jews to migrate from Germany to either Israel or to other countries. Such was not the case and therefore millions of Jews, including one and a half million Jewish children, died mercilessly at the hands of the Nazis.

After the war, a large segment of the European Jews who survived the Holocaust tried to immigrate to Israel where they hoped finally to find sanctuary from persecution. However, to appease the Arabs who lived in Israel, the British government resisted these efforts. There is an irony in this situation by the fact that during World War II, Jews helped the Allies to fight against the Germans while the Arabs sided with the Nazis. Nonetheless, the situation in Israel grew worse for the Jews after the war.

Finally, the British had enough of being in the middle of this turmoil and turned the issue over to another newly formed world-governing council, the United Nations. In November of 1947, the United Nations voted to partition the land of Israel into two sections, one for the Jews and the other for the Arabs. This partition plan also called for the British mandate to end on May 14, 1948. The Arab response to this vote was immediately to start attacking the Jews and their settlements in Israel.

On May 14, 1948, nearly eighteen hundred years after the Jewish nation of Israel ceased to exist it was reborn. However, there were "labor pains" before the existence of the new nation was assured. As soon as the last British troops left Israel, Arab armies from the countries surrounding Israel launched full-scale attacks against the Jews. By February 1949, the fighting had stopped and the Jews and Arabs agreed to an armistice. One result of this war was that Jerusalem was divided in half with the Arabs in eastern Jerusalem and the Jews in the newer, western part of Jerusalem. This left the Temple Mount and the Western Wall, which was part of the Second Jewish Temple complex, completely in Arab hands. They refused to allow the Jews to visit this holy site.

In June of 1967, the Arab nations were once again poised to attack Israel. This time the Jews defeated them overwhelmingly and gained control over all of Jerusalem, the Egyptian-held Gaza strip, and the Syrian-controlled Golan Heights on the eastern shore of the Sea of Galilee. The exultant Jews rushed to the Western Wall where they began praising and worshiping God. However, the Israeli Minister of Defense Moshe Dayan, reverted control of the Temple Mount to the Arabs almost immediately after this war ended. Though many Jews have complained that this has led to three decades of tensions between the Arab world and the Jews in Israel, I believe that it was not yet God's timing for the Temple Mount to be in Jewish hands.

In 1973 during the Jewish holy day of Yom Kippur, the Egyptians and Syrians again attacked Israel. After sustaining severe losses at the beginning, the Israeli army soon prevailed and once again defeated the Arab armies. This eventually led to a peace agreement between Egypt and Israel, which cost the Egyptian President, Anwar Sadat, his life at the hands of Arabs.

Since that time there have been several Arab and Muslim uprisings against Israel and its people. There has also been a call for the formation of a Palestinian state. It is very important to note that at no time in history has there ever been a country called Palestine. The ancient Romans referred to it by that name in an effort to denigrate further the Jews who were living there. When the Moslems had control of the land during the 600s A.D. through the 1000s A.D., they never created the country of Palestine. The British followed their Roman ancestors by also referring to the land of Israel as Palestine yet never formed such a nation. The United Nations gave the Arabs half the land of Israel under the control of Jordan, yet the Arab Jordanian government refused to establish a Palestinian state.

The modern call for the creation of the state of Palestine is a deceptive tactic by the Arabs and Muslims to destroy the nation of Israel. Since the rebirth of Israel, the Arabs have promised to "drive the Jews into the Sea". In Chapter 18, I will illustrate why I think that Satan is behind this endeavor.

I believe that the modern nation of Israel is a partial fulfillment of biblical prophecy. After eighteen centuries of the Jews losing their nation, God has miraculously brought them back to their land. They should have been assimilated into every culture where they were dispersed around the world, yet they maintained their Jewish identity throughout all this time. The agnostic writer, Mark Twain, wrote concerning the continuing existence of the Jews:

"If the statistics are right, the Jews constitute but one percent of the human race. It suggests a nebulous dim puff of star dust lost in the blaze of the Milky Way. Properly the Jew ought hardly be heard of; but he is heard of, has always been heard of. He is as prominent on the planet as any other people, and his commercial importance is extravagantly out of proportion to the smallness of his bulk. His contributions to the world's list of great names in literature, science, art, music, finance, medicine, and obtuse learning are also way out of proportion to the weakness of his numbers. He has made a marvelous fight in this world in all the ages, and has done it with his hands tied behind him. He could be vain of himself and be excused for it. The Egyptians, the Babylonians, and the Persians rose, filled the planet with sound and splendor, and faded to dream stuff and passed away. The Greeks and the Romans followed and made a vast noise and they are gone. Other peoples have sprung up and held their torch high for a time. But it burned out, and they sit in twilight now, or have vanished. The Jew saw them all. Beat them all, and is now what he always was, exhibiting no decadence, no infirmities of age, no weakening of his parts, no slowing of his energies, no dulling of his alert and aggressive mind. All things are mortal but the Jew. All other forces pass, but he remains. What is the secret of his immortality?"[5]

The answer to Mark Twain's question is *God.* God has a plan for the Jewish people and this plan included bringing them back to the land of Israel that He gave to them. God declared, through the prophet Amos, that one day He would bring the Jews back to the land of Israel forever:

> *"And I will bring again the captivity of My people of Israel, and they shall build the waste cities, and inhabit them; and they shall plant vineyards, and drink the wine thereof; they shall also make gardens, and eat the fruit of them. And I will plant them upon their land, and they shall no more be pulled up out*

of their land which I have given them, saith the LORD your God."[6]

I believe God fulfilled the first part of this prophecy when He brought the Jews back to Israel after eighteen hundred years of captivity throughout the world. Although the Jews have reclaimed large parts of the land and have made it bountiful since 1948, the complete fulfillment of this prophecy will occur during the Millennium.

I will discuss God's prophetic plans for the Jewish nation of Israel in more detail in Chapter 18. Before that however, I want to examine a teaching that has arisen in parts of the modern Christian Church.

---

1 *Daniel 7:7*
2 *Matthew 24:1-2*
3 *Luke 13:34-35*
4 *Numbers 24:17*
5 Mark Twain; Harpers Magazine; 1899
6 *Amos 9:14-15*

17 – Replacement Theology

There is a disturbing teaching that has gained momentum in the Christian Church since the rebirth of the modern nation of Israel. It is known as the doctrine of Replacement Theology. This is a teaching that I reject as completely unbiblical in nature. Regrettably, it is not just the modern, liberal Protestant churches that adhere to this belief but even some Evangelical churches subscribe to it.

This doctrine teaches that the Christian Church has *replaced* the Jewish nation of Israel in God's eyes. Therefore, the promises that God gave to the Jews now apply only to Christians. This leads those who support Replacement Theology to reject the idea that the Jews have a right to the land of Israel.

Although Replacement Theologians use various passages in the New Testament to support this doctrine, the foundation for it is a single verse written by the apostle Paul to the Christians in Galatia:

> *"As many as desire to make a fair show in the flesh, they constrain you to be circumcised; only lest they should suffer persecution for the cross of Christ. For neither they themselves who are circumcised keep the law; but desire to have you circumcised, that they may glory in your flesh. But God forbid that I should glory, save in the cross of our Lord Jesus Christ, by whom the world is crucified unto me, and I unto the world. For in Christ Jesus neither circumcision avails any thing, nor uncircumcision, but a new creature. And as many as walk according to this rule, peace be on them, and mercy, and upon the Israel of God."*[1]

It is the last verse in this passage that causes those to who adhere to Replacement Theology to reject the modern nation of Israel as the fulfillment of biblical prophecy. Paul here refers to believers in Jesus Christ as the *"Israel of God"*. Consequently, the Christian Church has replaced the Jews and their nation of Israel. However, Paul was addressing a serious issue that had reared up in the Church in Galatia.

Paul became aware of a situation that threatened to destroy the work that he had done the province of Galatia, which is located in modern southern Turkey. During three missionary trips to Galatia, Paul had led many Gentiles to accept Jesus Christ as the Messiah. There were also many Jews living in that region who believed that Jesus was the Messiah. However, they were telling the newly converted Gentile Christians that they had to accept the laws of Judaism as part of their salvation. These laws included the rite of circumcision that God had commanded the Jews to undergo as a sign of their relationship with Him. In this letter to the Christians in Galatia, Paul refutes this teaching as harmful and unbiblical.

Paul tells the believers that the Law of Moses does not justify people rather it is through faith in Jesus Christ that God saves a person:

> *"We who are Jews by nature, and not sinners of the Gentiles, Knowing that a man is not justified by the works of the law, but by the faith of Jesus Christ, even we have believed in Jesus Christ, that we might be justified by the faith of Christ, and not by the works of the law: for by the works of the law shall no flesh be justified."*[2]

He goes on in this letter to dispel the notion that the Gentiles have to keep the Law in order to be saved. He uses Abraham as an example of how God accepts a person as righteous because they believe in Him and His word:

> *"Even as Abraham believed God, and it was accounted to him for righteousness. Know you therefore that they which are of faith, the same are the children of Abraham. And the scripture, foreseeing that God would justify the heathen through faith, preached before the gospel unto Abraham, saying, In you shall all nations be blessed. So then they which be of faith are blessed with faithful Abraham. For as many as are of the*

works of the law are under the curse: for it is written, Cursed is every one that continues not in all things which are written in the book of the law to do them. But that no man is justified by the law in the sight of God, it is evident: for, The just shall live by faith. And the law is not of faith: but, The man that does them shall live in them. Christ has redeemed us from the curse of the law, being made a curse for us: for it is written, Cursed is every one that hangs on a tree: That the blessing of Abraham might come on the Gentiles through Jesus Christ; that we might receive the promise of the Spirit through faith. Brethren, I speak after the manner of men; Though it be but a man's covenant, yet if it be confirmed, no man disannulls, or adds thereto. Now to Abraham and his seed were the promises made. He says not, And to seeds, as of many; but as of one, And to your seed, which is Christ. And this I say, that the covenant, that was confirmed before of God in Christ, the law, which was four hundred and thirty years after, cannot disannul, that it should make the promise of none effect. For if the inheritance be of the law, it is no more of promise: but God gave it to Abraham by promise."[3]

Paul's whole point in this passage is that just as in Abraham's day and throughout the Old Testament, the Jews were saved by believing in God and His word, so too are Gentiles and Jews saved in New Testament times by believing that God sent His Son Jesus Christ to be the Savior of mankind. Paul mentions one of the covenants that God made with Abraham. He makes it clear that he is referring to the covenant whereby God was going to bless all nations through Abraham's seed or descendants. Paul points out that the coming of Jesus Christ fulfilled this promise of God. He calls it *"the promise of the Spirit"* which means that the covenant God made with Abraham had a spiritual aspect to it. Paul was definitely not referring to the other covenant that God made with Abraham to give the physical land of Israel to his Jewish descendants.

In the letter that Paul wrote to the Christians living in Rome, he expands further on Christians' relationship with the faith of Abraham:

> *"What shall we say then that Abraham our father, as pertaining to the flesh, has found? For if Abraham were justified by works, he has whereof to glory; but not before God. For what says the scripture? Abraham believed God, and it was counted unto him for righteousness...Blessed is the man to whom the Lord will not impute sin. Comes this blessedness then upon the Circumcision* [i.e., the Jews] *only, or upon the uncircumcision* [i.e., the Gentiles] *also? For we say that faith was reckoned to Abraham for righteousness. How was it then reckoned? When he was in circumcision, or in uncircumcision? Not in circumcision, but in uncircumcision. And he received the sign of circumcision, a seal of the righteousness of the faith which he had yet being uncircumcised: that he might be the father of all them that believe, though they be not circumcised; that righteousness might be imputed unto them also: And the father of circumcision to them who are not of the circumcision only, but who also walk in the steps of that faith of our father Abraham, which he had being yet uncircumcised. For the promise, that he should be the heir of the world, was not to Abraham, or to his seed, through the law, but through the righteousness of faith. For if they which are of the law be heirs, faith is made void, and the promise made of none effect: Because the law works wrath: for where no law is, there is no transgression. Therefore it is of faith, that it might be by grace; to the end the promise might be sure to all the seed; not to that only which is of the law, but to that also which is of the faith of Abraham; who is the father of us all, (As it is written, I have made you a father of many nations,) before him whom he believed, even God, who makes alive the dead, and calls those things which be not as though they were. Who against hope believed in hope, that he might become the father of many nations, according to that which was spoken, So shall your seed be."*[4]

Paul again declares that it is faith that saved Abraham. He states, *"to the end the promise might be sure to all the seed; not to that only which is of the law, but to that also which is of the faith of Abraham."* This means that everyone, whether Jew or Gentile, who believes God's word is a seed or descendant of Abraham. How can this be since Gentiles are not physically descended from Abraham? Paul is clearly speaking of Christians as a *"spiritual"* descendant of Abraham. Likewise, in the first passage in this section where Paul refers to Christians as the *"Israel of God"*, he is saying that Christians, as a body of believers, are the *"spiritual"* Israel of God. *This in no way means that the Christian Church has replaced the Jewish nation of Israel.*

No Divine Favor?

Another tenet of Replacement Theology is that in the age of grace through Jesus Christ, God shows no favor to anyone apart from their acceptance of His Son as the Savior and Messiah. Thus, God will not give the land of Israel to the Jews because to do so would be showing them favor because of their ethnicity. Since the majority of the Jews reject Jesus as the Messiah, supporters of Replacement Theology contend that they are no longer under God's heavenly blessing, which is true of anyone who rejects Jesus Christ as their Savior. However, Replacement Theologians also say that the Jews are no longer under God's earthly blessing. Thus, the covenant whereby God promised to give the land of Israel to the Jewish descendants of Abraham is null and void in the age of grace.

This tenet is as false as it is unbiblical. The apostle Paul, in the same letter to the Romans that I mentioned above, states the exact opposite of what the supporters of Replacement Theology say concerning God not showing the Jews any divine favor while they are in unbelief:

> *"For I would not, brethren, that you should be ignorant of this mystery, lest you should be wise in your own conceits; that blindness in part is happened to Israel, until the fullness of the Gentiles be come in. And so all Israel shall be saved: as it is written, There shall come out of Zion the Deliverer, and shall turn away ungodliness from Jacob: For this is My covenant unto them, when I shall take away their sins. As concerning the gospel, they are enemies for your sakes: but as touching the election, they are beloved for the fathers sakes. For the gifts*

and calling of God are irrevocable."[5]

Paul says that indeed the Jews are spiritually blind when it comes to accepting Jesus as their Messiah. However, he declares that although the Jews are the enemies of the gospel of Jesus Christ, they are *"beloved"* by God because of the fathers or patriarchs of the Jews. Even though they are outside the Christian faith, they still have God's divine favor of love upon them. Paul further states here that the gifts of God are irrevocable. Therefore, this means His promise to give the land of Israel to the Jews, even while they are in unbelief, is absolutely still in effect.

To drive home this point, Paul declares that another covenant God made with the Jews was to save them from their sins. He says however, the fulfillment of this covenant will not happen until the Gentiles have had enough time to turn to God and *then* all Israel *"shall be saved"*. From the time that Paul wrote this unto the present day, this covenant has still not been fulfilled. Yet according to Replacement Theology, this covenant too should be voided since the Jews are currently in unbelief. Thankfully, God will not void it because His gifts and callings are irrevocable. For the same reason, He will not void the covenant that He made with the Jews to give the land of Israel to them.

The term Paul uses here, "Israel", cannot refer to the Church. First, born-again Christians who make up the Church are already saved. Second, earlier in this chapter in Romans Paul makes a distinction between the Jews and the believing Gentiles:

> *"I say then, Has God cast away His people? God forbid. For I also am an Israelite, of the seed of Abraham, of the tribe of Benjamin. God ha not cast away his people which he foreknew. Know you not what the scripture says of Elijah? How he made intercession to God against Israel saying, Lord, they have killed your prophets, and dug down Your altars; and I am left alone, and they seek my life. But what says the answer of God unto him? I have reserved to Myself seven thousand men, who have not bowed the knee to the image of Baal. Even so then at this present time also there is a remnant according to the election of grace. And if by grace, then is it no more of works:*

otherwise grace is no more grace. But if it be of works, then it is no more grace: otherwise work is no more work. What then? Israel has not obtained that which he seeks for; but the election has obtained it, and the rest were blinded. (According as it is written, God has given them the spirit of slumber, eyes that they should not see, and ears that they should not hear;) unto this day. And David says, Let their table be made a snare, and a trap, and a stumbling block, and a recompense unto them: Let their eyes be darkened, that they may not see, and bow down their back always. I say then, Have they stumbled that they should fall? God forbid: but rather through their fall salvation is come unto the Gentiles, for to provoke them to jealousy. Now if the fall of them be the riches of the world, and the diminishing of them the riches of the Gentiles; how much more their fullness? For I speak to you Gentiles, inasmuch as I am the apostle of the Gentiles, I magnify my office: If by any means I may provoke to emulation them which are my flesh, and might save some of them. For if the casting away of them be the reconciling of the world, what shall the receiving of them be, but life from the dead? For if the firstfruits be holy, the lump is also holy: and if the root be holy, so are the branches. And if some of the branches be broken off, and you, being a wild olive tree, wert grafted in among them, and with them partake of the root and fatness of the olive tree; Boast not against the branches. But if you boast, you bear not the root, but the root you, You will say then, The branches were broken off, that I might be grafted in. Well; because of unbelief they were broken off, and you standby faith. Be not high-minded, but fear: For if God spared not the natural branches, take heed lest he also spare not you. Behold therefore the goodness and severity of God: on them which fell, severity; but toward thee, goodness, if you continue in His goodness: otherwise you also shall be cut off. And they also, if they abide not still in unbelief, shall be grafted in: for God is able to graft them in again. For if you wert cut out of the olive tree which is wild by nature, and were grafted contrary to nature into a good olive tree: how much more shall these, which be the natural branches, be grafted into their own olive tree? For I would not, brethren,

> *that you should be ignorant of this mystery, lest you should be wise in your own conceits; that blindness in part is happened to Israel, until the fullness of the Gentiles be come in. And so all Israel shall be saved"*[6]

The apostle states: Yes, spiritual blindness has come upon the Jews when it comes to Jesus being the Messiah. Therefore, God turned to the Gentiles who willingly believed that Jesus is God's Son and Savior. However, God has plans for the Jews whereby they will accept Jesus as the Messiah and then *"all Israel shall be saved!"* As I mentioned in Chapter 11 of this book, this salvation of the Jews will take place at Jesus' second coming when as the prophet Zechariah declared, *"[God] will pour upon the house of David, and upon the inhabitants of Jerusalem, the spirit of grace and of supplications: and they shall look upon Me whom they have pierced."*[7]

In Chapter 15, I discussed the covenant that God made with Abraham where He promised to give the land of Israel to Abraham's Jewish descendants. God confirmed this covenant by causing a deep sleep to fall on Abraham and then He, in the likeness of a flaming torch, moved between the halves of animals that Abraham had sacrificed. God placed absolutely no conditions on Abraham's part in order for this covenant to be fulfilled. Abraham was asleep and therefore could not agree to any conditions that God might have required. God did not tell Abraham that he or his descendants had to remain faithful to Him in order to receive this land. God, the Creator of Israel, would bestow a gift of the land upon the Jewish people. And as the apostle Paul wrote, *"the gifts and calling of God are irrevocable."*

No More Jewish Temples?

Another aspect concerning Replacement Theology rejects the idea that another Jewish Temple should be built. The death of Jesus Christ ended the necessity for animal sacrifices to atone for a person's sins. Therefore, a Jewish Temple is unnecessary since, through the means of the resurrection of Jesus, He became the true Temple of God. They quote the words of Jesus to support this:

> *"Jesus answered and said unto them, Destroy this Temple, and in three days I will raise it up. Then said the Jews, Forty and six years was this Temple in building, and will you rear it up in three days? But He spoke of the Temple of His body."*[8]

The irony here is that Jesus declares that He is speaking of a *spiritual* Temple concerning His resurrection. If Replacement Theologians are correct and the only Temple that exists now and forever is the Temple of Jesus' resurrected body, how will the *"abomination of desolation"* that Jesus spoke of enter into Him?

> *"And this gospel of the kingdom shall be preached in all the world for a witness unto all nations; and then shall the end come. When you therefore shall see the abomination of desolation, spoken of by Daniel the prophet, stand in the Holy place, (whoso reads, let him understand) Then let them which be in Judea flee into the mountains."*[9]

The Holy place or Temple that Jesus speaks of here cannot be the Temple that was standing when He was alive on the earth. He says that the gospel will be preached in *"all the world"* and then shall the end come. The gospel had not been preached in all the world by the time of this Temple's destruction in 70 A.D. Therefore, Jesus had to be referring to a future Temple that Replacement Theologians say should not be built. The apostle Paul also spoke of this future Temple in his letter to the Thessalonian Christians:

> *"Let no man deceive you by any means: for that day shall not come, except there come a falling away first, and that man of sin be revealed, the son of perdition; Who opposes and exalts himself above all that is called God, or that is worshipped; so that he as God sits in the Temple of God, showing himself that he is God."*[10]

Paul says that the *"man of sin"*, whom Christians call the Antichrist and Jesus calls the *"abomination of desolation"*, is going to sit in the Temple before the end of the current age. If Jesus is the only Temple that is going to exist from His resurrection through eternity, then how is the Antichrist going to enter into Him and declare himself God? When a person spiritualizes the plain meaning of the scriptures as the supporters of Replacement Theology do, the result will be one of absurdity.

Although it is true that there is no sacrifice apart from the sacrificial death of Jesus Christ whereby a person can be saved, it is not true that the Jewish Temple no longer served any purpose.

Neither did the apostle Paul agree with this belief. Many years after the death, resurrection, and ascension of Jesus, Paul still went to the Temple in Jerusalem to honor God:

> *"Then Paul took the men, and the next day purifying himself with them entered into the Temple, to signify the accomplishment of the days of purification, until that an offering should be offered for every one of them. And when the seven days were almost ended, the Jews which were of Asia, when they saw him in the Temple, stirred up all the people, and laid hands on him, Crying out, Men of Israel, help: This is the man, that teachs all men every where against the people, and the law, and this place: and further brought Greeks also into the Temple, and has polluted this holy place. (For they had seen before with him in the city Trophimus an Ephesian, whom they supposed that Paul had brought into the Temple.) And all the city was moved, and the people ran together: and they took Paul, and drew him out of the Temple: and forthwith the doors were shut. And as they went about to kill him, news came unto the chief captain of the troops, that all Jerusalem was in an uproar"*[11]

The apostle Paul, the Jewish author of a large segment of the New Testament and a Christian for many years by this time, thought it appropriate to make an offering to God in the Jewish Temple in Jerusalem. Yet Replacement Theologians would condemn him for such an action since the Temple was no longer necessary after the first advent of Jesus Christ.

In Part Two of this book, I demonstrated how the prophetic plans of God include not only the rebuilding of a third Jewish Temple in Jerusalem which the Antichrist will desecrate, but also a fourth

Temple in Jerusalem that Jesus will build and rule from during the Millennium.

Since, as Replacement Theology dictates, Christians do not need a Temple to worship God in, who is going to build the future third Temple in Jerusalem? The Muslims certainly do not want a Temple built on the Temple Mount. They already have their Dome of the Rock shrine standing there. Therefore, it has to be the Jews who will build this future prophetic Temple and for the Jews to build it they need to be in the land of Israel. As God declared many times in His word, He would bring the Jews back to Israel, which is the land that He gave to them and them alone. Then they will build the Temple according to His prophetic timing. As we read in the last chapter, God brought the Jews back to the land of Israel in 1948.

Bad Christian Theology

I read a public statement[12] that a seminary, which teaches Replacement Theology, issued in opposition to Christians who support the Jews' right to the land of Israel. In this statement they declared that bad Christian Theology concerning Israel led to the cruelty of the Crusades and that bad Christian Theology is leading to the oppression of the "Palestinians" in the modern, secular state of Israel. They are absolutely correct that bad Christian Theology led to the Crusades. That Theology taught that the Jews were no longer entitled to the land of Israel and therefore Christians had a right to conquer the land and persecute the Jews. Replacement Theology also teaches that the land of Israel does not belong to the Jews. That is one thing it has in common with those who initiated the Crusades against Jews.

I would ask those Christians who adhere to Replacement Theology two questions: Was God wrong for telling the Jews to conquer the land of Israel and destroy the Canaanites who were living there at the time of Joshua? If not, then was God wrong for bringing the Jews back to the land of Israel in modern times as He said repeatedly that He would?

For Replacement Theology to be tenable its adherents have to spiritualize every prophetic scripture in both the Old and the New Testament. Therefore, no prophecy written in the Bible is what it seems. They have to have a deeper, spiritual meaning for Replacement Theology to work. As I have shown however, it is not tenable because some prophetic scriptures cannot be "spiritualized" away.

I think it is lamentable that just as Paul had to deal with false teachings in his day, so too after two thousand years, Christians today have to deal with false teachings such as Replacement Theology.

Though the language and tone that I have displayed in this chapter might seem angry to some, there is a reason for that. The apostle Paul got angry with those who twisted the plain meaning of scripture. In the aforementioned letter to the Galatians, Paul used the strongest language possible in opposing those who were bringing false teachings into the Church:

> *"You did run well; who did hinder you that you should not obey the truth? This persuasion comes not of Him that calls you. A little leaven leavens the whole lump. I have confidence in you through the Lord, that you will be none otherwise minded: but he that troubles you shall bear his judgment, whosoever he be. And I, brethren, if I yet preach circumcision, why do I yet suffer persecution? Then is the offence of the cross ceased. I would they were even cut off which trouble you."*[13]

Paul says that those who were hindering Christians by insisting that to be a true Christian they had to circumcise themselves were changing the truth of God. He said that he wished these false teachers *would castrate themselves.* I too get angry with those who change the truth of God's prophetic word to support their own beliefs. I think that Christianity has done enough harm to the chosen people of God throughout its history. To oppose the unconditional covenant that God made with the Jews concerning their right to the land of Israel is harmful to the Jewish people.

In the statement issued by the seminary that I mentioned above, it said that Christians who support the modern state of Israel and the seizure and occupation of Palestinian land are in moral jeopardy of their own blood-guiltiness. On the contrary, those who would curse the Jews by denying them the land that God gave to them are the ones whose standing before God may be in question. To paraphrase the Jewish Pharisee Gamaliel who taught the apostle Paul, I say to those who oppose the Jews' right to the land of Israel, be careful, *"if it be God's will for the Jews to have the land, you cannot overthrow it; lest haply you be found even to fight against God."*[14]

---

1 *Galatians 6:12-16*
2 *Galatians 2:15-16*
3 *Galatians 3:6-18*
4 *Romans 4:1-3, 8-18*
5 *Romans 11:25-29*
6 *Romans 11:1-26*
7 *Zechariah 12:10*
8 *John 2:19-21*
9 *Matthew 24:14-16*
10 *II Thessalonians 2:3-4*
11 *Acts 21:26-31*
12 At the time of the writing of this book, this statement can be found at the following web site:
http://www.knoxseminary.org/Prospective/Faculty/WittenbergDoor/
The author's response to this public statement can be found at:
http://www.iesouschristos.com/openresponse.htm
13 *Galatians 5:7-12*
14 *Acts 5:39* (author's paraphrase)

18 – God's Timing For the End

In Part One of this book, I have shown how Jesus fulfilled the biblical prophecies concerning the suffering Messiah. In Part Two, I illustrated how Jesus will fulfill the biblical prophecies concerning the triumphant King Messiah in the end-times. Thus far in Part Three, I have demonstrated how Israel is the prophetic land that God gave to the Jews for their possession. In this penultimate chapter, I will discuss why I believe that the land of Israel is the key to the timing of when the end-times will occur. However, I want to preface this discussion by stating clearly that at no place in this book will you find a date and year as to when Jesus Christ is coming again. Jesus Himself stated:

> *"But of that day and hour knoweth no man, no, not the angels of heaven, but My Father only."*[1]

First, I will discuss some of the signs that the Bible mentions concerning the last days. Then I will conclude this chapter by examining what I believe is the key scripture passage in determining the timing of the end-time events.

The Last Days

The New Testament writers mention the end-times or Last Days several times in their writings. In the preface to this book I wrote about a question that Jesus' disciples asked Him concerning the last days:

> *"And as He sat upon the Mount of Olives, the disciples came unto Him privately, saying, Tell us, when shall these things be? And what shall be the sign of Your coming, and of the end of the world?"*[2]

In Chapter 9, I explained how the answer that Jesus gave to the disciples' question paralleled the end-time events listed in the Book of Revelation. Jesus told them several signs to watch for:

> *"And Jesus answered and said unto them, Take heed that no man deceive you. For many shall come in My name, saying, I am Christ; and shall deceive many."*[3]

Jesus issues a warning to those who are alive at the beginning of the end-times. False preachers are going to rise up and will deceive many with their message. They will claim to be Christians and some might proclaim themselves to be Jesus Christ come again. Some may teach that there are many ways to God or that they themselves are the way to God. Jesus states here that many will believe their false preaching. The ultimate deceiver is the Antichrist who will proclaim himself the Messiah.

The only way a person can keep from being deceived is to know what God says in His word, the Holy Bible. Jesus Christ said that He is the way, the truth, and the life; no one comes to the Father but through Him.[4] Anyone who teaches that no matter what religion a person follows, God will still accept them is contradicting the words of Jesus.

> *"And you shall hear of wars and rumors of wars: see that you be not troubled: for all these things must come to pass, but the end is not yet. For nation shall rise against nation, and kingdom against kingdom..."*[5]

Though humans have started many wars since the time of Jesus, the last two World Wars led to the creation of the Jewish nation of Israel, which as we will see, has tremendous end-time prophetic significance. However, I believe that the many wars Jesus speaks of here refers to those wars that affect the Jewish nation of Israel either directly or indirectly. During the end-times, Israel will be at the center of all the conflicts taking place at that time. The final war will end on the battlefields surrounding Jerusalem during the battle of Armageddon.

It is worth noting that from 135 A.D. until 1948, no war affected the *Jewish* nation of Israel. There was no Jewish nation during that time. The wars that were waged in the land of Israel during that period of history were between the Romans and Persians, the Byzantines and the Muslims, the Christian Crusaders and the Muslims, the Muslims and the Turks, and finally the Turks and the British. However, since 1948 and the rebirth of Jewish Israel, several wars have taken place in and around Israel and the Middle East.

Since Israel became a nation in 1948, conflicts and wars have been fought over it and its capital, Jerusalem. This does not come as a surprise to most Bible-believing Christians because God declared that this would happen in the last days:

> *"The burden of the word of the LORD for Israel, says the LORD, who stretches forth the heavens, and lays the foundation of the earth, and formed the spirit of man within him. Behold, I will make Jerusalem a cup of trembling unto all the people round about, when they shall be in the siege both against Judah and against Jerusalem. And in that day will I make Jerusalem a burdensome stone for all people: all that burden themselves with it shall be cut in pieces, though all the people of the earth be gathered together against it."*[6]

Although Jerusalem has been at the center of many wars for over three millennia, at no time has any war affected every nation in the world. However, God states that at the end He will make Jerusalem a "trouble spot" for the entire world. Jerusalem has indeed become the focal point of the world's attention in the last fifty years. This attention will culminate in the battle of Armageddon when Jesus will *"cut in pieces"* the armies of the Antichrist and the rest of the world.

"and there shall be famines, and pestilences, and earthquakes, in diverse places. All these are the beginning of sorrows."[7]

There have been many famines, plagues, and earthquakes since the time Jesus spoke these words. How could Jesus expect His followers to differentiate between the normal occurrences of the fallen world we live in and those that are the signs of the end? The answer has three aspects to it.

The first is that since Israel is the timing mechanism that God uses for the end-times we have to watch for any famines, plagues, or earthquakes that have happened since 1948. We could specifically point to such worldwide plagues as AIDS or influenza, famines in Africa, and the 9.0 earthquake in 2004. Are these enough to confirm that the end-times are near? I personally do not think so.

The second aspect concerns the last part of this passage: *"the beginning of sorrows"*. In the original Greek language of the New Testament this phrase literally means *"the beginning of labor pains"*. Jesus means that this is only the beginning of the troubles that are going to come on the world. The metaphor He uses is interesting because once labor pains start they occur closer and closer together and become more and more intense as they go on. Therefore, I believe that when the world starts seeing famines, pestilence, and earthquakes happening more frequently then these become the signs of which Jesus spoke.

The final aspect to the answer is that these signs may not occur until after the Antichrist comes on the world scene. The first sign Jesus gave above was that false Christs would appear and deceive many. Of course, as we read in Chapter 9, the world will not know that this world leader is the Antichrist at first. He will deceive many by seeming to be a man of peace. However, Jesus gave other signs by which His followers were to know that the end is near.

"Then shall they deliver you up to be afflicted, and shall kill you: and you shall be hated of all nations for My name's sake. And then shall many be offended, and shall betray one another, and shall hate one another. And many false prophets shall rise, and shall deceive many."[8]

In the last days, the world is going to increase its hatred for the followers of Jesus. This scenario will come about because of an intellectual rejection of the Bible and a propagation of the evolutionary theory by unbelievers. The apostle Peter spoke of this time in his second epistle:

> *"Knowing this first, that there shall come in the last days scoffers, walking after their own lusts, And saying, Where is the promise of His coming? For since the fathers fell asleep, all things continue as they were from the beginning of the creation. For this they willingly are ignorant of, that by the word of God the heavens were of old, and the earth standing out of the water and in the water: Whereby the world that then was, being overflowed with water, perished: But the heavens and the earth, which are now, by the same word are kept in store, reserved unto fire against the day of judgment and perdition of ungodly men."*[9]

This rejection of the truths of God will be the impetus for a worldwide persecution of Christians. They will arrest, torture, and execute Christians because of their belief that Jesus is the only way to God. False preachers will claim to speak in the name of God and will declare that the followers of Jesus are harming world unity because of their ideology. This persecution will reach its climax under the reign of the Antichrist.

> *"And because iniquity shall abound, the love of many shall grow cold."*[10]

Everywhere sin and lawlessness will increase while love among humans will decrease. The apostle Paul spoke of the breakdown of societal, personal, and familial relationships that will occur in the last days:

> *"This know also, that in the last days perilous times shall come. For men shall be lovers of their own selves, covetous, boasters, proud, blasphemers, disobedient to parents, unthankful,*

unholy, Without natural affection, trucebreakers, false accusers, incontinent, fierce, despisers of those that are good, Traitors, heady, high-minded, lovers of pleasures more than lovers of God; Having a form of godliness, but denying the power thereof: from such turn away."[11]

Paul gives a description of the abysmal human condition that will arise in the end-times. All the human behaviors that he lists here can be summed up by the motto: "If it feels good do it". The desire for pleasure will consume people at the expense of their families and their belief in God. Some will try to appear as godly persons yet deny the power of salvation through Jesus Christ. Everyone will do what seems right in his or her own eyes.

"But he that shall endure unto the end, the same shall be saved. And this gospel of the kingdom shall be preached in all the world for a witness unto all nations; and then shall the end come."[12]

There will be godly men who will continue to proclaim the truth of salvation in Jesus Christ until the end. Those who endure the persecutions and ungodliness of the last days by maintaining their faith in Jesus will be saved.

"When you therefore shall see the abomination of desolation, spoken of by Daniel the prophet, stand in the Holy Place (whoso reads, let him understand:) Then let them which be in Judea flee into the mountains: Let him which is on the housetop not come down to take any thing out of his house: Neither let him which is in the field return back to take his clothes. And woe unto them that are with child, and to them that give suck in those days! But pray you that your flight be not in the winter, neither on the Sabbath day: For then shall be great tribulation, such as was not since the beginning of the world to this time, no, nor ever shall be. And except those days should be shortened, there should no flesh be saved: but for the

elect's sake those days shall be shortened."[13]

The *"abomination of desolation"* takes place in the middle of the Tribulation Period. This event occurs when the Antichrist enters the Temple in Jerusalem and declares himself God. When that happens Jesus warns the Jews in Israel to flee because the Great Tribulation is about to begin. Conditions will become so horrible that if God did not limit the time frame of the Tribulation Period all humanity would be wiped out.

> *"Then if any man shall say unto you, Lo, here is Christ, or there; believe it not. For there shall arise false Christs, and false prophets, and shall show great signs and wonders; insomuch that, if it were possible, they shall deceive the very elect. Behold, I have told you before. Wherefore if they shall say unto you, Behold, he is in the desert; go not forth: behold, he is in the secret chambers; believe it not."*[14]

The false preachers will entice people to follow one leader or another, all in the name of God. These leaders will have demonic power to perform false signs and miracles in order to deceive humans. The apostle Paul also mentioned these false teachers arising in the last days:

> *"Now the Spirit speaks expressly, that in the latter times some shall depart from the faith, giving heed to seducing spirits, and doctrines of devils; Speaking lies in hypocrisy; having their conscience seared with a hot iron."*[15]

Evil spirits will seduce people away from the truths of God. They will deny that the Bible is the word of God and people will believe them. Jesus declares that He will protect those who are true believers in Him. If it were not for this protection, the power of the false leaders would deceive His elect followers.

> *"For as the lightning comes out of the east, and shines even unto the west; so shall also the coming of the Son of man be. Immediately after the tribulation of those days shall the sun be darkened, and the moon shall not give her light, and the stars shall fall from heaven, and the powers of the heavens shall be shaken: And then shall appear the sign of the Son of man in heaven: and then shall all the tribes of the earth mourn, and they shall see the Son of man coming in the clouds of heaven with power and great glory. And He shall send His angels with a great sound of a trumpet, and they shall gather together His elect from the four winds, from one end of heaven to the other."*[16]

Up to this point, Jesus has repeatedly warned against following the false messiahs and prophets that will rise up in the last days. Now He states that when He, the true Messiah, appears, the entire world will see it. This will occur at the end of the Tribulation Period with great signs in the cosmos and He will gather all His followers to Jerusalem.

> *"Now learn a parable of the fig tree; When his branch is yet tender, and puts forth leaves, you know that summer is nigh: So likewise you, when you shall see all these things, know that it is near, even at the doors. Truly I say unto you, This generation shall not pass, till all these things be fulfilled. Heaven and earth shall pass away, but My words shall not pass away. But of that day and hour knoweth no man, no, not the angels of heaven, but My Father only."*[17]

Jesus declares an important principle in this passage. Humans have the ability to tell when a natural process has begun by the signs that they observe taking place. In this case, He says that just as you can tell when a season is about to start, so too you will be able to tell when the "season" of the end-times is about to occur. Jesus states that when you see the signs that He has given beginning to occur, *know* that the end-times are not just near but *even at the doors.*

The generation that sees these signs will not perish before the end-times comes to fruition. However, unlike the "seventy weeks" prophecy of Daniel which gave the specific day of Jesus' first coming, no one will know the exact day and year of His second coming. He did tell us that we are to *know* the season of His second appearance.

The apostle Paul tells Christians that they need to watch for these signs and recognize them as the beginning of the end:

> *"But of the times and the seasons, brethren, you have no need that I write unto you. For yourselves know perfectly that the day of the Lord so comes as a thief in the night. For when they shall say, Peace and safety; then sudden destruction comes upon them, as travail upon a woman with child; and they shall not escape. But you, brethren, are not in darkness, that that day should overtake you as a thief. You are all the children of light, and the children of the day: we are not of the night, nor of darkness. Therefore let us not sleep, as do others; but let us watch and be sober."*[18]

Paul states that the world will not be looking for the second coming of Jesus. Instead, they will be looking for a peaceful world to live in. Their declaration of *"Peace and safety"* may occur when the Antichrist makes a peace treaty with Israel and the world. Then sudden destruction will come upon the world. However, Paul admonishes Christians not to be caught off guard by the beginning of the Day of the Lord. As children of God's light and by the light of His prophetic word, Christians should be watching for that Day so that it doesn't overcome them like a thief in the night.

I believe that these signs could not take place until the Jewish nation of Israel was in existence. If there were no Jewish Israel then there would be no Temple in Jerusalem for the Antichrist to enter. Neither would there be any Jews in Israel to heed Jesus' warning to flee from Israel when the Antichrist appears in the Temple.

I also believe that God has given a time frame during which the end-times are to occur. This period revolves around the Jewish nation of Israel.

Ezekiel's Dry Bones

The Old Testament prophet Ezekiel began his ministry around the year 593 B.C. God had given to him several visions concerning the fate of the Jews and the nation of Israel. I believe that one of these visions is the key to the timing of God's plans for the last days:

> *"The hand of the LORD was upon me, and carried me out in the spirit of the LORD, and set me down in the midst of the valley which was full of bones, And caused me to pass by them round about: and, behold, there were very many in the open valley; and, lo, they were very dry. And He said unto me, Son of man, can these bones live? And I answered, O Lord GOD, You know. Again He said unto me, Prophesy upon these bones, and say unto them, O you dry bones, hear the word of the LORD. Thus says the Lord GOD unto these bones; Behold, I will cause breath to enter into you, and you shall live: And I will lay sinews upon you, and will bring up flesh upon you, and cover you with skin, and put breath in you, and you shall live; and you shall know that I am the LORD. So I prophesied as I was commanded: and as I prophesied, there was a noise, and behold a shaking, and the bones came together, bone to his bone. And when I beheld, lo, the sinews and the flesh came up upon them, and the skin covered them above: but there was no breath in them. Then said He unto me, Prophesy unto the wind, prophesy, son of man, and say to the wind, Thus says the Lord GOD; Come from the four winds, O breath, and breathe upon these slain, that they may live. So I prophesied as He commanded me, and the breath came into them, and they lived, and stood up upon their feet, an exceeding great army. Then He said unto me, Son of man, these bones are the whole house of Israel: behold, they say, Our bones are dried, and our hope is lost: we are cut off for our parts. Therefore prophesy and say unto them, Thus says the Lord GOD; Behold, O my people, I will open your graves, and cause you to come up out of your graves, and bring you into the land of Israel. And you shall know that I am the LORD, when I have opened your graves, O My people, and brought you up out of your graves, And shall*

put My Spirit in you, and you shall live, and I shall place you in your own land: then shall you know that I the LORD have spoken it, and performed it, says the LORD. The word of the LORD came again unto me, saying, Moreover, you son of man, take you one stick, and write upon it, For Judah, and for the children of Israel his companions: then take another stick, and write upon it, For Joseph, the stick of Ephraim and for all the house of Israel his companions: And join them one to another into one stick; and they shall become one in your hand. And when the children of your people shall speak unto you, saying, Will you not show us what you mean by these? Say unto them, Thus says the Lord GOD; Behold, I will take the stick of Joseph, which is in the hand of Ephraim, and the tribes of Israel his fellows, and will put them with him, even with the stick of Judah, and make them one stick, and they shall be one in Mine hand. And the sticks whereon you write shall be in your hand before their eyes. And say unto them, Thus says the Lord GOD; Behold, I will take the children of Israel from among the heathen, where they be gone, and will gather them on every side, and bring them into their own land: And I will make them one nation in the land upon the mountains of Israel; and one King shall be King to them all: and they shall be no more two nations, neither shall they be divided into two kingdoms any more at all. Neither shall they defile themselves any more with their idols, nor with their detestable things, nor with any of their transgressions: but I will save them out of all their dwelling places, wherein they have sinned, and will cleanse them: so shall they be My people, and I will be their God. And David My Servant shall be King over them; and they all shall have one Shepherd: they shall also walk in My judgments, and observe My statutes, and do them. And they shall dwell in the land that I have given unto Jacob my servant, wherein your fathers have dwelt; and they shall dwell therein, even they, and their children, and their children's children for ever: and My Servant David shall be their Prince for ever. Moreover I will make a covenant of peace with them; it shall be an everlasting covenant with them: and I will place them, and multiply them, and will set My Sanctuary in the midst of them for evermore. My Tabernacle also shall be with them: yea, I will be their God, and they shall be My people. And the heathen shall know that I the LORD do sanctify Israel, when My Sanctuary shall be in the midst of them for evermore."

- Ezekiel 37:1-28

In this vision God reveals to Ezekiel the future of the Jewish nation Israel. He shows Ezekiel a valley full of very dry bones that represent Israel. God speaks to these bones and tells them that He is going to put breath into them so that they may come to life. However, this process is going to occur in stages.

First, He will cause the bones to come up out of their graves. Then He will put sinews or muscles on them. Next, He will cause flesh to grow upon them and then cover them with skin. Lastly, He will put His breath or Spirit upon them that they may come to life.

In Chapter 17, I discussed Replacement Theology which denies that the Jews have a right to live in the land of Israel. This teaching states that the modern nation of Israel is not a fulfillment of prophecy because the Jews are in unbelief when it comes to accepting Jesus as the Messiah. I illustrated how God still keeps His covenants with the Jews even while they are in unbelief. It is interesting that the description Ezekiel gives of these bones that represent the Jewish nation of Israel is that they are *very dry*. In other words, they are spiritually dry or dead. It isn't until the end of the process that they become spiritually alive. That the Jews do not currently believe that Jesus is the Messiah is actually a fulfillment of this part of Ezekiel's prophecy.

God says that He will begin the process of restoring the Jews to the land of Israel by taking them up out of their graves and bringing them into the land of Israel. The metaphor God uses here probably refers to the "graves" that the Jews were in when He dispersed them to the nations around the world. He declares that He will take them from every nation and bring them back to the land of Israel. However, I believe that there is also a literal aspect to this metaphor.

In the 1930s and 1940s, the Nazi government of Germany tried to exterminate the Jewish people from the face of the earth. They did succeed in killing more than 6,000,000 Jews before the world stopped them. The Allied armies discovered the concentration camps and the gas ovens and mass graves that contained these Jews. Two years after World War II ended, the countries of the world, via the United Nations, gave the land of Israel back to the Jews. In this case, the Jews were literally taken from their graves and brought back to the land of Israel.

There has been a debate in certain theological circles as to why God allowed the Holocaust to occur. Some say that it was the Jews' punishment for rejecting God's Son, Jesus Christ, as the Messiah. I do not believe that at all. Rather I believe the Holocaust was an attempt by Satan to thwart God's end-times plans.

I mentioned earlier in this book how that just before God was going to fulfill His plans, Satan tried to stop them. God was going to use Moses to deliver the Jews from bondage in Egypt. Satan's plan was to have Moses killed as a baby by inciting the pharaoh to issue a decree ordering the Jews to kill all their newborn male babies. This tactic failed and Moses did fulfill God's plan. Next, God sent His Son to deliver humanity from its bondage to sin. Satan incited King Herod to kill all the newborn male babies in Bethlehem in order to kill Jesus. This attempt failed and Jesus fulfilled the mission that God gave Him. I believe that Satan knew God was about to fulfill His plan of bringing the Jews back to the land of Israel in 1948 and used the Nazis to try and stop this from occurring. Again, Satan's diabolical plan failed and God brought the Jews back to Israel after eighteen hundred years. Though Satan may have been behind the Holocaust, he found willing human servants in the Nazi regime. (Likewise, I believe Satan is still trying to hinder God's plan through the conflict between the Jews and the Arabs. The fact that many Arabs want to "drive the Jews into the sea" is illustrative of his influence to harm God's chosen people).

Thus, in 1948 I believe that God raised the Jews from their "graves" and returned them to the land of Israel as a dry, secular nation. The next stage in the process involves putting sinews or muscles on the nation of Israel. This is mere speculation on my part but it may be that the powerful Israeli military may be a partial fulfillment of this part of Ezekiel's prophecy. Muscles are an indicator of the strength of a body and the Israeli army has been an indicator of the strength of the Jews' will to survive and live.

The next phase of the dry bones vision stated that the nation of Israel would have flesh and skin put on it. The Bible does not speak highly of human flesh. It uses "flesh" as a metaphor for our sinful natures, which try to please God by good works or rebel against Him by evil works. I believe it is possible that when the Jews rebuild the third or Tribulation Temple, this will fulfill the flesh stage of their rebirth as a nation. They will believe they are honoring God with their new Temple and sacrifices yet the Antichrist will actually be using them for his purposes.

This brings us to the final stage of the dry bones vision. God declared that He will put His breath or Spirit in the nation of Israel and they will be His people and He will be their God. This will take place at the second coming of Jesus Christ. The prophet Zechariah spoke of this event:

> *"And it shall come to pass in that day, that I will seek to destroy all the nations that come against Jerusalem. And I will pour upon the house of David, and upon the inhabitants of Jerusalem, the Spirit of grace and of supplications: and they shall look upon Me whom they have pierced, and they shall mourn for Him, as one mourns for his only son, and shall be in bitterness for Him, as one that is in bitterness for his firstborn."*[19]

This passage is a reference to the second coming of Jesus Christ when the whole world will look on Him whom they pierced. God at that time will pour out His Spirit upon Israel and they will receive God's Servant Jesus Christ as their Lord and Savior.

The last part of this vision of Ezekiel's declares that God's Servant will be King over the Jews and the land of Israel. Again, this refers to the Messianic Kingdom over which Jesus will reign.

The Clock Has Started

With the creation of the modern state of Israel, I believe God's end-times timepiece has started ticking. The time frame appears to have begun with the raising up of the spiritually dry bones of the modern secular nation of Israel. It will conclude with the salvation of all Israel when they shall look upon Him whom they pierced. At that time they will receive the Spirit that God breathes or pours out on them and will begin the Messianic Kingdom Age.

How long will it take this process to be completed? Trying to ascertain the time frame for this prophecy in years is fruitless. Some may say that since God uses the formation of a man to represent the rebirth of the Jewish nation of Israel, we could use the biblical lifespan of a human as the time frame. Therefore, since the Psalm of Moses[20] declares that the lifespan of a post-patriarchal human is seventy to eighty years, this is the length of time that God will use for the complete regeneration of the Jewish nation of Israel. However, in this vision of Ezekiel's it appears that this newly formed man is an adult, not a baby, so Adam's situation parallels more closely this metaphor. God created Adam from dust just like these "dry bones" and He created Adam as an adult. Since Adam lived to be 930 years old, the time frame of this prophecy could be 930 years. The truth is that God did not specify how long it would be from the rebirth of the nation Israel until the completion of this prophecy.

I believe the key to determining the time that it takes for the completion of this prophecy lies in the rate at which the different stages of the regeneration occur. If the sinews or muscles do represent Israel's military strength, we could be in the second stage.

The next phase would be the rebuilding of the third Temple. When that occurs it will be around seven years until the second coming of Jesus Christ and the completion of dry bones vision given to Ezekiel. With regards to the rebuilding of the third Temple, there are Jewish organizations that have already created the utensils to be used in it and the garments that are to be worn by the priests in the performance of their Temple duties. As soon as it is built the Jews will be able to perform animal sacrifices and fulfill the other activities associated with the Temple.

I have stated several times that I cannot give the date and year of Jesus' second coming. As a Christian though, I can keep my eyes open to what God is doing in the world and in the land of Israel. I believe Jesus when He said that His followers would *know* when the end was near, even at the doors. If it were not possible for Christians to know this, then why did Jesus and His servant Paul indicate that it was?

Many times God declared that He would bring the Jews back to the land of Israel forever. When He did that in 1948, why should I not see that as the leaves of a fig tree getting tender? During the Jews' eighteen-hundred year absence from the land of Israel, they were dispersed throughout the world. They should have been assimilated into every culture where they went and disappeared as a people. Yet miraculously, after eighteen centuries of wandering, they are finally back in Israel. I would be blind indeed not to see the hand of God in this.

Therefore, I do believe that the return of Jesus Christ is in the near future. How long exactly I cannot say. I do know that every human being has their own end-times which as Moses wrote, may come after only seventy or eighty years. I may go to Jesus before He comes to me but that will not keep me from heeding the words of the apostle Paul:

> *"Therefore let us not sleep, as do others; but let us watch and be sober. For they that sleep, sleep in the night; and they that be drunken are drunken in the night. But let us, who are of the day, be sober, putting on the breastplate of faith and love; and for an helmet, the hope of salvation. For God has not appointed us to wrath, but to obtain salvation by our Lord Jesus Christ, Who died for us, that, whether we wake or sleep, we should live together with Him."*[21]

Thus, I conclude with the final words of Jesus Christ in the Bible:

"He which testifieth these things saith, Surely I come quickly. Amen. Even so, come, Lord Jesus. The grace of our Lord Jesus Christ be with you all. Amen."

- Revelation 22:20-21

---

[1] *Matthew 24:36*
[2] *Matthew 24:3*
[3] *Matthew 24:4-5*
[4] *John 14:6*
[5] *Matthew 24:6-7a*
[6] *Zechariah 12:1-3*
[7] *Matthew 24:7b-8*
[8] *Matthew 24:9-11*
[9] *II Peter 2:3-7*
[10] *Matthew 24:12*
[11] *II Timothy 3:1-5*
[12] *Matthew 24:13-14*
[13] *Matthew 24:15-22*
[14] *Matthew 24:23-26*
[15] *I Timothy 4:1-2*
[16] *Matthew 24:27-31*
[17] *Matthew 24:32-36*
[18] *I Thessalonians 5:1-6*
[19] *Zechariah 12:10*
[20] *Psalm 90:10*
[21] *I Thessalonians 5:6-10*

19 - Today Is The Day Of Salvation!

Although all the chapters in this book are important because they give the biblical foundation for God's complete plan for humanity, this is the *most* important chapter in this book. The reader's response to the biblical truths I discuss in this chapter will determine where they fit in the prophetic plan of God.

There are only two spiritual conditions in which a human being can die. Either they can die in their sins or they can die sinless by accepting the sacrificial death of Jesus Christ through the grace of God.

Many people teach and believe that if you are a good person and live a good life then God will accept you. This leads to the belief that most people will go to heaven. However, Jesus contradicts this teaching when He declares that most people will not enter into heaven:

> *"Enter you in at the strait gate: for wide is the gate, and broad is the way, that leads to destruction, and many there be which go in thereto. Because strait is the gate, and narrow is the way, which leads unto life, and few there be that find it."*[1]

Jesus states that few people are on the narrow path that leads to eternal life. Most are on the wide path that leads to Hell. The reason for this is that life *seems* easier when we are accountable to no one. For the most part we can do whatever we want. Conversely, Jesus said that He is the way that leads to Heaven yet this *seems* like a more difficult path to take.

The truth is that giving your life to Jesus Christ is the easier way to live. If we live our lives according to God's truths then we are completely in His hands and what happens to us is up to Him. If we live our lives without God then whatever happens to us is either in our hands or in the world's hands. I have told my children that if I obey the traffic laws then I do not have to look over my shoulder wondering where the police are. On the other hand, if I drive fast or drive intoxicated, then I may kill myself or someone else and the police would arrest me. Just as the easier way is to follow the traffic laws, so too is it easier to follow God's ways.

However, just because a person accepts Jesus Christ as their Savior does not insure that their life will become perfect. I have heard people say, "How could God allow some tragedy to happen to that person?" The answer to this is that we live in a "fallen" world and that sin and the Devil affect the circumstances of our lives. Yet, I can control *one* circumstance in my life. If I accept Jesus Christ as my Savior then it does not matter what the world or other people may do to me. I am completely in the hands of God and if a criminal harms me or kills me, I still belong to the Lord for eternity. I cannot control what another person may do to me but I can control what I can do for myself.

In Part One I illustrated how Jesus accurately fulfilled the Old Testament prophecies concerning the suffering Messiah. Likewise, He will fulfill the prophecies of the royal Messiah and the end-times that will usher in His Millennial Kingdom. This should lead you to ask where you fit into God's plans for your life and for the last days.

I remember reading a newspaper account of the gunfight at the O.K. Corral in Tombstone, Arizona in 1881. An editor for the Tombstone Epitaph[2] used a very insightful phrase in describing the fate of those men who died during the gun battle:

"Three Men Hurled into Eternity in the Duration of a Moment."

When those three men arose the day of the gunfight they did not know that they would be leaving this world and entering into the eternal dimension. Likewise, we also do not know when our last day on earth will occur.

Whether or not humanity is indeed approaching the end-times as I believe, each one of us can decide today where we will spend eternity.

God has declared that He does not want anyone to die and incur separation from Him forever:

> *"The Lord is not slack concerning His promise, as some men count slackness; but is longsuffering to us-ward, not willing that any should perish, but that all should come to repentance. But the day of the Lord will come as a thief in the night."*[3]

He loves His human children so much that He sent His Son to die for us so that we wouldn't perish:

> *"For God so loved the world, that He gave His only begotten Son, that whosoever believeth in Him should not perish, but have everlasting life. For God sent not His Son into the world to condemn the world; but that the world through Him might be saved. He that believeth on Him is not condemned: but he that believeth not is condemned already, because he hath not believed in the name of the only begotten Son of God."*[4]

Many people have a wrong concept of the nature of God. They see Him as an angry, demanding deity. Although He does show His anger and will express it during the end-times, the basis of His nature is love. He directs His anger toward those who harm others or even themselves because they reject the truth about Him and His ways. However, His overwhelming quality is love as the apostle John wrote:

> *"He that loves not knows not God; for God is love. In this was manifested the love of God toward us, because that God sent His only begotten Son into the world, that we might live through Him. Herein is love, not that we loved God, but that He loved us, and sent His Son to be the propitiation for our sins. Beloved, if God so loved us, we ought also to love one another. No man has seen God at any time. If we love one another, God dwells in us, and His love is perfected in us. Hereby know we that we dwell in Him, and He in us, because He has given us of His Spirit. And we have seen and do testify that the Father sent the Son to be the Savior of the world.*

Whosoever shall confess that Jesus is the Son of God, God dwells in Him, and he in God. And we have known and believed the love that God has to us. God is love; and he that dwells in love dwells in God, and God in him."[5]

Because God does love His children He made a way for us imperfect, sinful humans to dwell in His perfect, holy presence forever.

Born from Above

Jesus made two *absolute* statements concerning salvation:

"Jesus said unto him, I am the way, the truth, and the life: no man comes unto the Father, but by Me."[6]

With this statement, Jesus declares that all other forms of religion are invalid. These false religions started out when humankind rebelled against the truth of God at the tower of Babel. God dispersed humanity throughout the world where they quickly turned from His truths and created false gods to worship:

"Sing unto the LORD, bless His name; show forth His salvation from day to day. Declare His glory among the heathen, His wonders among all people. For the LORD is great, and greatly to be praised: He is to be feared above all gods. For all the gods of the nations are idols: but the LORD made the heavens."[7]

The world would have people believe that there are many paths and religions that lead to God. However, Jesus makes it clear that He alone is the way to God. If you reject this truth then you reject God, Jesus, and the Bible.

Jesus made a second absolute statement concerning salvation, yet in a somewhat enigmatic way:

"Jesus answered and said unto him, Truly, truly, I say unto you, Except a man be born again, he cannot see the kingdom of

> *God...Except a man be born of water and of the Spirit, he cannot enter into the kingdom of God. That which is born of the flesh is flesh; and that which is born of the Spirit is spirit."*[8]

Jesus states that a person *has* to be *"born-again"* to enter the kingdom of God. There is no other way. What does it mean to be born-again?

I believe the key to understanding this passage lies in the spiritual essence of God. Jesus described the nature of God to a woman who was seeking to understand the truth about God:

> *"But the hour comes, and now is, when the true worshippers shall worship the Father in spirit and in truth: for the Father seeks such to worship Him. God is a Spirit: and they that worship Him must worship Him in spirit and in truth. The woman said unto Him, I know that Messiah comes, which is called Christ: when He is come, He will tell us all things. Jesus said unto her, I that speak unto you am He."*[9]

Jesus the Messiah, being God in human flesh, declares that God as a whole is Spirit. To truly know God a person has to know Him spiritually. We humans do have the capacity to know Him on a spiritual level as the Bible makes clear the true essence of our being:

> *"And God said, Let us make man in Our image, after Our likeness...So God created man in His own image, in the image of God created He him; male and female created He them."*[10]

God created humans in His image and since He is a spiritual being, we are spiritual beings. The problem is that our sin nature has quenched our spiritual nature so that we live as carnal beings. We seek only to fulfill the desires of our flesh which leads us to sin.

Jesus states that even though we are born of human flesh our spirits need to be born also. Another translation of the Greek phrase for "born again" is "born from above". I believe this second translation is the more accurate of the two because it makes clear that our new spiritual birth comes from God in Heaven. How do we achieve this new birth experience?

The New Birth

The apostle Peter wrote concerning the new birth process in his first epistle:

> *"Because it is written, Be ye holy; for I am holy. And if you call on the Father, who without respect of persons judges according to every man's work, pass the time of your sojourning here in fear: Forasmuch as you know that you were not redeemed with corruptible things, as silver and gold, from your vain conversation received by tradition from your fathers; But with the precious blood of Christ, as of a lamb without blemish and without spot: Who truly was foreordained before the foundation of the world, but was manifest in these last times for you, Who by Him do believe in God, that raised Him up from the dead, and gave Him glory; that your faith and hope might be in God. Seeing you have purified your souls in obeying the truth through the Spirit unto unfeigned love of the brethren, see that you love one another with a pure heart fervently: Being born again, not of corruptible seed, but of incorruptible, by the word of God, which lives and abides for ever. For all flesh is as grass, and all the glory of man as the flower of grass. The grass withers, and the flower thereof falls away: But the word of the Lord endures forever. And this is the word which by the gospel is preached unto you."*[11]

The first issue Peter addresses is the issue of holiness. We can only attain holiness through our belief in Jesus by which we will then have *"purified [our] souls in obeying the truth through the Spirit"*.

Peter then says that God judges every person according to his or her works. However, Jesus declared that only one work is acceptable to God:

> *"Jesus answered and said unto them, This is the work of God, that you believe on Him whom He has sent."*[12]

Everyone who rejects Jesus will have his or her works judged by God at the Great White Throne judgment.

The last issue Peter deals with is the "born again" experience. He states that we are born again by the incorruptible word of God. This means that when we believe what God says about the sacrificial death of His Son and ask God to use Jesus' sacrifice as atonement for our sins, then our spirits will come alive and will be able to receive the truths of God. The principle at work here is the same that God used with Abraham:

> *"And [Abraham] believed in the LORD; and He counted it to him for righteousness."*[13]

The basis for a spiritual relationship with God is that we believe what God says. Peter states that this occurs when we accept *"the word which by the gospel is preached unto you."*

Sin

What does it mean to believe the gospel? The first issue that a person has to deal with is their sins. The Bible states that sin separates us from God:

> *"Behold, the LORD's hand is not shortened, that it cannot save; neither His ear heavy, that it cannot hear: But your iniquities have separated between you and your God, and your sins have hid His face from you, that He will not hear."*[14]

Sin hinders any relationship with God that we may desire. Humans need a way to have their sins removed so that we can fellowship with God and abide in His presence.

In the Old Testament God set up a sacrificial system so that the Jews could have their sins atoned for in order to maintain a relationship with Him. However, as the writer of the Book of Hebrews points, out these animal sacrifices were not a permanent solution to the problem for a person's sins:

> *"For the law [of Moses] having a shadow of good things to come, and not the very image of the things, can never with those sacrifices which they offered year by year continually make the ones who drew near thereunto perfect. For then would they not have ceased to be offered? Because that the worshippers once purged should have had no more conscience of sins. But in those sacrifices there is a remembrance again made of sins every year. For it is not possible that the blood of bulls and of goats should take away sins."*[15]

If animal sacrifices were an acceptable, permanent solution to humankind's sin then why did God require the Jews to offer them every year? The Jewish high priest had to enter the Temple once a year on the Day of Atonement and sprinkle the blood of a sacrificed animal on the mercy seat of the Ark of the Covenant to cover the sins of all the Jews. However, these sacrifices were just a shadow of the good things to come.

Sacrifice

The writer of Hebrews explains how Jesus is the permanent, acceptable sacrifice for human sin:

> *"Neither by the blood of goats and calves, but by His own blood He entered in once into the holy place, having obtained eternal redemption for us. For if the blood of bulls and of goats, and the ashes of an heifer sprinkling the unclean, sanctifies to the purifying of the flesh: How much more shall the blood of Christ, who through the eternal Spirit offered Himself without spot to God, purge your conscience from dead works to serve the living God? And for this cause He is the mediator of the new testament, that by means of death, for the redemption of the transgressions that were under the first testament, they which are called might receive the promise of eternal inheritance...For Christ is not entered into the holy places made with hands, which are the figures of the true; but into heaven itself, now to appear in the presence of God for us: Nor yet that He should offer himself often, as the high priest*

entered into the holy place every year with blood of others; For then must He often have suffered since the foundation of the world: but now once in the end of the world has He appeared to put away sin by the sacrifice of Himself. And as it is appointed unto men once to die, but after this the judgment: So Christ was once offered to bear the sins of many; and unto them that look for Him shall He appear the second time without sin unto salvation."[16]

Jesus Christ entered into the heavenly Temple to sprinkle His blood on the mercy seat of the Ark of the Covenant. This then became the one and only sacrifice that God would accept as atonement for a human's sins.

The apostle John confirms that Jesus is the fulfillment of the Old Testament sacrificial system:

"...if any man sin, we have an advocate with the Father, Jesus Christ the righteous: And He is the atonement for our sins: and not for ours only, but also for the sins of the whole world."[17]

Therefore, the gospel of salvation declares that a human being can become righteous and holy through believing God's word concerning the sacrificial, atoning death of His Son Jesus Christ for their sins. With this understanding let us now look at how a person can attain personal salvation.

Salvation

A man asked the apostle Paul the most straightforward question concerning salvation found in the Bible:

"Then he called for a light, and sprang in, and came trembling, and fell down before Paul and Silas, And brought them out, and said, Sirs, what must I do to be saved? And they said, Believe on the Lord Jesus Christ, and you shall be saved, and your house. And they spoke unto him the word of the Lord, and to all that were in his house."[18]

Paul answers the man's question by stating the same principle that God used in Abraham's case: ***Believe!*** Believe what God says about His Son and His sacrificial death as atonement for your sins.

As we read above an unsaved person needs first to address their sin. You need to acknowledge that you are a sinner and that you want to repent from your sinful ways. The apostle John declares that if you do this God will be faithful to forgive you of all your sins:

> *"This then is the message which we have heard of Him, and declare unto you, that God is light, and in Him is no darkness at all. If we say that we have fellowship with Him, and walk in darkness, we lie, and do not the truth: But if we walk in the light, as He is in the light, we have fellowship one with another, and the blood of Jesus Christ his Son cleanses us from all sin. If we say that we have no sin, we deceive ourselves, and the truth is not in us. If we confess our sins, He is faithful and just to forgive us our sins, and to cleanse us from all unrighteousness. If we say that we have not sinned, we make Him a liar, and His word is not in us."*[19]

To have fellowship with God we have to confess our sins to Him. This shows that we are willing to put our pride behind us and submit humbly to God's will for our lives. The apostle Paul also addressed the issue of sin:

> *"Even the righteousness of God which is by faith of Jesus Christ unto all and upon all them that believe: for there is no difference: For all have sinned, and come short of the glory of God; Being justified freely by His grace through the redemption that is in Christ Jesus: Whom God has set forth to be an atonement through faith in His blood, to declare His righteousness for the remission of sins that are past, through the forbearance of God; To declare, I say, at this time His righteousness: that He might be just, and the justifier of him which believes in Jesus."*[20]

Every person who has ever lived has sinned. However, we can have our sins removed completely and forever by believing and accepting that Jesus' blood cleanses us from all unrighteousness according to the word of God.

Therefore, after confessing your sins you should ask God to forgive and cleanse you through the sacrificial death of His Son. Having done this you may rest assured that you are saved because God *always* keeps His word. Your salvation does not depend on any "good works" that you might perform. There is only one work that your salvation requires: To believe in the saving work of Jesus' death.

The evidence of God's promise to give you eternal life is the resurrection of Jesus Christ. The apostle Paul stated that more than *five hundred* persons saw the resurrected Jesus Christ:

> *"Moreover, brethren, I declare unto you the gospel which I preached unto you, which also you have received, and wherein you stand; By which also you are saved, if you keep in memory what I preached unto you, unless you have believed in vain. For I delivered unto you first of all that which I also received, how that Christ died for our sins according to the scriptures; And that He was buried, and that He rose again the third day according to the scriptures: And that He was seen of Cephas* [i.e., Peter], *then of the twelve: After that, He was seen of above five hundred brethren at once; of whom the greater part remain unto this present, but some are fallen asleep. After that, He was seen of James; then of all the apostles. And last of all He was seen of me also, as of one born out of due time. For I am the least of the apostles, that am not meet to be called an apostle, because I persecuted the church of God."*[21]

There is no doubt that Jesus Christ rose from the dead. Many of these witnesses died horrible deaths because they *knew* that Jesus had risen from the grave. Believers in Jesus Christ will also rise from their graves to eternal life.

The seal of God's promise to save you is the gift of the Holy Spirit:

> *"Blessed be the God and Father of our Lord Jesus Christ, who has blessed us with all spiritual blessings in heavenly places in*

Christ: According as He has chosen us in Him before the foundation of the world, that we should be holy and without blame before Him in love: Having predestinated us unto the adoption of children by Jesus Christ to Himself, according to the good pleasure of His will, To the praise of the glory of His grace, wherein He has made us accepted in the beloved. In Whom we have redemption through His blood, the forgiveness of sins, according to the riches of His grace; Wherein He has abounded toward us in all wisdom and prudence; Having made known unto us the mystery of His will, according to His good pleasure which He has purposed in Himself: That in the dispensation of the fullness of times He might gather together in one all things in Christ, both which are in heaven, and which are on earth; even in Him: In Whom also we have obtained an inheritance, being predestinated according to the purpose of Him who works all things after the counsel of His own will: That we should be to the praise of His glory, who first trusted in Christ. In Whom you also trusted, after that you heard the word of truth, the gospel of your salvation: in Whom also after that you believed, you were sealed with that Holy Spirit of promise."[22]

When you ask God to forgive your sins and accept Jesus into your heart, He fills you with His Holy Spirit. Jesus gave the reason for the indwelling of the Holy Spirit in a person:

"I have yet many things to say unto you, but you cannot bear them now. Howbeit when He, the Spirit of truth, is come, He will guide you into all truth: for He shall not speak of Himself; but whatsoever He shall hear, that shall He speak: and He will show you things to come. He shall glorify Me: for He shall receive of Mine, and shall show it unto you."[23]

God gives us the Holy Spirit to guide us into all truth. Even though we have accepted Jesus as the Messiah and Savior, we will continue to sin until the day we put off our corruptible flesh. The Spirit will convict us when we are in sin and will speak through us to lead others to salvation. He will place the truths of God's word, the Holy Bible, in our spirits to help throughout our life.

If you accept the salvation of Jesus Christ, do not be fooled into thinking that everything will be perfect from now on. We still live in a fallen, sinful world, which will affect us for the rest of our lives. The good news is that you will no longer have to go through life's trials and tribulations alone. Jesus Christ will be alive in you through His Holy Spirit.

The alternative to this is horrific. Jesus told those religious leaders who rejected Him as the Messiah that they would die in their sins. This means that God will judge them according to their works, which will not measure up to His standard of perfection. He will then have no choice but to cast them into Hell for eternity where they will no longer be able to sense His presence. You however, still have a choice of where you will spend eternity.

Do not make the mistake of thinking that you are too horrible a person to ever be able to accept the grace of God. The apostle Paul gives a small list of those unsaved persons who will not inherit eternal life:

> *"Know you not that the unrighteous shall not inherit the kingdom of God? Be not deceived: neither fornicators, nor idolaters, nor adulterers, nor effeminate, nor abusers of themselves with mankind, Nor thieves, nor covetous, nor drunkards, nor revilers, nor extortioners, shall inherit the kingdom of God. And such were some of you: but you are washed, but you are sanctified, but you are justified in the name of the Lord Jesus, and by the Spirit of our God."*[24]

Notice the last sentence in this passage. Paul said that some of His fellow Christians had indulged in the sinful behaviors he listed here, yet the blood of Jesus Christ cleansed them all. Paul himself was responsible for the deaths of Christians before God saved him.

Therefore, nothing should hinder you from coming to Jesus Christ and asking Him to save you. He declared how important the salvation of your soul is:

> *"For what shall it profit a man, if he shall gain the whole world, and lose his own soul? Or what shall a man give in exchange for his soul? Whosoever therefore shall be ashamed of Me and of My words in this adulterous and sinful generation; of him also shall the Son of man be ashamed, when He comes in the glory of His Father with the holy angels."*[25]

You could become the richest person in the world but you will still die within a hundred years or so. What good will all your wealth and pleasure do you in eternity when you are separated from the presence of God? As we have read, Jesus Christ is coming to the earth again to judge the world. It is up to you whether He will be ashamed at seeing you or blessed by seeing you.

If you are interested in giving your life to Jesus Christ but are unsure as to where to start, you may begin your walk with Him by saying the following prayer from your heart:

"Heavenly Father God, I know that I am a sinner and have led a sinful life. I want to stop struggling with my sin. I ask you to cleanse me and forgive me of all my sins through the shed blood of your Son, Jesus Christ. I believe you raised Jesus from the dead. I accept Jesus as the Messiah and as my Lord and as my Savior for now and eternity. It is in Jesus' name that I pray and ask these things. *Amen.*

You now have God's promise that you are saved. I would begin reading the Bible (start with the Gospel of John) and praying to God that He would give you an understanding of it by the guidance of the Holy Spirit. You definitely need to find a Bible-believing church. Remember that many churches out there deny the truths and miracles of God. You should ask to be baptized in accordance with Jesus' instructions. Your sins are already washed away but baptism is a public declaration that you identify with the death, burial, and resurrection of Jesus Christ.

If you do become a follower of Jesus Christ, your eternal life has begun. You may even be alive when Jesus comes to rapture the Church in the end-times. The important thing is that you will spend eternity with your Heavenly Father who created you.

---

[1] *Matthew 7:13-14*
[2] "The Tombstone Epitaph"; October 27, 1881
[3] *II Peter 3:9-10a*
[4] *John 3:16-18*
[5] *I John 4:8-16*
[6] *John 14:6*
[7] *Psalms 96:2-5*
[8] *John 3:3, 5-6*
[9] *John 4:23-26*
[10] *Genesis 1:26-27*
[11] *I Peter 1:16-25*
[12] *John 6:29*
[13] *Genesis 15:6*
[14] *Isaiah 59:1-2*
[15] *Hebrews 10:1-4*
[16] *Hebrews 9:12-15 , 24-28*
[17] *I John 2:1b-2*
[18] *Acts 16:29-32*
[19] *I John 1:5-10*
[20] *Romans 3:22-26*
[21] *I Corinthians 15:1-9*
[22] *Ephesians 1:3-13*
[23] *John 16:12-14*
[24] *I Corinthians 6:9-10*
[25] *Mark 8:36-38*

Epilogue: Present Day

Armageddon, Doomsday, End of the World, Apocalypse are all terms used to describe the end of the present age. In 1947, atomic scientists created a "Doomsday Clock" by which they would let the world know how close humanity was to nuclear annihilation. The ethnic, environmental, economic, and epidemic turmoil that the world is experiencing continues to spiral downward seemingly leading to a point of no return. Racial tensions, natural disasters, ever-increasing costs of living, and plagues such as AIDS and influenza indicate that the world is in dire straits. Global terrorism based on religious grounds is putting fear into the hearts of men and women. Strife in the Middle East is escalating every day. The rejection of a God that created humans and instilled them with a conscience for doing right and condemning wrong is widespread. Are these signs that the Apocalypse is about to begin?

Skeptics say that these problems have always existed in mankind's history and that the present troubles are nothing new. Up to a point, their skepticism has some validity. It is true that since the First Century, Christians have predicted that the end was near because they were experiencing some of the troubles listed above. However, the Bible states that there are some specific circumstances that need to take place for the End-Times scenario to begin.

When the disciples asked Jesus what would be the sign of the end of the world in chapter 24 of the Gospel of Matthew, He gave them some general signs to look for which included earthquakes, famines, pestilences, and wars. Yet He also gave them some specific signs such as:

"When ye therefore shall see the abomination of desolation,

> *spoken of by Daniel the prophet, stand in the holy place, (whoso readeth, let him understand:) Then let them which be in Judea flee into the mountains."*[1]

Jesus said that when His followers saw the abomination standing in the "holy place", He meant standing in the Temple in Jerusalem. He also told His followers to flee from Judea to the mountains. This is significant because for both of these events to occur the Jews have to be living in the land of Israel and the Temple has to be rebuilt in Jerusalem. From 135 A.D. until 1948, the Jews as a nation did not live in the land of Israel. Now that the Jews are residing back in the land these prophecies can be fulfilled. It also means that all the other end-time prophecies can take place at any time. Consequently, the key to understanding Biblical prophecies for the last days revolves around the nation of Israel.

Is the world's current state of affairs indicating that it is indeed near the end of the present age? To answer this I will use two prophetic passages in the Old Testament.

A Burdensome Stone

The first is found in the Book of Zechariah where God declares what will happen in the last days:

> *"The burden of the word of the LORD for Israel, saith the LORD, which stretcheth forth the heavens, and layeth the foundation of the earth, and formeth the spirit of man within him. Behold, I will make Jerusalem a cup of trembling unto all the people round about, when they shall be in the siege both against Judah and against Jerusalem. And in that day will I make Jerusalem a burdensome stone for all people: all that burden themselves with it shall be cut in pieces, though all the people of the earth be gathered together against it."*[2]

Nations and Empires have fought over Jerusalem numerous times over the past three thousand years. Yet at no time was Jerusalem a *"burdensome stone for all people"* nor were ever *"all the people of the earth gathered together against it."* That situation changed dramatically in the last half of the Twentieth Century and the first part of the Twenty-First Century. With the importance of oil coming to the forefront as nations became more and more reliant on it to sustain their economies, the Middle East became the focal point of the world's attention. Nations as diverse as China, Russia, the European countries, and the Americas all had a vested interest in what happened in that area of the world. However, within the Middle East itself there was an underlying dilemma. The oil-rich Arab/Islamic countries had a deeply ingrained hatred for the Jews and the nation of Israel. Consequently, the nations of the world have tried to intervene in this conflict in order to bring stabilization to the area and the peaceful transfer of oil to their respective countries. Presently, this situation has not been resolved though there have been various attempts to achieve peace in the region. As a result of this lack of success Jerusalem has become a *"burdensome stone"* and a *"cup of trembling"* for all the nations of the world.

Gog and Magog

The second prophetic passage comes from the Book of Ezekiel where God declares in the latter days after the Jews have come back to the land of Israel, armies from surrounding countries will come against Israel:

> *"And the word of the LORD came unto me, saying, Son of man, set thy face against Gog, the land of Magog, the chief prince of Meshech and Tubal, and prophesy against him, And say, Thus saith the Lord GOD; Behold, I am against thee, O Gog, the chief prince of Meshech and Tubal: And I will turn thee back, and put hooks into thy jaws, and I will bring thee forth, and all thine army, horses and horsemen, all of them clothed with all sorts of armour, even a great company with bucklers and shields, all of them handling swords: Persia, Ethiopia, and Libya with them; all of them with shield and helmet: Gomer, and all his bands; the house of Togarmah of the north quarters, and all his bands: and many people with thee. Be thou prepared, and prepare for thyself, thou, and all thy company that are assembled unto thee, and be thou a guard*

unto them. After many days thou shalt be visited: in the latter years thou shalt come into the land that is brought back from the sword, and is gathered out of many people, against the mountains of Israel, which have been always waste: but it is brought forth out of the nations, and they shall dwell safely all of them. Thou shalt ascend and come like a storm, thou shalt be like a cloud to cover the land, thou, and all thy bands, and many people with thee. Thus saith the Lord GOD; It shall also come to pass, that at the same time shall things come into thy mind, and thou shalt think an evil thought: And thou shalt say, I will go up to the land of unwalled villages; I will go to them that are at rest, that dwell safely, all of them dwelling without walls, and having neither bars nor gates, To take a spoil, and to take a prey; to turn thine hand upon the desolate places that are now inhabited, and upon the people that are gathered out of the nations, which have gotten cattle and goods, that dwell in the midst of the land. Sheba, and Dedan, and the merchants of Tarshish, with all the young lions thereof, shall say unto thee, Art thou come to take a spoil? hast thou gathered thy company to take a prey? to carry away silver and gold, to take away cattle and goods, to take a great spoil? Therefore, son of man, prophesy and say unto Gog, Thus saith the Lord GOD; In that day when My people of Israel dwelleth safely, shalt thou not know it? And thou shalt come from thy place out of the north parts, thou, and many people with thee, all of them riding upon horses, a great company, and a mighty army: And thou shalt come up against My people of Israel, as a cloud to cover the land; it shall be in the latter days, and I will bring thee against My land, that the heathen may know Me, when I shall be sanctified in thee, O Gog, before their eyes. Thus saith the Lord GOD; Art thou he of whom I have spoken in old time by My servants the prophets of Israel, which prophesied in those days many years that I would bring thee against them? And it shall come to pass at the same time when Gog shall come against the land of Israel, saith the Lord GOD, that My fury shall come up in My face. For in My jealousy and in the fire of My wrath have I spoken, Surely in that day there shall be a great shaking in the land of Israel; So that the fishes of

> *the sea, and the fowls of the heaven, and the beasts of the field, and all creeping things that creep upon the earth, and all the men that are upon the face of the earth, shall shake at My presence, and the mountains shall be thrown down, and the steep places shall fall, and every wall shall fall to the ground. And I will call for a sword against him throughout all My mountains, saith the Lord GOD: every man's sword shall be against his brother. And I will plead against him with pestilence and with blood; and I will rain upon him, and upon his bands, and upon the many people that are with him, an overflowing rain, and great hailstones, fire, and brimstone. Thus will I magnify Myself, and sanctify Myself; and I will be known in the eyes of many nations, and they shall know that I am the LORD."*[3]

God declares that in the *"latter years"* and *"latter days"* an army consisting of several countries will come against Israel. The result of this invasion is *"all the men that are upon the face of the earth, shall shake at My presence, and the mountains shall be thrown down, and the steep places shall fall, and every wall shall fall to the ground...pestilence and with blood; and I will rain upon him, and upon his bands, and upon the many people that are with him, an overflowing rain, and great hailstones, fire, and brimstone."* As you read earlier in this book, this is an accurate description of what is going to take place during the Tribulation Period. Thus, this invasion will occur around that time.

Many Biblical scholars and historians (going all the way back to Josephus in the First Century) have identified the countries listed in this passage with their modern counterparts. They are as follows:

Magog:	Russia
Meshech:	Moscow
Tubal:	Tobolsk
Persia:	Iran
Ethiopia:	Ethiopia
Libya:	Libya
Gomer:	Germany
Togarmah:	Turkey/Aremenia

After Togarmah, Ezekiel refers to *"many people with thee"* which may indicate countries surrounding the ones specifically mentioned may also be part of this attack. It is worth mentioning that after the breakup of the Soviet Union many of its southern provinces became Islamic countries. This fact, along with the inclusion of Iran, Turkey, and Libya, indicates that this invasion may have an overtly Islamic rationale for attacking Israel.

Does the current global situation avail itself to allow for this invasion to take place soon? Iran is threatening to develop nuclear weapons and to wipe Israel off the face of the earth. Islam, which is spreading throughout the world, by its very nature threatens the extinction of Israel. Would oil-hungry countries like China and Russia align themselves with oil-deficient Israel or oil-sufficient Islamic countries? The Book of Revelation mentions the fact that the "*kings of the east*" will cross the Euphrates River on their way to the Middle East. This seems to be a reference to China and other Asian nations. However, as long as the United States supports Israel it seems that such an undertaking would not occur. The problem is that as Abraham Lincoln stated (paraphrasing Jesus) "A house divided against itself cannot stand." America is becoming an increasingly divided and immoral country and may one day lose its superpower status and thereby be unable to defend Israel. Nevertheless, the fact remains that the countries aligning themselves against Israel in this passage are very close to completing the necessary alliances needed to fulfill this prophecy.

The United Nations and the European Union

In 1947 the United Nations voted to return the Jews to their ancient land of Israel. I believe there was a temporal reason and a spiritual reason this event took place. The temporal reason was that the nations of the world felt guilty for allowing the holocaust that killed over six million Jews to take place. The spiritual reason was that it fulfilled God's plan to restore the Jews to the land of Israel as He declared to the prophet Amos: *"And I will bring again the captivity of My people of Israel, and they shall build the waste cities, and inhabit them; and they shall plant vineyards, and drink the wine thereof; they shall also make gardens, and eat the fruit of them. And I will plant them upon their land, and they shall no more be pulled up out of their land which I have given them, saith the LORD thy God."*[4] Since that time however, the United Nations has set its face against Israel by passing hundreds of resolutions condemning Israel. This alone tells me that God intervened to use the nations of the world to fulfill His purpose for the Jews and their land. There is no way the UN would vote to create the state of Israel today.

The European Union (EU) is made up of countries that have been historically anti-Semitic and therefore anti-Israel. An EU poll taken in 2003 declared that Israel was the biggest threat to world peace. In 2005 it condemned Israel for building a security wall to protect Israelis from terrorist bombers. Their role in future events may include presenting the Antichrist to the world.

These two organizations are further evidence that the world is coming against Israel and that the situation will never improve in any beneficial way for it.

Israel

Israel is currently taking steps that seem contrary to God's purpose for them as a nation. The government is in the process of unilaterally withdrawing it citizens by force from various parts of their country. They are redrawing the borders of Israel in the hope that they may attain peace with their Arab/Islamic neighbors. This appears to be an exercise in futility. The European Union declared they would not recognize any change to the pre-1967 borders other than those arrived at by agreement between the parties. Consequently, if Israel doesn't revert their country back to the borders they had before 1967 without the approval of the Arab/Islamic parties, the EU would not support this unilateral disengagement plan. To acquiesce to the demands of the EU would mean that Israel would have to relinquish control of the Temple Mount and the Wailing Wall to the Arab/Islamic powers. I do not see Israel surrendering this holy site back to Islam. Thus, peace will not be achieved through natural means.

On the Palestinian side of the issue, the people have elected members of the terrorist organization Hamas to the Palestinian Authority government to represent them to Israel and to the world.

Though most of the world's reaction to this election was negative they will eventually have to negotiate with whomever is leading the Palestinian Authority if they ever hope to achieve peace and bring stability in the Middle East.

The problem is that the Bible makes it clear that true peace in the Middle East and the rest of the world will not occur until the Messiah is reigning from Jerusalem.

Seducing Spirits

I want to mention one final prophecy concerning the last days and how it pertains to the present time.

The apostle Paul was coming to the end of his life. One of the last letters he wrote was to a young Christian named Timothy whom he had mentored in the faith. He gave Timothy many instructions concerning those who would serve in the Church as leaders. He also exhorted him to teach the people how to live with one another in Christian love. Then Paul gave him a prophetic warning:

> *"Now the Spirit speaketh expressly, that in the latter times some shall depart from the faith, giving heed to seducing spirits, and doctrines of devils; Speaking lies in hypocrisy; having their conscience seared with a hot iron."*[5]

Paul declares that in the last days, people will pay attention to *"seducing spirits"*. Although demonic activity has been influencing humans since the beginning, these spirits will increase their efforts in the end-times. I believe that we are now experiencing the final assault on humanity by these seducing spirits.

Prior to the late 1960s there were some human activities that society considered to be shameful. Since that time however, these behaviors have become mainstream in our culture. They may have existed throughout history but now are looked upon as activities to be tolerated and in some cases encouraged.

Pornography is rampant in today's world. With the growth of the Internet, access to sexual imagery has grown exponentially. Lives are being ruined by this evil manifestation. It is an addiction that has destroyed marriages and shattered the innocence of children. No one can deny that there is an evil power that drives humans to engage in this dehumanizing activity.

Another indication of the rise of sexual immorality is the homosexual movement around the world. God calls homosexuality an abomination[6] yet society declares that we have to be tolerant of this "alternative" lifestyle. If you resist these efforts to normalize homosexuality, you are labeled a "homophobe" and are declared to be an intolerant bigot. Homosexuals parade down main streets around the world in open defiance of God. In 2006, there is a planned march through the holy city of Jerusalem that may involve thousands or even hundreds of thousands of homosexual activists. Many activists demand that the Christian Church accept their lifestyles as having the approval of God. The fact that the Bible never *commends* homosexuality but only *condemns* it does not influence homosexuals to reexamine their chosen lifestyle as harmful to themselves in the eyes of God. Tragically, their consciences may have indeed become seared. There is no doubt that a spirit of rebellion against God is influencing the homosexual movement.

Lastly, a movement known as Liberal Theology made tremendous inroads into the Christian Church in the Twentieth Century. Its adherents deny the miracles of the Bible and the right of the Jews to live in the modern state of Israel. They deny the divinity of Jesus Christ and the inerrancy of the Bible. Many will be lost in eternity because the teachers of this false doctrine have kept them from hearing the truths of God.

In 2003, a book[7] that sold more than 40 million copies around the world denied the historical claims of Christianity. Though the author claims his book is a novel, many people believe that it is factual. Some of the ideas it expresses include the denial that Jesus Christ is divine, Jesus and Mary Magdalene were husband and wife and had a child, and the Bible is the product of man and not God. The author writes *"Almost everything our fathers taught us about Christ is false."* Some people may discount the truths of the Bible because of books like this. As the apostle Paul said, *"in the latter times some shall depart from the faith."*

It is clear that seducing spirits are active in the world today. Their goal is to turn people away from God before He begins His end-times judgments.

The End?

From a global point of view it does seem that the stage is set for God to implement His plan for the end of the present age. Even if there was no God I wonder how much longer humanity can continue on the destructive path it has taken in the past few decades. For the first time in history we have the power to destroy the world. Hatred, immorality, and human abuses are increasing. Evolution continues to dehumanize man and thereby devalue human life. Globalization to bring humanity together through commerce and information is reminiscent of man's earliest attempt to unify and make a name for themselves without recognizing God as their Creator at the Tower of Babel. It is interesting that even these behaviors are the subject of end-times prophecy:

> *"This know also, that in the last days perilous times shall come. For men shall be lovers of their own selves, covetous, boasters, proud, blasphemers, disobedient to parents, unthankful, unholy, Without natural affection, trucebreakers, false accusers, incontinent, fierce, despisers of those that are good, traitors, heady, highminded, lovers of pleasures more than lovers of God; Having a form of godliness, but denying the power thereof: from such turn away."*[8]

Yet, as I have pointed out in this chapter, this is the first time in history that God's declared plan for the End-Times can take place. The Jews are back in the land of Israel and world events and attitudes are approaching the final stage of this plan.

---

1 *Matthew 24:15-16*
2 *Zechariah 12:1-3*
3 *Ezekiel 38:1-23*
4 *Amos 9:14-15*
5 *I Timothy 4:1-2*
6 *Leviticus 18:22*
7 "The Da Vinci Code" by Dan Brown [Random House, a division of Doubleday; 2003]
8 *II Timothy 3:1-5*

I want to thank you for taking the time out of your life to read my book. If you are a believer, I hope it has been a blessing to you and encouraged you. If you are not a believer, I hope you will take the subject of this book seriously. Many people have tried throughout the centuries to discredit the Bible yet have been unsuccessful in doing so. As each year goes by history, archaeology, geography, science, and the study of human behavior continue to provide evidence that the Bible is true. As Jesus proved by His first coming, the Bible is also prophetically accurate. *Therefore, do not doubt that the future events discussed in this book will happen.* I leave you with the words of the apostle Peter:

"For we have not followed cunningly devised fables, when we made known unto you the power and coming of our Lord Jesus Christ, but were eyewitnesses of His majesty. For He received from God the Father honor and glory, when there came such a voice to Him from the excellent glory, This is My beloved Son, in Whom I am well pleased. And this voice which came from heaven we heard, when we were with Him in the holy mount. We have also a more sure word of prophecy; whereunto you do well that you take heed, as unto a light that shines in a dark place, until the day dawn, and the day star arise in your hearts."

- II Peter 1:16-19

www.ingramcontent.com/pod-product-compliance
Lightning Source LLC
LaVergne TN
LVHW050929080826
845145LV00001B/271

* 9 7 8 0 6 1 5 1 7 3 1 0 8 *